Historical Perspectives on Business Enterprise Series

The Passenger Train in the Motor Age

California's Rail and Bus Industries, 1910–1941

Gregory Lee Thompson

Ohio State University Press
Columbus

Copyright © 1993 by the Ohio State University Press.
All rights reserved.

Library of Congress Cataloging-in-Publication Data

Thompson, Gregory Lee, 1946–
 The passenger train in the motor age: California's rail and bus industries, 1910–1941 / Gregory Lee Thompson.
  p. cm. — (Historical perspectives on business enterprise series)
 Includes bibliographical references and index.
 ISBN 0-8142-0609-3 (alk. paper)
 1. Railroads—California—Passenger traffic—History—20th century. 2. Buses—California—History—20th century. I. Title. II. Series.
HE2583.T47 1993
385'.262'09794—dc20   93-10723
                                                          CIP

Text and jacket design by Mike Jaynes.
Type set in Times Roman and Serifa by Tseng Information Systems, Durham, NC.
Printed by Thomson-Shore, Inc., Dexter, MI.

The paper in this book meets the guidelines for permanence and durability of the Committee on Production Guidelines for Book Longevity of the Council on Library Resources. ∞

9 8 7 6 5 4 3 2 1

For my parents,
Virginia A. and Karl W. Thompson

Contents

List of Maps	ix
List of Figures	xi
Preface	xiii
Introduction	1
1. Passenger Service and the Seeds of Decline, 1856–1920	9
2. Management and Its Ability to Change, 1910–1920	39
3. Troubles during Prosperity, 1920–1929	63
4. Pacific Greyhound Lines and the Southern Pacific, 1929–1936	91
5. Rising Deficits in a Rebounding Market: Rail Passenger Strategy, 1930–1941	113
6. What Went Wrong	135
7. Conclusion	152
List of Abbreviations	163
Appendix	165
Notes	201
Index	235

Maps

1.1	California rail lines, ca. 1880	12
1.2	Mainlines of the Atchison, Topeka & Santa Fe, ca. 1915	20
1.3	Mainlines of the Southern Pacific and the Union Pacific, ca. 1915	24
1.4	Southern Pacific and Santa Fe lines in California, ca. 1915	25
4.1	Pacific Greyhound Lines, routes in central California, 1931	100
4.2	Pacific Greyhound Lines, routes in central California, 1936	102

Figures

1.1	Southern Pacific passenger train services in central California, ca. 1915	26
1.2	Population growth in California regions, 1860–1910	28
2.1	California passenger revenues as a percentage of California income, 1911–1920	52
3.1	California passenger revenues as a percentage of California income, 1911–1930	72
3.2	Southern Pacific passenger train services in central California, ca. 1920	74
3.3	Southern Pacific passenger train services in central California, ca. 1925	75
3.4	Southern Pacific passenger train services in central California, ca. 1930	76
3.5	Passenger fare yields in U.S. regions, 1922–1930	81
5.1	Southern Pacific passenger train services in central California, ca. 1935	116
5.2	Passenger fare yields in U.S. regions, 1922–1935	117
5.3	Indices of growth of Los Angeles to San Francisco passenger train revenues, area population, and area income, 1934–1941	130

5.4	California passenger revenues as a percentage of California income, 1911–1941	131
6.1	Gross earnings for major trains on the Southern Pacific, Pacific Lines, 1938	146

Preface

Governments of many of the world's advanced countries took a leading, proactive role in intercity transportation development. In the United States, however, the intercity transportation system, consisting of facilities, vehicles, services, and institutions, arose from contests between disparate private interests in markets and political arenas. Developers, transportation corporations, automobile manufacturing concerns, urban regions, industrial conglomerates, and private individuals, among others, created the system as they maneuvered in pursuit of profit and advantage. Governments played reactive, supporting roles.[1]

Over the past three-quarters of a century, this contest went badly for intercity rail passenger service in the United States. Little of it survived into the 1970s, and I began writing this book intending to explain why. I particularly wanted to examine the extent to which passenger train disappearance reflected consumer tastes, political interference in markets, or unwise decisions by railroad corporations.

As I proceeded, I discovered that America's golden age of the passenger train occurred not in the 1950s, as many people believe, but during the first decade of the twentieth century. By 1941 passenger trains already appeared headed for extinction. Although airlines offered only limited competition, and passenger trains still figured importantly in the popular imagination, they lost money. More ominously, the railroads that made the heaviest investments to improve passenger service before World War II lost as much if not more money than those that made few improvements. At the same time, bus companies made money carrying passengers. Reflecting on these results and the likelihood of better and cheaper airline service in the postwar era, thoughtful observers during World War II predicted the demise of rail passenger service.

The fact that the passenger branch of the railroad business was failing even before airlines offered serious competition suggests that railroad managers unsuccessfully adapted the passenger train to the automobile age. I wanted to discover why. Accordingly, I changed my study's focus to the thirty-year period after 1910, when America adopted the automobile.

This book addresses how railroad corporations made decisions during those important three decades. I examine the sensitivity of railroad management structures to market signals, how regulation constrained managers, how fairly or unfairly they were treated by government policy, and why government policy evolved as it did. I originally did not intend to address intercity bus management, but I found that it had become so intertwined with rail management by the 1930s that I could not ignore it. Likewise, I examine highway and, to a lesser extent, steamship development.

This work rests on a foundation of sources that historians rarely use, case files of regulatory commissions. A brief description of what case files are will illustrate their value as primary source material. Unless historians make greater use of this type of source, it likely will disappear.[2]

Shortly after Congress formed the Interstate Commerce Commission in 1887, Thomas M. Cooley, the first chief commissioner, defined the new agency's procedures for administrative regulation. Drawing upon his own experience as a supreme court justice in Michigan, Cooley adopted an adversarial judicial model. When a complaint was brought against a railroad, a presiding hearing examiner methodically prepared a record through examination and cross examination. Counsel for the plaintiff presented evidence by examining qualified witnesses. Testimony often centered on exhibits, consisting of charts, tables, company records, specially conducted surveys, or other material bearing on the argument. Counsel for each of the protesting parties poked holes in the arguments and exhibits through cross examination. They then presented rebuttal arguments in like manner.[3]

The complete record of such a case is called a case file and is identified by a docket number. It contains transcripts of testimony, exhibits, abstracts, briefs, correspondence, and opinions and decisions. Important cases sometimes dragged on for two or three years, producing transcripts in excess of 20,000 pages and exhibits reaching into the thousands.

Case files are a remarkably rich repository of contemporary views and data shedding light on a nation in change. New competitive pressures, new technologies, changing social conditions, or decline or expansion of different parts of the country affected railroad profits and losses. Such change often provoked railroad corporations to initiate new ways of doing business, which in turn threatened to upset social and economic relations within communities and sectors of the country. Threatened interests used regulatory bodies to protect their positions; the case file is the record of their efforts.

Although they do not all do so equally or sometimes at all, case files may offer insight into groups and institutions reacting to change. They can reveal the internal decision-making structure of railroads and sometimes other agencies of transportation. They also can reveal values, fears, and decision-making procedures of community, regional, and national associations of businesses.

Case files are also useful to historians because of their adversarial foundation, which ensures at least two views on controversial issues. Trying to understand the inevitable contradictions and paradoxes in the evidence that this approach creates, the historian gains considerable insight into conflict.

The focus of case files offers a third advantage. Contending parties pulled evidence from their records or created it with special surveys to buttress their point of view. The historian who finds a case whose questions are of intellectual interest will benefit from the work of knowledgeable employees who decades earlier culled relevant company records. A case file assembled between 1936 and 1938, for example, will contain abundant relevant evidence for those years and sparser relevant evidence bearing on the case for up to twenty-five years before.

The file for the *Santa Fe Case,* heard by the California Railroad Commission between 1935 and 1938, provided much of the source material for this book. Faced with a mounting passenger deficit despite increasing traffic, the Atchison, Topeka & Santa Fe Railway used a bus subsidiary in 1935 to file applications with the commission to establish statewide bus service in competition with the West Coast bus monopoly, Pacific Greyhound Lines. The railroad also promised to inaugurate new streamlined trains to compete with the Southern Pacific Company, the dominant railroad in California. The Southern Pacific, with a 39 percent stake in Pacific Greyhound, bitterly fought the Santa Fe applications, as did Pacific Greyhound. Their efforts produced the longest case in California's regulatory history to that time. The case's 17,000 pages of transcript and 850 exhibits proved a rich find illuminating transportation modernization in California.[4]

I supplemented the file of the *Santa Fe Case* with several other case files from the California Railroad Commission and the Interstate Commerce Commission. In 1942, in a labor of love, the chief clerk of the Washington, D.C., Union Station, Clyde H. Freed, summarized ICC decisions pertaining to passenger fares. His work prompted me to spend the summer of 1983 researching several ICC case files.[5]

Railroad annual reports to the California Railroad and Interstate Commerce commissions, employee magazines, *California Highways and Public Works,* railroad timetables, and railroad records found in private collections provided additional source material. In a few instances I made use of primary source material published in railroad enthusiast books. Enthusiasts perform a valuable service in saving historical material that otherwise would not survive. Where I gained insight from such material, I credited the source.

I also benefited from the work and insights of numerous other historians cited throughout this book. In some instances their work, read in the context of the primary sources that I examined, led me to different conclusions than they had reached. This does not imply disrespect for their work, without which I could not have reached my own perspective. Numerous individuals and institutions assisted me with this work, and to each of them I am deeply indebted. As my committee co-chairs during dissertation work, out of which this book grew, James J. Flink and Gordon J. Fielding at the University of California, Irvine, deserve special thanks. I also appreciate the help of committee members Charles Lave and David Brownstone. Peter Lindert and Alan Olmstead from the Agricultural History Center at the University of California, Davis, deserve thanks for encouraging me to pursue the costing of railroad passenger service. During a year-long postdoctoral fellowship at the Hagley Museum and Library in Wilmington, Delaware, I benefited from additional critiques from Glenn Porter, Maury Klein, and Brian Gratton. After becoming aware of my use of ICC case files, Leonard Rapport, recently retired from the National Archives, discussed at length with me his insights on their great value, for which I am most grateful. Many of the ideas in this book matured as I prepared transportation planning courses at Florida State University. I thank my colleagues, with whom I discussed developing thoughts, for their insights, and in particular I thank James Frank and Mark Ellis for helping me refine my argument on the growth machine.

I am especially indebted to the several individuals who opened their private collections to me. In particular, William A. Myers of Anaheim Hills and James Seal of Santa Monica most generously loaned me the entire file from the *Santa Fe Case,* which they obtained when the Public Utilities Commission discarded it in the early 1980s. I am grateful to Mr. Seal for making me aware of the importance of the file, which at first did not interest me. After finally traveling to Santa Monica to inspect it, I realized immediately its richness. Back home, I spent the next three years poring over this copious source. Subsequently, Mr. Myers donated to me photocopies of all transcripts and exhibits from the case, to which I have referred repeatedly since. Mr. Myers and Mr. Seal also made available to me files from two Sacramento Northern abandonment hearings.

I also thank Richard Tower of San Francisco and Vernon Sappers of Oakland for allowing me access to their files from the passenger department of the Southern Pacific Company and from the Sacramento Northern Railway. Arthur Jenkins, the hearing examiner for the *Santa Fe Case,* allowed me access to his personal papers concerning the case, and William Billings, James Gibson, Robert Burroughs, and the late John Hoschek of the Motor Bus Society of New Jersey generously provided me with materials and insights on intercity bus service in California. Pat Erigero graciously assisted in checking sources. To all of them, many thanks.

Libraries, archives, and museums also aided my efforts. Ellen Schwartz, Stephen Drew, and Walter Gray III of the California Railroad History Museum provided invaluable assistance, as did Edee Darknell and Carol Gilbert from the library of the California Department of Transportation. I also am indebted to Liz Kogen, Heddie Richter, Chris Baer, and other members of the staff of the Hagley Museum and Library. I also thank Patricia Holbauch of the Tulare County Museum. Lynn Long of the library of the Institute of Transportation Studies at the University of California, Irvine, provided me with tireless, ongoing assistance over several years, and I also received assistance from the library's counterpart at Berkeley. Finally, I thank the staffs of the California State Archives, the Bancroft Library, the archives of the Automobile Club of Southern California, the National Archives, the Washington National Record Center, the map room of the Library of Commerce, and the docket room of the Interstate Commerce Commission for their assistance in obtaining case files and other archival materials.

The Southern Pacific Company kindly allowed me to photocopy annual reports to the Interstate Commerce Commission from the 1930s. I thank the company for this privilege.

I also wish to thank Fred Matthews, Tom Matoff, Austin Kerr, Mansel Blackford, and an anonymous referee for reading and critiquing earlier drafts of my manuscript. I also extend thanks to George and Linda Paine for assisting me during my summer of research in Washington, D.C.

Finally, but certainly not least, I extend copious thanks to my research assistant, Wade White, for redrawing the tables, figures, and maps that appear in this book. His efforts greatly raised its quality.

Several organizations provided financial support for this effort. The Pacific Coast Chapter of the Railroad and Locomotive Historical Society extended me a generous grant, administered by the Agricultural History Center at the University of California, Davis, and the California Railroad History Museum. The George Krambles Foundation and the Institute of Transportation Studies at the University of California, Irvine, provided me with additional support during my doctoral studies. I began writing the book while in residence at the Hagley Museum and Library, financed by a year-long Andrew W. Mellon/National Endowment for the Humanities advanced research fellowship.

Several paragraphs in this book were published originally in different form in the *Business History Review* and the *Journal of Transport History*. I extend thanks to the editors of these journals for allowing me to include them.

Introduction

For several decades beginning in the 1860s the passenger train dominated American intercity passenger transportation and figured importantly in the evolving American economy. Beginning about 1910 the automobile challenged the passenger train's dominance. Whether railroad managements responded inappropriately, or whether the automobile's appeal proved irresistible, the automobile quickly triumphed, relegating the passenger train to unimportance and unprofitability. In this book I examine the automobile challenge and railroad management's response to determine whether managements did their best to adapt the passenger train to the automobile age.

The examination focuses on the California operations of the Southern Pacific Company and the Atchison, Topeka & Santa Fe Railway. Both companies typified large American railroads during a period when California's rapid automobile, population, and economic growth was presenting their managements with a business environment undergoing greater than average change. Because buses figured importantly in railroad passenger strategies after the mid-1920s, I also examine the development of the intercity bus industry in California and its relations with railroads.

In evaluating how well railroad managements adapted to changing passenger markets, I challenge three generally accepted tenets of business and railroad history. The most basic of these tenets views the history of business decision making as a rational process in which managements acted to earn maximum possible profits. When confronted with a changing market, they altered their products to meet new consumer desires at the lowest possible cost.

Under this paradigm the noted business historian Alfred D. Chandler, Jr., explains how railroad entrepreneurs created the modern business hierarchy in response to the unprecedented scope and complexity of early railroad trunk lines. The completion of interregional trunk lines in the 1840s challenged railroad leaders to coordinate the safe operation and maintenance of scores of trains on tracks spanning hundreds of miles. Railroad leaders also had to make financial sense of organizations offering diverse freight and passenger services taking in revenues and making expenditures at hundreds of geographically dispersed points. To meet these challenges railroad leaders pioneered the modern business bureaucracy, which separated professional managers from owners. Cost accounting figured prominently in the new structure as the means by which top managers controlled their vast enterprises. By knowing the revenue and cost consequences of their actions and acting to maintain or increase profits, railroad managers could adapt their enterprises to changing conditions.[1] The elegance of this argument stimulated the recent synthesis on the rise of big business.[2]

Although they preceded the Chandler paradigm, several explanations for the decline of the American passenger train support it. George W. Hilton's analysis of Amtrak explains the historic decline of the passenger train as the result of decreasing demand, to which railroad management responded reasonably well. However, the service and cost virtues of the automobile and airplane overwhelmed management's best efforts. Railroad managements tried to make passenger trains more appealing to an increasingly auto-conscious public, while they did their best to improve the productivity of the technology. If management erred on the side of emotion, it was in sticking with passenger trains far too long. John R. Meyer's and Clinton V. Oster, Jr.'s, recent analysis of airline deregulation also views rail passenger decline in this manner. They claim that railroad managers made a valiant attempt in the 1930s to lower costs and improve service with the introduction of streamliners. Despite such efforts, which Meyer and Oster claim succeeded for a while, trains in the post–World War II environment again became a high-cost mode of travel. By this time managements had exhausted the technological possibilities for economically improving passenger trains, which consequently were doomed.[3]

In challenging the view that railroad managers met the auto challenge by offering the most profitable service they could have, I side with the noted American business historian Thomas C. Cochran. Cochran explains business evolution by allowing for sometimes irrational managerial behavior. His analysis of railroad executive correspondence between 1845 and 1890 finds organizational change occurring more slowly and haphazardly than Chandler claims. Cochran gives more weight to institutional precedent, primarily from the military, as well as to a long period of trial and error in finding out what practices were and were not socially acceptable. He finds little evidence that railroad managers paid much attention to outside industry analysts promoting organizational and accounting innovation, and he reports that accounting information often misdirected management. Railroad entrepreneurs and managers had at best only vague ideas about the profitability consequences of their actions. They made major investments in order to relieve traffic congestion on lines and in terminals, to operate longer and heavier trains, or to open new territory before a competitor might. They had little interest in innovation. Drawing on the darker side of Weberian theory, Cochran sees weaknesses as well as strengths within railroad bureaucracies that sometimes prevented rational responses to changing business environments.[4]

Stephen Salsbury's history of the collapse of the Penn Central lends considerable support to the Cochran view, as does James J. Flink's recent history of the automobile in American life.[5] My work also supports it. I argue that although railroad managers generally pursued the profit motive, they did not do so for much of their passenger operations. They ran many passenger trains as a self-imposed social obligation or to promote freight service, particularly on routes where they competed with other railroads. This sometimes led to questionable investments. The investment by one railroad in a bright new passenger train often compelled its competitor to similarly invest, even though the service was unprofitable by the railroad's limited definition of profitability. Meanwhile the railroad neglected to invest in more promising passenger routes where freight competition was not significant.

I also argue that managers acted inappropriately because most of them misunderstood the costs of running trains. In his broadly based, sweeping history of the railways of England and Wales, the British historian Jack Simmons notes that as nearly as he could determine, Victorian railroad managers had no notion of the profitability of their various services. Simmons remarks that the subject, because of its obvious historical implications, warrants closer study. In this work I provide such a closer examination for the case of railroads in the United States, confirming and offering insight into Simmons's conclusions.[6]

In the American context, managers thought that most of their costs were fixed, meaning that costs did not increase much when managers added cars to already existing trains. This belief led to strategies for reducing the passenger deficit by eliminating local and branch line trains, which grossed little revenue. At the same time, managers improved heavy mainline trains, which grossed considerable revenue. Unfortunately such actions failed to improve the profitability of passenger service. I argue that this was because costs behaved differently than management believed. Rather than remaining fixed, costs went up significantly when management added cars to trains. Management's cutting of little-used trains reduced costs while not significantly reducing revenues, but its improving of mainline trains added substantially to costs as well as to gross revenues. In many cases costs rose faster than revenues, causing passenger train profitability to decline and eventually go into the red at the end of the 1920s. Because costs behaved contrary to management beliefs, the passenger deficit increased rather than declined in the later 1930s as management succeeded in carrying much larger passenger volumes.

Another historical view of railroad decline, popularized by Albro Martin in *Enterprise Denied,* holds regulation responsible for the railroad industry's chronic financial problems since about 1910. Martin argues that regulation stripped management of its prerogative to set freight and passenger rates in accordance with changing market conditions. Yielding to pressure from shippers, Congress transferred rate authority to the Interstate Commerce Commission between 1906 and 1910. Subsequently holding down rates in a period of inflation, the ICC caused rail profit margins to wither, discouraging investment in tracks, structures, and rolling stock and driving managerial talent from the industry. Martin blames shortsighted government policy for the decline of the American railroad industry.[7]

Martin's view could explain chronic passenger train unprofitability after the automobile severely cut into its markets. Because of unfair government treatment of the railroads, managements may have invested far less in their viable passenger markets than they would have in a free market environment. Underinvestment would have made passenger service less competitive with the auto. Once the auto began to reduce passenger train demand, regulation also may have prevented managements from adjusting passenger services to new markets by discontinuing money-losing trains or raising fares.

My examination of the passenger train's decline in California supports some of these points but puts a new twist on them. Other points it contradicts. While government policy unfairly favored highways over railroads and hindered management's ability to compete with the auto, I contend that railroad management, rather than government policy, must take the blame for this condition. Transportation users in California, particularly development interests, wanted more and cheaper service than private rail corporations could provide at a profit. This fundamental incompatibility of interests underlay the conflict between the American railroad industry and its users during the Progressive Era. It explains why business interests so enthusiastically promoted both railroad regulation and tax-supported highways, whose bureaucracies thought in terms of service to users rather than profits. Railroad managements bridled at the resulting inequity, but their desired remedy of a return to laissez-faire enthused no other interest group. The only other option for eliminating the inequity was to publicly finance railroads under the control of users. This option may have found wide support but for the vehement opposition of railroad managers. The United States' seemingly irrational policy of favoring highways while regulating railroads thus resulted from the failure of railroad managers to appreciate the social context in which they operated, which was one in which users dominated transportation policy. Railroad management's concession to this reality by running some unprofitable services to benefit more important users proved ineffective.

I also argue that regulation interfered remarkably little in the day-to-day management of passenger service prior to World War II, and that self-destructive practices attributed to regulation came instead from within railroad management and resulted from management's attempts to appease users. The practice of subsidizing money-losing passenger service with freight revenues offers a good example. It is commonly assumed that regulatory bodies compelled railroads to finance money-losing passenger service with freight revenues. To the contrary, I argue that the ICC opposed this practice before and after World War I and prodded the railroads to improve their cost accounting so that they could recognize passenger subsidies when they occurred. The railroad industry fought the ICC every inch of the way on this issue, primarily because it did not want the ICC or shippers to have knowledge of its cost structure, which would have further eroded management's already weak political position. This is one reason why the railroad industry made so little progress in cost accounting.

In general the ICC also welcomed railroad efforts to experiment with passenger fares. It encouraged railroads to raise fares in 1920, and it allowed them to lower fares in the 1930s. As passenger service lost ever larger quantities of money, railroad managements failed to raise fares not because of pressure from the ICC, but because the market would not stand higher fares. In 1936, when the ICC forced the eastern railroads to lower fares against their will, gross revenues subsequently rose substantially, indicating that fares had been too high from the market's perspective. I argue that the cause of the passenger deficit was not a regulatory structure that refused to approve fare increases, but a passenger service that cost too much to operate in comparison to the fares that the public was willing to pay. Management failed in not confronting its high cost structure with strategies and investments oriented to reducing the cost per passenger mile.

I also show that the California Railroad Commission readily permitted railroads to discontinue money-losing passenger trains during the interwar period. In the many instances where California railroads knowingly operated unprofitable passenger service, I argue that they did so out of their sense of social obligation rather than fear of regulatory proceedings.

Finally, I challenge the conspiracy explanation for passenger train decline. Bradford Snell, an often-quoted critic of American transportation policy, charged in the early 1970s that the railroad industry increased its profits by getting rid of many successful passenger trains in the 1930s. It did this, he claimed, by conspiring with the Greyhound Corporation and General Motors to replace profitable trains with General Motors-built buses. This move ultimately led disgusted passengers to abandon inferior buses in favor of autos. The railroad industry benefited from increased freight revenues associated with the construction of more autos, more than compensating for the loss of profitable passenger trains.[8]

In looking at rail and bus passenger practices in California, I examine the development of the largest and most profitable of the Greyhound operating subsidiaries, Pacific Greyhound Lines. After first forming its own bus subsidiary, the Southern Pacific Company actively participated in the formation of Pacific Greyhound Lines, of which it owned a 39 percent interest. I argue that the Southern Pacific and Pacific Greyhound Lines diverted no important passenger markets from rail to bus. On the contrary, Pacific Greyhound fare policy protected important rail markets during the early 1930s. The corporation's astounding profitability during the 1930s came not from the few rail passengers who were diverted to buses, but from bus managers who strove to make it ever more efficient.

In short, I discount three widely held beliefs about the decline of the American passenger train. In their place I offer the following explanation. California's development interests, whose economic and political power eclipsed that of the railroads by 1910, demanded plentiful and cheap intercity transportation. They did so because their prosperity depended on economic growth, which in turn depended on plentiful and cheap transportation, among other things. To achieve their transportation objectives, they resorted to railroad regulation and subsidized construction of transportation infrastructure, including ports, canals, and highways. By 1915 their efforts rendered the private provision of railroad passenger service in California not only unprofitable but increasingly unnecessary. In the new era (after 1910) of subsidized competition, railroad passenger service could survive only if railroad managers developed better passenger service at lower cost. Managers partly succeeded in doing this by eliminating rural passenger train services and by speeding up and improving the comfort of remaining trains. Their successes demonstrated that there was an automobile-era market for fast, comfortable, and low-priced trains linking the larger cities. However, their failures in other areas prevented such trains from developing as they could have. Managers failed to improve their infrastructure to keep up with the dramatic highway improvements that the California state government made. Even with government subsidies to roads, a market existed for improved rail routes in the most important corridors. Managers could have invested in rail improvements themselves, or they could have recognized the sentiment of the state's business interests that transportation infrastructure should be publicly provided and subsidized. In the latter event, they could have attempted to broker deals whereby the rail infrastructure would have been taken over by an arm of the government and improved. They attempted neither strategy, but chose instead to publicly decry subsidies to other forms of transportation, a move that interested no one other than railroad managers. Consequently, the new streamliners of the 1930s ran over rail alignments made obsolete by indirect routes. Managers also failed to price their trains appropriately during the 1920s, which alienated all but business travelers. In the 1930s they tried and partly regained nonbusiness travelers through ultra-low fares, but they lost money on the traffic because their costs were too high. Low cost operation did not figure in their objectives for designing their passenger service, partly because they failed to understand how passenger costs behaved.

I begin this chronicle by examining the conflict between California's railroads and the development interests in the state. In chapter 1 I describe the interrelated development of the Southern Pacific and Santa Fe railroad lines and the development of the state between 1860 and 1910. I show the passenger train's extraordinarily rapid growth, its profitability, its largely local nature, and its importance to the state prior to 1910. I demonstrate that railroad managements performed superbly in modernizing California's transportation system in the decade prior to 1910, but I also show that railroad corporations were disliked by most business and development interests in the state. I examine why this was so and the consequences up to 1920: regulation and tax-supported competition.

Business hostility to the railroads and the not unrelated development of competition rapidly created a nasty environment for the passenger train. In chapter 2 I examine how the railroad managements reacted. I trace how they made decisions, look at their objectives for operating passenger services, and examine how they changed strategy between 1910 and 1920, including the two-year period of federal control of the railroads.

In chapter 3 I continue tracing the evolution of passenger strategy during the prosperous 1920s as passenger demand continued to decline. During this time the Santa Fe decided to quit most of its intrastate business, while the Southern Pacific decided to replace much of its local trains with its own buses.

The Southern Pacific's bus initiatives at the end of the decade set the stage for the 1929 formation of Pacific Greyhound Lines, which became one of the two largest and most profitable bus systems in the United States during the 1930s. In chapter 4 I look at the formation of Pacific Greyhound Lines, its ownership and control, its management methods producing its large profits, and its relations with the Southern Pacific. In this chapter I lay the Snell thesis to rest.

While Pacific Greyhound Lines made large profits during the Depression, neither the Southern Pacific nor the Santa Fe did, despite passenger trends similar to those of the bus company. The railroads failed not for the want of trying bold initiatives, including streamliners, even lower fares, and a new statewide bus system to compete with Pacific Greyhound Lines. In chapter 5 I examine their initiatives and results, and in chapter 6 I evaluate what went wrong. In the evaluation I consider how railroad cost analysis changed since 1910, contributing to the financial difficulties of the 1930s. Finally, in the conclusion I tie the various threads together.

1
Passenger Service and the Seeds of Decline, 1856–1920

At the peak of its influence around 1910, California's railroad system provided few clues to its impending decline. Since the end of the business depression in 1897 railroad traffic had mushroomed throughout the United States, but it grew particularly fast in wealthy and rapidly urbanizing California. During the thirteen-year period, California passenger traffic tripled and freight traffic doubled, challenging rail managers with the enviable problem of finding ways to accommodate growth. Managers met the challenge by employing thousands of workers to rebuild and expand trains, tracks, and terminals, essentially scrapping the primitive system of 1897 and replacing it with a larger and more efficient one. Such efforts, according to the 1914 *Census of Manufacturers,* furnished California with "excellent transportation facilities by land."[1] The state's 8,368 miles of steam and 2,382 miles of electric railroad lines provided a high level of freight and passenger service, attracted heavy traffic, and made money for investors.

Despite such favorable indicators, California's railroads began to decline around 1910. The amount of money that the typical Californian spent on passenger service peaked about 1910 and fell rapidly after 1914. The demand for freight service also slowed after 1910, and profits shrank as well. With a few exceptions, physical improvements under way or planned for the railroad system in 1910 turned out to be the last until recent years. As the historian Fred Matthews observed, California's railroad plant of the late 1940s took shape largely between 1897 and about 1915, a period sometimes referred to as the Harriman Era.[2]

Railroads in other regions of the country also began to decline about the same time. Business historian Albro Martin, one of the few scholars to study the sudden turnaround of railroad fortunes, attributes it to a punitive regulatory regime that ensued from Congress's 1906 passage of the Hepburn Act and 1910 passage of the Mann-Elkin Act. Subsequent shortsighted rate regulation depressed railroad earnings, which in turn shattered investor confidence and dried up investment.[3]

I argue for a more fundamental cause in California: the business community's hostility toward the corporations running the railroads. By 1910 the hostility was evident to those who looked beyond the railroads to their users. California business interests, particularly those associated with land development, showed little appreciation for the accomplishments of railroad managers and increasingly vilified the corporations operating the railroads. By 1910 the business community was winning the battle against the railroads for political control of the state and also was promoting various private and government-supported competitors to railroads. While both punitive regulation and subsidized competition, of which the automobile was but one example, precipitated railroad decline, business displeasure constituted the more fundamental cause.

Business hostility played a large role in shaping the nature of the passenger system of 1910, and it defined the business environment in which railroad managers continued to work. To adapt the passenger train to the automobile age, managers would had to have done a better job of ameliorating such hostility. This chapter sets the foundation for analyzing how well rail managements did their jobs by describing the complementary evolution of the railroad system and the society that it served in California, paying particular attention to the conflict between business and railroad corporations that was a part of that evolution. I argue that the conflict arose from a paradox of laissez-faire America in which privately owned and operated railroads were incompatible with a society that highly valued the unconstrained exploitation of land. Private railroad operation required profits. Unconstrained land exploitation demanded more transportation than railroads could provide at a profit. Railroad managers initially tried to resolve the conflict by subsidizing the strongest development interests, encouraging their further growth, while extracting profits from other regions. This approach worked for a while, but those who were left out turned bitter and eventually formed a coalition powerful enough to topple railroad dominance. Whom the railroad managers chose to benefit, the responses of those less fortunate, and railroad reaction to those responses constituted a dialectic that shaped the development of California and its railroads. It also contained the seeds of railroad decline.

Jack Simmons suggests that a similar dialectic may have partly shaped the evolution of English railways, but its intensity was greater in the United States, where land exploiters played a much larger role in business and national life.[4] Edmund Morgan, Merritt Roe Smith, and Thomas C.

Cochran, among other prominent American historians, comment on the rise and importance of land speculation during the colonial and early national periods.[5] The urban historian Sam Bass Warner, Jr., and Cochran both document how the courts between the 1790s and the 1830s gradually sanctified the private right to exploit land, even if public purposes were harmed by so doing. Cochran states further, "Throughout our history, 'real estate' has been the biggest business."[6] He also notes that the American business in western lands had no European counterpart, and that the frontier West was a region of business enterprise where some of the highest profits came from town promotion. Robert R. Dykstra's excellent case study of Kansas cattle towns underscores this point.[7]

Collectively, these historians suggest that a potent economic and political force centered on land speculation and development helped mold the history of the United States. Some contemporary observers call this force the growth machine.[8] Its power was the greatest in those areas with the greatest potential for growth. During the time of westward expansion desirable areas of the frontier provided such opportunity. The greatest opportunity lay in California.

The unfolding of conflict between California's growth machines and pioneer railroads began in the 1860s with the construction of the first transcontinental railroad. At the end of the 1850s Theodore Judah, the chief engineer of a short line railroad that extended from Sacramento, obtained financial backing from four Sacramento merchants to survey a railroad route across the Sierra Nevada. He succeeded in finding a favorable route, and to arouse interest in building it, he and the merchants, who later became known as the Big Four or the Associates, incorporated the Central Pacific Railroad in 1861. They then persuaded Congress to designate the Central Pacific as the western half of the proposed Pacific Railroad that would terminate in Sacramento. With the benefit of large federal subsidies and land grants, they subsequently built the Central Pacific and connected it with the Union Pacific and the eastern rail network in 1869.[9]

When the Associates incorporated the Central Pacific, California contained but 380,000 people and few cities. San Francisco (map 1.1) was the largest and grew because it commanded the most convenient location for transhipping goods between oceangoing sailing ships and river steamers bound for interior mining activity. Around the city's docks sprang up warehouses, wholesale trading houses, and financial, legal, and labor institutions. These activities supported a population of 57,000 people in 1860. The state contained only a few other cities of significance. Sacramento's state government and trading activities supported 13,800 inhabitants. Be-

1.1 California rail lines, ca. 1880

tween 3,500 and 4,500 people resided in Los Angeles and Stockton, while Oakland, San Diego, and Visalia each contained fewer than 1,500 people.[10]

Most California commercial groups initially opposed the Central Pacific Railroad from fear that it would undermine their standing in relation to interests in Sacramento. Having the most to lose, established San Francisco interests voiced their objections the loudest, and the Associates attempted to placate them. The Pacific Railroad Acts of 1862 and 1864 redesignated San Francisco as the western terminal of the railroad, and through construction and the purchase of short lines, the Associates extended tracks to Oakland and San Francisco by 1869. They persuaded Oakland to grant the railroad monopoly rights for the development of port facilities, while San Francisco and the state granted the railroad the choicest sites for terminal and port facilities in that city. By the early 1870s the Associates monopolized all rail and water transportation in the Bay Area, but through that decade they generally acted in the interests of San Francisco merchants. In 1873 they relocated the railroad headquarters to San Francisco. Most importantly, they established a system of freight tariffs that discriminated in favor of San Francisco and against most other points in California.[11]

Geographic rate discrimination was common at the time and arose from the way that railroad managers viewed the economics of railroading.[12] To managers, railroads were huge, expensive machines that incurred vast capital and labor charges whether or not they carried any traffic. Debt interest, stock dividends, the salaries of managers, and the wages of maintenance forces in shops and on the line were thought to go on day after day during times of slack or heavy traffic. Managers viewed such supposedly constant expenses as overhead, which from the 1850s into the 1930s they figured at about 75 percent of their total annual expenses.[13]

Because managers believed that most of their expenses came from overhead and not from the operation of trains, they set rates regardless of the distance that the traffic moved. They faced only three constraints. First, rates had to at least cover the variable costs of moving the traffic. As the business historian Alfred D. Chandler observed, "Any rate that covered more than the variable costs of transporting a shipment brought the road extra income."[14] Second, total revenues from all rates had to cover all variable and overhead costs and provide a profit; otherwise, the railroad could not stay in business. This meant that if managers discounted rates for shippers in one geographic area to the point that they barely covered operating costs, shippers in most other areas had to pay much higher rates. Third, no rate could be so high as to stop the flow of traffic or hinder the prosperity of the regions that the railroad served.[15]

Holding such views, Central Pacific managers lowered rates for San Francisco interests in the early 1870s to appease hostile San Francisco merchants as well as to meet the competition provided by sailing ships from the eastern seaboard. Once they did so, however, they resisted pressure from other geographic areas to similarly lower rates. If the managers yielded to all interests for lower rates, the heavy overhead burden would go unpaid, taking the railroad into bankruptcy court.[16]

By the early 1870s these practices resulted in freight rates that had two components between eastern and California points. The first component was a relatively low transcontinental rate between eastern points to San Francisco. The remainder of the move from San Francisco to other places in California was covered by a much higher local rate, which was moderated to some extent where there was coastal or river steamer competition. Local traffic within California also moved at the high rates.[17]

During the 1870s the discriminatory rate structure benefited San Francisco wholesale houses and their jobbers, who ordered goods from eastern manufacturers for resale to retail outlets in other towns in the West. As the rails of the Central Pacific and the affiliated Southern Pacific [18] spread north and south from San Francisco, the trade area of San Francisco jobbers also spread. In most other California regions, development interests anticipated prosperity from the railroad, but the actual arrival of the railroad generally left them disappointed. Except for San Francisco, rates remained too high for dramatic growth.[19]

The 1876 arrival of the Southern Pacific in Los Angeles illustrates this point. After completing the Central Pacific in 1869, the Associates began extending mainlines north into Oregon and south to Texas and New Orleans. The mere extension of Central Pacific and Southern Pacific rails [20] south through the San Joaquin Valley set off a land boom in Los Angeles in 1873 and 1874. The boom quickly collapsed, but promoters expected that the actual arrival of the tracks in Los Angeles would precipitate a new boom.[21]

They were disappointed. The Associates announced that rather than detouring the mainline through Los Angeles, they would serve the town with a branch line. Los Angeles interests wanted the mainline so badly that the city voted a large subsidy for the Associates to change their mind. However, no great commercial boom ensued after the eagerly anticipated mainline reached the city, and disappointment quickly turned to bitterness. Town boosters resented the railroad's rate structure that discriminated in favor of San Francisco, making Los Angeles merchants more subservient to wholesale houses located in San Francisco.[22]

The passage of the mainline through the San Joaquin Valley had the same disappointing results. About five years before the railroad arrived in 1871, extensive wheat farming began replacing cattle production in the valley. Wagons carried the grain to tidewater at Stockton, from which sailing ships transported it to world markets. The arrival of the railroad quickly replaced wagon movement to Stockton, but it failed to replace sailing ships taking the grain to the eastern United States and to other parts of the world. Lower freight rates compared to those for wagons hastened the expansion and intensification of wheat farming, which fostered population growth. However, the rate of growth between 1870 and 1880 actually was less than that between 1860 and 1870, before the railroad arrived. Some new towns formed along the line of the railroad, Fresno being the most important, but the pre-existing town of Visalia, which was bypassed by the railroad, also continued to grow. Overall, the coming of the railroad in 1871 intensified trends already under way but brought no economic revolution to the San Joaquin Valley. Freight rates remained too high.[23]

Although San Francisco's growth rate fell off compared to the 1860s, when the city commanded water transportation in the state, no other California region came close to matching San Francisco's absolute growth of 127,000 people during the 1870s.[24] San Francisco's good fortune angered development interests in other parts of the state because they believed that the city grew at their expense through rate discrimination. The respected Berkeley economist Stuart Daggett reported that most communities in California believed railroads discriminated against them and therefore sought political and economic redress. He also observed that each town sought to gain advantage over other towns in terms of railroad service and rates, concluding that "city ambitions are limitless, and impossible to satisfy."[25] Research by the California historian Ward McAfee supports this position. McAfee noted that entire communities, and not particular economic interests within the communities, fought the Southern Pacific.[26] In his analysis of the evolution of California's business institutions, the historian Mansel Blackford viewed hostility toward the railroads as a clash of emerging business interests with established railroads, a consequence of geographic rate discrimination.[27]

Disaffected town boosters adopted two strategies for redressing their grievances. They tried to regulate the railroad, and they promoted competition. The latter bore the tastiest fruit.

Regulation was tried early but failed dismally. Before 1876 more groups opposed regulation than favored it. The Associates and San Francisco interests opposed regulation because they benefited from the rate structure as it then existed. Communities without railroad service (most notably Los Angeles) also opposed regulation because they feared that it would cripple railroad expansion. However, as more communities received rail service and were disappointed in the lack of subsequent economic growth, the balance swung in the other direction. After 1876 Los Angeles led the pro-regulation camp, and a state constitutional convention was called in 1878. The convention created a three-person elected railroad commission to regulate rates. Anti-railroad delegates to the convention, led by those from Los Angeles, reasoned that an elected commission would circumvent the corrupt state legislature, whose members appeared to be routinely manipulated by the railroad. As it turned out, during the next twenty years the elected commission did nothing to harm Southern Pacific's interests.[28]

Competition appeared more slowly but eventually wrought the desired results. In 1885 the Atchison, Topeka & Santa Fe Railroad opened a direct route between Kansas City and both Los Angeles and San Diego. In 1887 it opened an extension from Kansas City to Chicago. Almost at once the San

Francisco-based rate structure of the Southern Pacific toppled south of the Tehachapi Mountains, which separated Los Angeles from the San Joaquin Valley. Los Angeles interests now enjoyed low rates and fast service directly to Chicago, and Chicago jobbers displaced San Francisco jobbers in the southern California counties. A rate war also broke out between the Southern Pacific and the Santa Fe, which drove down transcontinental passenger rates to absurdly low levels. In their battle to capture the market, each railroad outdid the other in hiring artists and writers to romanticize the region's ideal climate and dramatic beauty.[29]

The competitive war between the Southern Pacific and the Santa Fe touched off the population and commercial boom that Los Angeles promoters long had awaited. The perceptive California historian Carey McWilliams called this the Pullman car migration, the first of many population explosions in southern California. Not only did tourists flock to the region, but wealthy professional families began to relocate there from small towns in the Northeast. McWilliams reported that in 1887 the Southern Pacific transported 120,000 people to Los Angeles, while the Santa Fe operated four passenger trains a day into Los Angeles from the East. Town promoters took advantage of the influx by laying out sixty new towns in southern California between 1887 and 1889. Most of the town sites quickly were abandoned, but a few attracted substantial numbers of the new migrants and grew.[30]

Most developers in southern California and the rest of California learned the lesson of 1887–88 well. Outside of San Francisco, a region served by only one railroad prospered little more than a region served by no railroad at all. Prosperity required railroad competition and lower rates. Henceforth development interests outside of San Francisco, led by those in Los Angeles, worked to undermine the political dominance of the Southern Pacific in California as they also sought to bring more railroad competition to the state.

The Los Angeles Chamber of Commerce led in this fight. Even before the boom of 1887–88 several of the city's leaders foresaw the unlimited drawing power of Los Angeles's ideal climate. However, they also realized that in almost every other respect nature had endowed their hated competitor to the north with far better assets necessary for growth. San Francisco possessed one of the world's finest natural harbors, a vast, rich hinterland drained in part by navigable rivers that funneled into the harbor, plenty of water, and a national railroad system that focused on the city. In contrast, Los Angeles had a sparse hinterland, no navigable rivers, no harbor, little water, no obvious source of power, and before the arrival of the Santa Fe, inadequate rail facilities with rates that were far too high.

To compensate, the city's developers organized the Los Angeles Chamber of Commerce in 1888 under the leadership of Los Angeles *Times* owner Harrison Gray Otis. This group of remarkable, if reactionary, men intended to coerce the powers of government into providing their region with endowments that nature so thoughtlessly had neglected, while ensuring that labor costs remained far below those in northern California. In so doing, they intended to systematically remove obstacles to development. In their minds, the Central Pacific/Southern Pacific constituted one of the biggest constraints to their freewheeling desires. They intended that in the future they, and not private railroad corporations, would dictate major policy on infrastructure affecting their region.

In 1891 the chamber engaged the Associates in a bitter battle, from which it emerged victorious six years later. Both groups lobbied the United States Congress to finance the construction of a large, artificial harbor to serve Los Angeles, but they differed on the issue of access. The Associates wanted the new harbor in Santa Monica, where the Southern Pacific controlled all access. The chamber wanted it in San Pedro. Although the Southern Pacific served San Pedro, interests affiliated with the chamber also owned terminal facilities there, together with a local railroad running to downtown Los Angeles, the Los Angeles Terminal Railroad. The chamber knew that a third transcontinental railroad might be built into Los Angeles from a connection with the Union Pacific at Salt Lake City. It hoped to encourage such construction by offering the Terminal Railroad and its San Pedro facilities to the railroad promoters. If Congress designated San Pedro as the new harbor site, the chamber's enticement had tremendous value.[31]

The chamber won this critical fight. In 1897 Congress designated San Pedro as the new harbor, which the city of Los Angeles then annexed. The congressional decision not only prevented the Southern Pacific from monopolizing harbor access, but it also stimulated construction of the San Pedro, Los Angeles & Salt Lake, which absorbed the Terminal Railroad and completed its line between its namesake cities in 1905.[32]

Overall, the strategy of the Los Angeles Chamber of Commerce proved remarkably successful. By 1910 vast public works that it had conceived in the 1890s were completed, and others were under way. Those completed included the nation's most ambitious privately and publicly built hydroelectric system, which transmitted power over hundreds of miles at high voltages. They included the construction of a public aqueduct bringing water three hundred miles from the Owens Valley. They included the private construction of street railways as well as a vast system of local interurban electric railways that interlaced the inhabitable parts of Los Angeles, Orange, Riverside, and San Bernardino counties with more than one thousand miles of track. They included the marshaling of federal and state governments to build the world's largest artificial harbor, and one of the busiest.[33] These facilities supported the beginnings of one of the largest migrations in the history of the United States. By 1910 more than 500,000 people lived in Los Angeles County, and migrants continued to flood in. As Carey McWilliams remarked, Los Angeles did not just grow; rather, the Los Angeles Chamber, and particularly Otis, conjured the metropolis into existence. They did so with the benefit of subsidized infrastructure, both public and private. Taxpayers and railroad shippers in other parts of the state and country provided the subsidies; the area's developers reaped the rewards.[34]

The beneficent effects that the Santa Fe had for the developers of Los Angeles, and the muscle of the Los Angeles Chamber of Commerce, attracted attention in other parts of the state. Commercial interests in San Francisco reacted most strongly and in a way that greatly enhanced the state's further railroad development. From the end of the 1870s the freight rate favoritism that the Southern Pacific gave San Francisco gradually eroded under competitive pressure from the Santa Fe and increasing political pressure from other communities in California. By 1890 the Southern Pacific granted many California towns terminal status, meaning that the railroad would ship eastern goods to the towns so designated at relatively low rates. This condition applied not only to points in southern California served by the Santa Fe, but to points monopolized by the Southern Pacific, such as Fresno. Because high local freight rates still prevailed, the lower rates to eastern points from smaller California towns weakened the power of San Francisco wholesale houses. By the late 1880s many towns could do business more cheaply with houses in Chicago, who began muscling out San Francisco jobbers. San Francisco merchants turned their anger on the hapless Southern Pacific.[35]

To regain their position, San Francisco merchants organized the California Board of Trade in 1890. The board had two objectives. One was to operate clipper ships to New York at rates much lower than those charged by the Southern Pacific-influenced steamship lines. The idea was to force transcontinental rail rates to San Francisco down to a level much lower than to any other point in the West. The second objective was to build a railroad from San Francisco through the San Joaquin Valley to a connection with the Santa Fe at Mojave. This line would compete with the Southern Pacific, forcing down local rates. With ultra-low transcontinental rates to San Francisco, and with low local rail rates from San Francisco to towns such as Fresno, San Francisco wholesale merchants hoped to protect their territory from Chicago jobbers.

The board quickly realized its first objective, but for several years it could not obtain sufficient backing for the more ambitious task of building a railroad. San Francisco's merchant community would not provide the necessary funds. Little progress was made until communities in the San Joaquin Valley began looking to Los Angeles for a direct railroad connection. In 1893 the newly formed Kings County in the southern San Joaquin Valley petitioned the Los Angeles Chamber of Commerce to sponsor a new, direct railroad over Tejon Pass into the San Joaquin Valley. Although the valley's southernmost town of Bakersfield was no further than ninety-nine miles from downtown Los Angeles, two formidable mountain ranges stood between the two cities. Even worse, because serving Los Angeles had been only an afterthought when the Southern Pacific built its mainline in 1876, the rail route between Los Angeles and Bakersfield was 170 miles long, and the fastest passenger train required more than seven hours to make the trip. Freight trains took more than sixteen hours. Understandably, Kings County not only wanted a new railroad to drive down rates, but a direct railroad to bring it closer to the fabulous new riches of Los Angeles. Other valley points also looked to Los Angeles rather than to San Francisco for competing rail service.[36]

To lessen valley pressure for a Los Angeles rail connection, real estate interests in San Francisco, under the direction of sugar magnate Claus Spreckles, took control of the Board of Trade in 1895 and provided the financial support to build the railroad. They evidently hoped that a Santa Fe connection to San Francisco would not only stop valley interests from agitating for a direct rail line to Los Angeles, but would provide the same development impetus to San Francisco that it had to Los Angeles. Construction began almost immediately on the San Francisco & San Joaquin Railroad, and in 1897 the company opened service between Stockton and Bakersfield. In 1898 the San Francisco interests sold the line to the Santa Fe, which completed the extension between Stockton and San Francisco via a ferry connection from Richmond. The Santa Fe also obtained permission to use Southern Pacific tracks between Bakersfield and its own system at Mojave. The first Santa Fe train ran through the San Joaquin Valley to San Francisco in 1900 (map 1.2).[37]

The Santa Fe ended up with an extremely circuitous 284-mile connection between Los Angeles and Bakersfield via Barstow. Despite this liability, the Santa Fe extension to San Francisco brought a new competitive order to central California whose result could not have differed more from what the California Board of Trade intended. The extension temporarily, at least, lowered local valley rates, but more importantly it resulted in permanently lower rates between valley points and both Los Angeles and Chicago.[38]

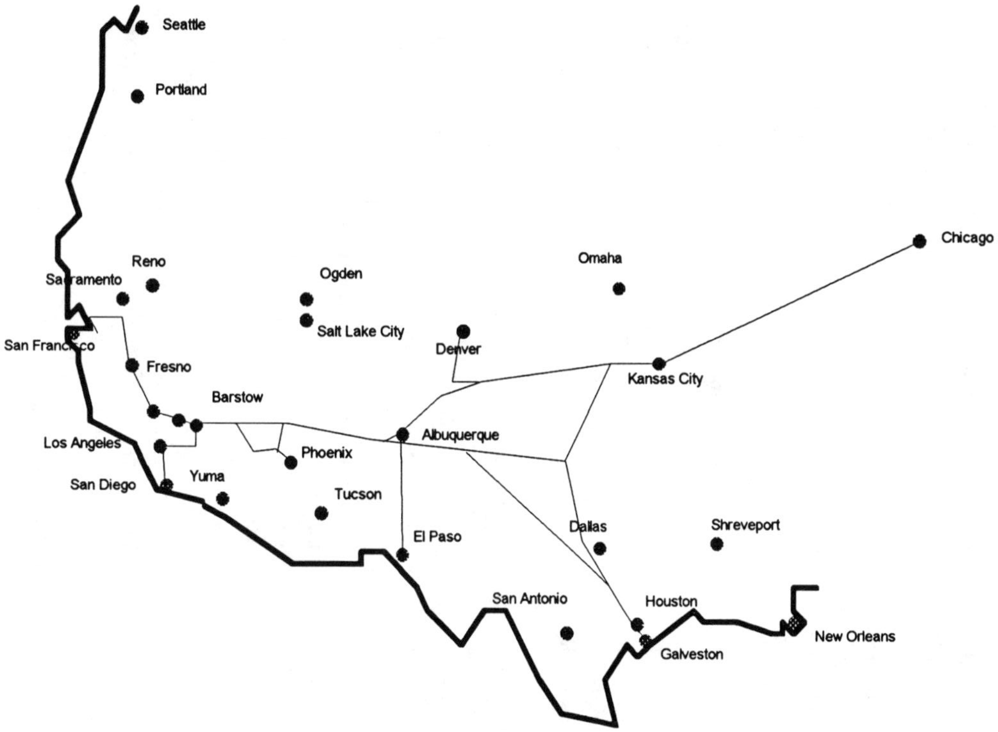

1.2 Mainlines of the Atchison, Topeka & Santa Fe, ca. 1915.

The lower rates quickly changed the economy of the San Joaquin Valley. While the valley's first large-scale agriculture, extensive wheat farming, required only local railroads to take grain to tidewater, the far more profitable but perishable products of fruit farming required the speed of transcontinental rail service. In addition, they necessitated the adoption of refrigerator cars and interrail competition to bring down rates. Not until the late 1890s had all of these requirements fallen into place. Thereafter, fruit and nut farming rapidly displaced wheat and at the same time increased wealth and urbanization. This was because the capital and labor intensiveness of the new mode of agriculture demanded new financial, labor, legal, and marketing institutions. It also required ancillary packing and canning industries. These institutions and industries located in cities, not only in the major metropolises of San Francisco and Los Angeles, but in the valley. Between 1897 and 1910 the valley experienced a wave of new town formations, accompanied by an almost doubling of its population.[39]

Out of the dialectic between railroad entrepreneurs and development interests in California there emerged by 1910 a populous, increasingly complex, and wealthy society. Some 2.4 million people lived in the state, and although agriculture, particularly the growing of fruit and vegetables, grossed more than any other state industry, the 1910 U.S. Census classified only 36 percent of the state's residents as rural. Only 20 percent of employed persons in the state worked in agricultural activities. Most other Californians lived in cities, suburbs, and smaller towns, where they worked in a variety of trades. Manufacturing employed 27 percent of the work force and was growing rapidly, facilitated in part by the increasing availability of cheap electrical power. Between 1900 and 1910 the value of manufactured products doubled in California, and in the next four years it grew almost as much again. Trade, personal services, the professions, and government accounted for another 35 percent of California's work force in 1914; taking its population into consideration, California had about 50 percent more people employed in these occupations as did the nation as a whole. Rail transportation employed another 9 percent of the work force, a representation about 40 percent heavier than for the nation as a whole. Californians also earned more than most Americans. In 1929, the first year for which the census published comparative figures, the average Californian earned $995, which was 41 percent more than the average American and higher than citizens in all but three eastern states.[40]

California's expanding economy demanded increasingly large amounts of transportation, particularly after the end of the national business depression in 1897. Measured as a passenger riding one mile in nonsuburban service, Southern Pacific passenger traffic tripled between 1899 and

1910, while freight traffic almost doubled. The remarkable passenger traffic growth derived in equal proportions from local and through passengers, as evidenced by the fact that the average trip length of Southern Pacific non-commuter passengers did not vary much from seventy-five miles between 1899 and 1914.[41]

Such passenger and freight traffic growth reflected the increasing complexity of California's internal economy as well as its integration into that of the nation. It also reflected the relative wealth of Californians, who spent more on rail travel than most Americans. In 1911, the first year for which California figures are available, Californians spent more than $9.40 per capita on just Southern Pacific and Santa Fe intercity railroad trains, compared to the national average of $7.02 spent on all intercity trains.[42]

To better manage their sprawling transportation enterprises, the remaining Associates reorganized them in the early 1890s into the new Southern Pacific Company. This company directly operated all of its lines between Portland, Ogden, and El Paso, which it called its Pacific System. Included in the Pacific System was the original Central Pacific Railroad, which remained as a separate company that was leased to the Southern Pacific Company and directly operated by it. In addition, the Southern Pacific Company held subsidiary railroads in Texas and Louisiana, as well as steamship lines operating along the West Coast, from San Francisco and Los Angeles to the Orient, and from Galveston and New Orleans to New York. Overall, it owned 9,441 miles of track and was the largest transportation enterprise in the world.

As impressive as it was, by about 1900 its managers realized that the Southern Pacific needed modernization. The business historian Maury Klein quotes Southern Pacific chief engineer William Hood observing in 1901 that he had a good nineteenth-century railroad adequate to the traffic of the time.[43] However, its facilities could not accommodate growth. During the last few years of the nineteenth century, the most capable and the last survivor of the Associates, Collis P. Huntington, began the herculean task of improving the facilities, but his unexpected death in August 1900 cut the program short. The financier and owner of the Union Pacific, Edward H. Harriman, then bought control of the Southern Pacific Company and combined it with his Union Pacific. Harriman continued the modernization program with a vengeance. Under him, Southern Pacific management upgraded mainlines, extended branch lines and electrified some of them, purchased additional local electric railways, added signal systems, and purchased more powerful new locomotives and new steel rolling stock. It also greatly expanded the volume of service. By the end of their reign in 1912, the Harriman interests had invested $247 million in physical improvements to properties owned by the Southern Pacific Company. This amount was more than half as much as the $450 million that had been invested to build and upgrade the 9,441-mile system to 1900 (map 1.3).[44]

Harriman directed a large part of the improvements toward handling local traffic. In writing on the evolving complexity of California's economy and business institutions between 1890 and 1920, Mansel Blackford correctly stresses the importance of the eastern market and the role railroads played in opening it.[45] Over time, however, the swelling local market contributed as much if not more to the emerging business interests of the state. Because the flood of wealthy tourists and migrants demanded luxury hotels, restaurants, and above all else, homes, they spurred the development of domestic manufactures, financial and legal institutions, and an increasingly interdependent society. Such intense local interactions could not have occurred without the concurrent development of the state's rail routes oriented to local travel. As new towns appeared in the San Joaquin Valley after 1897, for example, both the Southern Pacific and the Santa Fe extended branch lines and, more importantly, greatly expanded the volume of local trains using these lines (map 1.4). Vast steam and electric suburban and interurban train lines germinated and interlaced both the Los Angeles and the San Francisco areas during this period. In 1910 Harriman bought control of the last of several separate interurban companies in Los Angeles and reorganized them into the thousand-mile Pacific Electric Railway, the largest suburban electric system in the world. He also improved and electrified his suburban lines in the San Francisco East Bay area, improved and electrified longer distance local train services centered on Portland, and bought smaller electric interurban and streetcar companies in California.

At the height of the passenger era between 1910 and 1915 a wide variety of passenger trains served California, but the overwhelming majority of them served local passengers. While numerous luxury limited trains catered to transcontinental and transcoastal travel demands, for every such train about fifty steam locals shuttled between the smaller towns of the state. At the maximum extent of passenger service, the Southern Pacific lines between Portland and El Paso operated about 20 million train miles per year in passenger service. Local trains, mostly operating in California, accounted for 50 percent of these, while suburban trains in the San Francisco Bay area accounted for another 19 percent. Mainline limited trains accounted for only 31 percent of the service.[46] These figures do not reflect passenger trains using the Pacific Electric or other local subsidiaries of the Southern Pacific.

The Santa Fe also operated more local than through train service in California. In 1910 the company scheduled 3.1 million passenger train

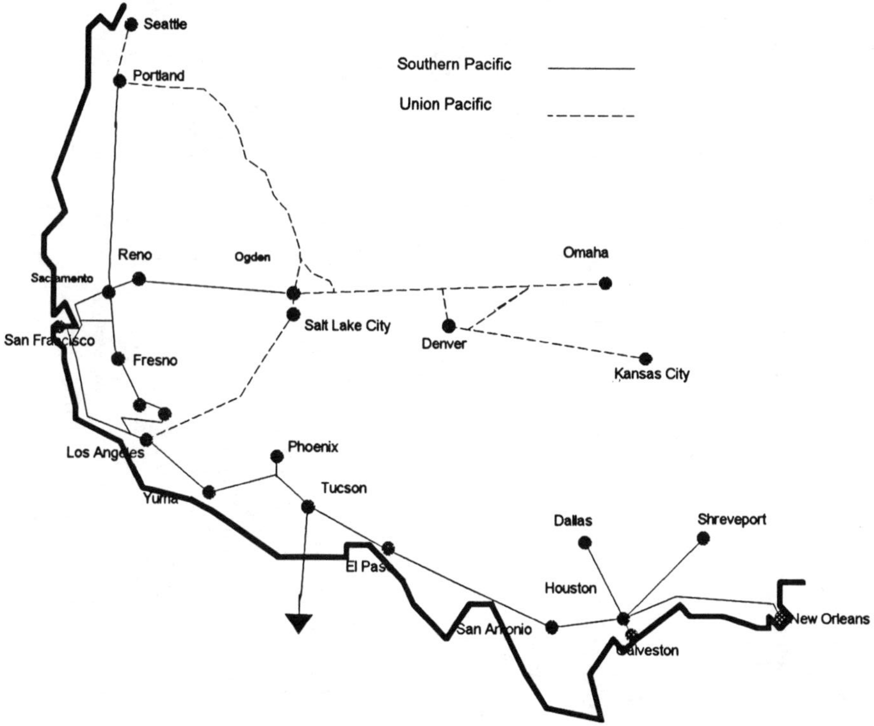

1.3   Mainlines of the Southern Pacific and the Union Pacific, ca. 1915.

1.4   Southern Pacific and Santa Fe lines in California, ca. 1915

miles in California, 71 percent of which operated for intrastate passengers. Service expanded rapidly, reaching its peak of 4.9 million train miles in 1916. Of this amount, 68 percent operated for the benefit of intrastate passengers.[47]

Figure 1.1 shows a schematic of local and through Southern Pacific passenger train services in the San Joaquin Valley in 1915. The schematic illustrates the remarkable extent to which passenger service developed in the valley in a very short period of time.[48] Passenger train density on some of the secondary lines actually exceeded that on the north-south mainline, and moreover, more passengers used the local trains. The Exeter *Sun* reported in 1944, for example, that at the peak of the passenger train era more passengers rode the east side line through Porterville and Exeter than the mainline via Tulare.[49]

Passengers had good reason to ride these trains; although they were

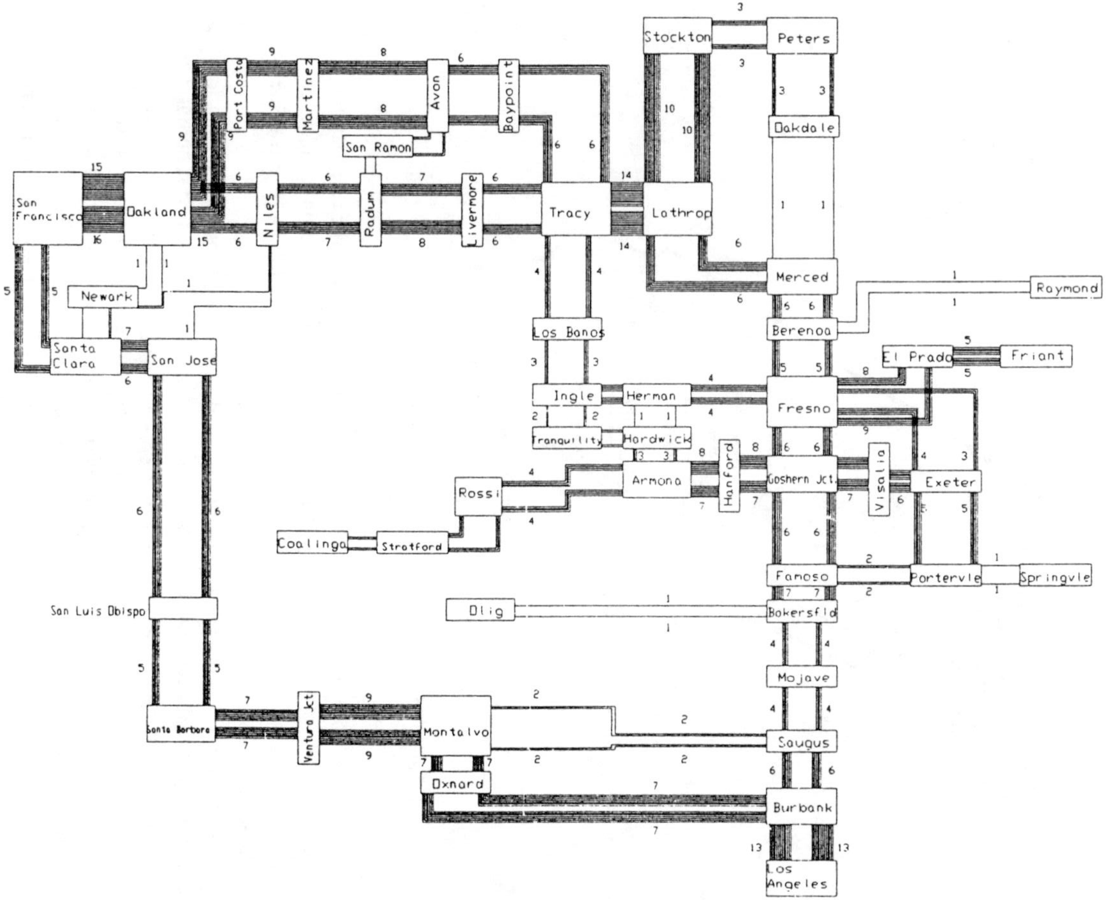

1.1   Southern Pacific passenger train services in central California, ca. 1915. Source: SFC, exhibit 626

slow, averaging 20 to 25 miles an hour, they offered relatively comprehensive service.[50] An examination of employee timetables from the period shows relatively good spacing of the local and through steam and electric trains and good scheduled connections between intersecting trains at Goshen Junction and at Exeter. From many of the towns in the San Joaquin Valley a person could travel to many other towns, conduct business or visit, and return the same day.

Many transportation commentators believe that local trains always lost money. This was not so in California, where, as Stuart Daggett notes, the Southern Pacific's enviable earning power around the turn of the century derived from its heavy local California traffic.[51] Daggett referred primarily to freight, but evidence suggests that local passengers also contributed to company coffers. In the appendix, I estimate the revenues and the fully allocated costs for Southern Pacific steam through trains and steam locals in 1911. These calculations show that on average through trains netted about $1.29 per train mile, while local trains netted about $0.79. Because through trains operated 6 million miles of service and local trains 9.7 million miles of service, both types of trains each contributed about $8 million in net revenue in 1911.

Despite dramatic improvements to the rail system between 1897 and 1910, regions of the state monopolized by the Southern Pacific stagnated in comparison to those with rail competition. The difference in the development history of the Sacramento region compared to those of Los Angeles, San Francisco, and the San Joaquin Valley underscores this point, as shown in figure 1.2. The Sacramento area possessed perhaps the most fertile combination of soil, water, and climate in the state, and it also received the first rail service. Yet the Southern Pacific monopolized transportation to the region, and the Sacramento region's growth lagged behind that of the other parts of the state. The lesson was clear. To grow, an area needed cheap transportation. The more transportation the area got, and the cheaper the transportation was, the faster the area would grow. It can be inferred that this was the reason that the state's development and business interests continued their attacks on the Southern Pacific and fostered the development of alternative and redundant forms of transportation.

Regulation and competition continued to be the weapons with which development and business interests fought the railroad corporations. The regulatory movement gained considerable strength when San Francisco interests finally realized that the Southern Pacific could no longer discriminate in their favor. Between 1897 and 1910 they and most other major interest groups in the state decided that railroad political influence had to end.[52] These sentiments culminated in the 1910 elections, when Hiram Johnson

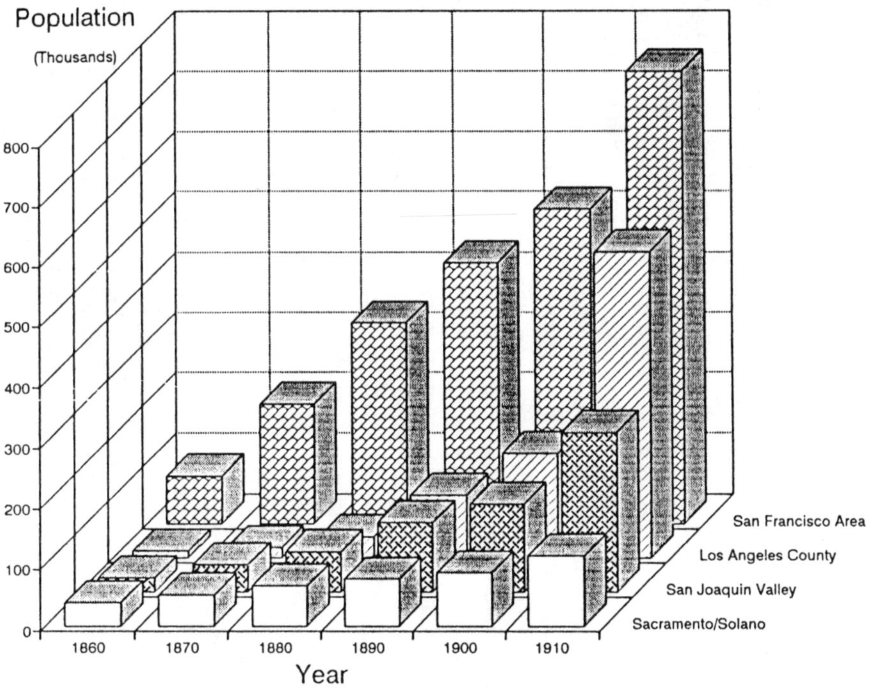

1.2 Population growth in California regions, 1860–1910

campaigned for California's governorship on just one substantive issue—kick Southern Pacific out of politics. To flaunt his independence from the railroad, the San Francisco lawyer shunned the customary campaign train in favor of a bright red Locomobile, which his son navigated over California's rutted dirt roads. Ringing a large cowbell as he entered each town, Johnson called the faithful to his side to harangue them about the evils of railroad influence in the state. If elected along with an anti-railroad and insurgent legislature, he promised that he would sponsor the creation of a people's railroad commission that would tame the octopus, as the railroad was popularly known. Although another anti-railroad Republican candidate out-polled him in San Francisco, Johnson's margin in southern California was so large that he carried the primary. Capitalizing on strong anti-railroad sentiment from almost all organized business groups in the northern and southern parts of the state, Johnson went on to win the election. On his coattails rode an insurgent-majority legislature. In 1911 they created a new, strong railroad commission, and beginning that year the Southern Pacific ceased its overt political activities.[53]

Under Johnson's general leadership, members from the new legislature and the old railroad commission drafted constitutional amendments and legislation defining a powerful new railroad commission. Perhaps viewing the political tide as irreversible, the Southern Pacific surprisingly submitted to these changes without a fight.[54] In 1911 the legislature submitted to the voters three constitutional amendments that transformed the California Railroad Commission into a five-member, governor-appointed body. Simultaneously, the commission organized itself into departments to discharge its enlarged responsibilities for rates, legal matters, administrative affairs, statistics and accounting, service, and stocks and bonds. The legislature also adopted the Stetson-Eshleman Bill, granting the commission maximum powers authorized under the amended constitution. The new California Railroad Commission took office in March 1912.[55]

During the same period coalitions of national shippers gained control of the Interstate Commerce Commission with the passage of the Hepburn Act of 1906 and the Mann-Elkins Act of 1910. The shippers used their power to freeze freight and passenger rates during a period of price inflation. These measures weakened the earning power of the nation's railroads and crippled their ability to raise capital.[56]

In California the new railroad commission exacerbated this condition. While it had jurisdiction only over intra-California rates, these provided California railroads with much of their profits. This was particularly so for the Southern Pacific, because of its favorable position in the large intra-California market. After the Santa Fe entered California, the importance of local earnings fell, but at the end of the 1890s they still elevated Southern Pacific's earnings per mile of track considerably above those of all other western railroads.[57]

The new railroad commission set about ending geographic rate discrimination in California, which meant generally reducing intra-California rates.[58] It also denied railroad-requested rate increases. After Southern Pacific rebuilt and electrified its Oakland, Alameda, and Berkeley suburban lines in 1911–12, for example, it discovered that the services lost money and petitioned the railroad commission for rate increases. In spite of need, the commission denied the petition.[59]

After interests opposed to railroad corporation policies breached the railroads' political defenses, the railroads proved politically powerless to defend themselves from unreasonable attacks. Refusing to even consider the railroad viewpoint on the matter, the 1911 legislature required California's railroads to add an extra brakeman to trains. The stated purpose was to improve railroad safety, but the addition had no effect on safety and it increased operating costs.[60] In 1913–14, after having been denied local rate increases by the California Railroad Commission, Southern Pacific sought to implement more efficient work rules on its newly electrified East Bay suburban train operation to take advantage of the safer and more efficient technology. When labor refused the company's initiative, the matter was referred to arbitration, pursuant to new federal legislation. The local arbitration panel ruled against the railroad, and as a consequence, the company could not operate the new service profitably.[61] These actions compounded the effects of the Interstate Commerce Commission's refusal to increase railroad freight rates in the inflationary period prior to World War I.

Another serious government attack started in December 1912 when the U.S. Supreme Court upheld a ruling by the Justice Department that the combined Union Pacific/Southern Pacific violated anti-trust statutes. The court ordered Union Pacific to divest itself of all Southern Pacific stock, a ruling that deprived the Southern Pacific of easy access to capital. Even more damaging, the Union Pacific unmerger case led into the Central Pacific unmerger case. On 11 February 1914 the Justice Department brought suit against the Southern Pacific and Central Pacific, charging that the combination of the two systems constituted restraint of trade of the Sherman Anti-Trust Act. Southern Pacific bitterly fought this case but did not win until 1923. The ten-year fight deeply scarred the company, as Southern Pacific historian Don Hofsommer documents.[62]

Development interests also fostered transportation competition. Most of the electric interurban railways that spread rapidly between 1897 and 1914 were promoted by local interests.[63] Coastal water transportation also made a dramatic comeback during this era, facilitated by growing transportation demand, improved steamship technology, and large public expenditures in harbor improvements. Prior to 1900 the Southern Pacific-controlled Pacific Coast Steamship Company monopolized service between Seattle, San Francisco, Los Angeles, and San Diego. Although it continued to expand service on these routes during the first decade of this century, by 1912 it had to fight with five competitors for the market. By 1914 the competitors increased to eleven. At that time the fastest steamers beat Southern Pacific passenger trains between San Francisco and Portland and took a large part of the passenger market. In the Los Angeles to San Francisco market the fast *Harvard* and *Yale*, with their nineteen-hour overnight schedules, could not match the fastest train schedules of fourteen hours, but their very much lower fares combined with luxurious accommodations attracted several hundred passengers per night, about as many as were carried by rail.[64] In 1912 the United States government completed the Panama Canal, and almost immediately this vast public works project increased the competitiveness of transcontinental steamship service. Congress prohibited railroad-owned steamship lines from using the canal. In his history of the Union Pacific, the business historian Maury Klein vividly portrays how quickly and deeply the canal cut into transcontinental rail traffic, while further lowering rates. By 1921 the overwhelming majority of freight leaving Los Angeles and San Francisco went by water.[65] As late as 1927 coastal steamers carried 60 percent of the freight moving between California and Oregon.[66]

Other public works projects sponsored by California development interests increased competition to rail services even more. Since the 1890s the good roads movement attracted zealous adherents in California, who in the latter part of that decade persuaded the state legislature to adopt a master plan for a statewide system of improved wagon roads.[67] No funding or administrative apparatus was created to build the system, but the plan remained a goal that business interests gradually embraced.

The 1906 San Francisco earthquake provided a wonderful opportunity for transforming the state highway dream into reality. To repair quake damage, local governments demanded emergency engineering services from the state, including road repair and reconstruction. Nathan Ellery, who recently had been appointed state road commissioner, strongly advocated road development. He used the pressure from local jurisdictions to persuade the legislature in 1907 to create a new department whose responsibilities included roads. Ellery headed the new Department of Engineering, administrative ancestor to today's California Business and Transportation Agency. The legislation permitted counties to sell bonds for highway repairs and construction and specified that the state engineer's office would coordinate county road work. This act led to the passage of bond issues amounting to $7.3 million for road construction in San Diego, Los Angeles, San Joaquin, and Sacramento counties by 1910, as well as the establishment of county highway commissions to carry out the work.[68]

After 1907 San Francisco interests pushed particularly hard for the construction of a state road system patterned after the 1896 plan. State engineer Ellery, soon to become chief engineer for the city and county of San Francisco, worked with Governor James N. Gillett, the San Francisco Commonwealth Club, and the Automobile Club of California (a San Francisco organization) to draft a statewide road plan, which the legislature adopted in 1909. A scaled-down version of the 1896 roads master plan, the State Highway Act of 1909 provided $18 million in state-supported bonds to construct 3,082 miles of paved highways. Two north-south trunks would run the length of the state and generally parallel the state's main rail routes. A series of east-west laterals would connect all county seats and major cities and towns to the north-south routes.[69] The legislature put the act on the 1910 ballot for acceptance or rejection by the public.

That San Francisco interests intended to benefit from the road plan is indicated not only by the groups who supported the act, but also by the vote for its adoption. At the time the legislature recognized that $18 million could build only a fraction of the road system, but it set the price tag low in order to obtain voter approval.[70] Obviously some areas would not obtain state highways until the legislature provided additional funding. The 1910 election revealed that voters in southern California viewed the program as something designed to further San Francisco's interests, most likely by assigning construction priority to roads linking San Francisco with the territory it dominated. They voted three to one against the measure, while Bay Area counties voted by equally large margins in favor of it. In the San Joaquin Valley the vote was evenly split. The issue narrowly passed.[71]

The regional nature of the highway vote suggests that popular enthusiasm for automobiles had little influence on the drafting of the initial highway act. If newspaper accounts are any indication, by 1910 the auto had already captured the public's imagination in all parts of the state. In the weeks before and after the passage of the act in 1909 and the election the following year, the San Francisco *Chronicle* and the Los Angeles *Times* widely and enthusiastically reported automobile shows and races, most likely because automobile ownership was beginning to soar. The state's equitable climate made year-round driving possible even before the widespread adoption of the enclosed automobile in the early 1920s. As recently as 1906 only three out of every thousand Californians owned autos, but by 1910 this figure increased fivefold to fifteen per thousand (see table 3 in the appendix). At the time of the election, however, both papers carried no editorials, advertisements, or stories, save one, either in favor of or opposed to the state highway act. The *Chronicle* merely noted four days following the election that the measure had barely passed, with most opposition centered in southern California. The *Times* did not mention even that much. The lack of popular enthusiasm for the state highway program suggests that its support was narrowly based and largely behind the scenes.

This finding is consistent with the work of the auto historian James J. Flink, which shows that auto diffusion before 1910 failed to correlate with commitments for highway improvement.[72] In most of the United States farming and bicycle interests swelled the ranks of good roads movements, which agitated for good farm-to-local-market roads. In California urban interests, most notably those in San Francisco, pushed for intercity roads most likely to better link San Francisco with its market area. Given the area's role in transportation development to that time, the motivation likely was the attainment of comparative advantage for purposes of trade and development.[73]

Despite San Francisco's initial interest in the road plan, Los Angeles interests captured the nascent highway bureaucracy. Led by Los Angeles County, southern California counties purchased more highway bonds than any other group. The Chandler Act of 1911 also created a new administrative structure for road building that took control away from San Francisco personnel. The act created a new three-member advisory panel that became known as the California Highway Commission and that initially was headed by an energetic thirty-seven-year-old civil engineer from Los Angeles, Newell Dyke Darlington. Darlington previously served on the Board of Public Utilities of the City of Los Angeles. For its first highway engineer, the commission chose Austin B. Fletcher, previously secretary-engineer of the San Diego County Highway Commission.[74]

The California Highway Commission first met in 1911, and by 1912 Fletcher had staffed the organization with professional engineers, adopted specific routes and construction standards, and begun construction. The commission's objective was to provide free roads with no barriers to their use. Initial road standards included fifteen-foot concrete pavements with maximum grades of 6 percent in mountain passes and minimum curvature of one hundred feet. These contrasted with the unkept, narrow, rutted surfaces, the twenty-foot radius curves, and the 20 to 30 percent grades that then typified California roads.[75]

Next to free roads, the most important policy of the highway commission was the routing of roads as directly as practicable between large population centers. In 1913 the commission pronounced that the new state highways would not deviate even short distances from direct routes to serve intermediate population centers, even those of considerable magnitude, nor would they serve a farm-to-local-market function. The time of through travelers, and the cost of shipping through goods, would not be sacrificed for local needs. Within this general principle, the commission stated that one of its most important objectives was to link Los Angeles more closely to the San Joaquin Valley and the northern part of the state.[76]

Most of the state highways followed already existing county roads, to which the state took title and upgraded. The commission boldly departed from this practice in laying out the route between Los Angeles and Bakersfield. Known as the Ridge Route, the 125-mile road over Tejon Pass was 45 miles shorter than the rail route and 50 miles shorter than the old dirt road. It opened in 1915, and in that year the state engineering office observed that even with a lunch stop, motor stages traveled the still unpaved road more quickly than the train traveled between Los Angeles and Bakersfield. Just a year earlier motorists had had to allow as much as two days to make this trip. By 1916 the Automobile Club of Southern California observed that travel between Los Angeles and the San Joaquin Valley had increased greatly and predicted that the new link would bring the southern San Joaquin Valley into the social and economic sphere of Los Angeles. The club called the Ridge Route the magnum opus of southern California road construction.[77]

As the state highway program's backers predicted, the California Highway Commission ran out of money long before it completed the 1909-mandated state highway system. In 1916 the commission asked the voters for more money, and this time they responded enthusiastically. Rising auto ownership had created support for road improvements. In 1914, 42 people out of a thousand owned cars; the number per thousand increased to 97 in 1917 and 150 by 1920 (see table 3). In the 1916 election, voters approved the issuance of $15 million worth of additional highway bonds by a four-to-one margin.[78]

When the highway commission exhausted that money in 1919, it still had not completed all of the state routes included in the 1909 plan. California voters then approved another $40 million in bonds. The additional monies also failed to complete the system, but they provided enough support to link all of California's population centers with concrete roads by 1920.[79]

While the state highway system took shape, networks of local roads also developed. Between 1914 and 1920 county road expenditures reached $104.2 million, compared to $42.2 million for state roads (see table 4). The densest networks developed in southern California, which, according to the Automobile Club of Southern California, was constructing more roads than any area of the world circa 1914.[80]

During the period that California's paved highways took form California's intercity bus industry also emerged. According to most histories of the industry, intercity bus service began in 1913 or 1914 when a Swedish immigrant, Carl Eric Wickman, started shuttling passengers in a Hupmobile between Hibbing and Alice, Minnesota, two miles apart. Becoming progressively more successful with his bus operations, Wickman founded the Greyhound Corporation in the late 1920s.[81]

Actually, intercity bus services already existed in California by 1910, and by 1914 they were flourishing. As Albert E. Meier's and John P. Hoschek's short but excellent history of the intercity bus industry in the United States shows, the industry expanded faster in California than elsewhere in the United States. While Wickman and his earliest associates did indeed found the holding company that became the Greyhound Corporation, much of its substance and leadership came from California bus pioneers W. E. "Buck" Travis and Fred Ackerman and their efforts at finding accommodation with California's rail industry.[82]

George Tatterson may have pioneered what then was known as interurban jitney service. By 1910 he was driving a touring car and open-air trailer in regular service for paying passengers between Ripon, Manteca, and Stockton, the county seat of San Joaquin County. According to Tatterson, similar services soon operated in all directions from Stockton.[83]

In the first phase of California intercity bus development, small entrepreneurs bought various types of autos or small truck chassis, which they modified to carry additional passengers. They operated the vehicles along relatively short routes over dirt roads, charging fares for passengers. Speaking of a service that he started in 1911 between Brawley and Calexico in California's Imperial Valley, Tom Morgan recalled, "During the first three years there I drove during the daytime and repaired the cars at night and kept the books on Sundays."[84]

Such services grew spontaneously not only in the San Joaquin and Imperial valleys but in most parts of the state where towns existed. By 1915 the California Railroad Commission estimated that five hundred interurban jitneys operated in the state, and by 1917 the number ballooned to more than seventeen hundred.[85] These operators covered a large proportion of the state and county roads and thrived on travelers making very short trips.[86]

As more Californians owned cars and found that they could drive them where they wanted on the rapidly expanding state highway system, their demand for all forms of public transportation declined. By 1915 steam train, electric interurban railway, and interurban jitney operators found themselves competing for a market that no longer was expanding. In that year the Western Association of Short Line Railroads and the United Railroads of San Francisco (an urban streetcar company) filed complaints with the California Railroad Commission over, respectively, unregulated truck and bus competition.[87] Some of the interurban jitney operators also organized in an attempt to restrict entry to the field. Tatterson, the Stockton-area bus pioneer, captured the spirit of the times when he later wrote, "The earlyday operation was quite competitive—everybody for himself and to control the situation the Star Stage Association was formed and at one time had 67 members and any newcomers were run off the road." [88]

Not only did jitney owners form operating associations, but in 1915 they also formed a political association.[89] The short line and street railroad complaints, as well as the efforts of the association of interurban jitney operators, all worked to the same purpose, which was to bring trucks and interurban jitneys under the jurisdiction of the California Railroad Commission. They succeeded with the Auto Truck and Stage Act of 1917. Thereafter, the commission regulated the entry of new bus services. Operators existing in 1917 were given grandfather rights to continue operation; newcomers could enter the business only by obtaining commission permission either to purchase the rights from an already existing operator or to be issued a new certificate.[90]

From the outset, the railroad commission refused to issue new certificates for services duplicating already existing bus services. This policy effectively prevented bus competition within California, and until a U.S. Supreme Court ruling in 1925, it restricted interstate bus service, as well. Between 1925 and 1935, when Congress passed the Motor Carrier Act, interstate service was unregulated, and during the late 1920s and early 1930s various long distance services competed for traffic from the East to and from Los Angeles and San Francisco, and from the North to San Francisco. However, the railroad commission forbade these services to carry California intrastate passengers.[91]

Only three years after passage of the act, the interurban jitney industry of owner-operators evolved into the intercity bus industry, characterized by regional corporate monopolies. Through mergers and buyouts of operating rights, certain entrepreneurs rose to dominate different regions of the state.[92] They consciously pursued policies of what now is known as economies of scope. That is, they attempted to create networks of routes, which simultaneously served a large number of origin-destination pairs, in order to fill up empty seats (i.e., achieve a high load factor) in a declining market. Through trial and error, they developed a strategy of connecting major cities with trunk bus routes that offered frequent service and stops on demand. The completion of long distance concrete highways made long distance bus service a practical proposition. The more alert bus entrepreneurs discovered that such services attracted both price-sensitive long distance travelers and frequency-sensitive short distance riders. During the 1920s and 1930s, bus operators found they needed the symbiosis between the two types of riders in order to remain profitable. Bus operators outside of metropolitan areas who catered only to long distance or to short distance riders went out of business. So did those who were not cost-conscious.[93]

W. E. "Buck" Travis would eventually emerge from this transition as California's dominant bus entrepreneur. Travis bought his way into the business in 1920, but unlike most of the original owner-operators, he came from a business family and had years of experience running large-scale transportation enterprises. His father operated stage lines throughout the West, and after growing up on the family ranch in Nevada and then attending Harvard, Travis took over the business. He prospered, but around 1907, as a consequence of government restrictions, he transferred his investments to urban taxis, first in Chicago and later in San Francisco. Travis not only operated taxis, he built them; and he soon found that the emerging interurban jitney operators demanded his vehicles. When the owner-operators began consolidating after the passage of the 1917 bus and truck act, Travis saw an opportunity for increasing his investment. He later testified that the act ended cutthroat competition "and created a semblance of stability for investments that might be made in equipment, terminals or improvements of any character."[94] In 1920 Travis bought the operating rights from the fifty-four owner-operators who remained in the Star Auto Stage Association, which he erroneously believed was profitable. Intending to reorganize and tighten up its operations, he incorporated the Star Auto Company, which later in 1920 he renamed the California Transit Company.[95]

By 1920 seven regional bus systems such as the California Transit Company covered the settled areas of the state. Hundreds of owner-operators also continued in service, but they increasingly operated on the fringes as the larger systems purchased the more lucrative certificates.[96] In that year intercity buses using state highways, excluding those between Los Angeles and Santa Ana in the Los Angeles basin, carried about 117 million passenger miles, or about one-sixth the volume of intrastate, non-commuter traffic riding the rails. Of the 103 routes surveyed, four exceeded one hundred miles in length.[97]

As the United States began adjusting to the postwar world of 1920, California's rapidly evolving intercity bus services added but one additional element of competition to California's rail passenger services. The groundwork for such competition was laid from almost the beginning of the rail era in California and stemmed from conflict between California's various development communities, who wanted subsidized transportation, and the promoters of private railroads, who needed profits to survive. Until the

1890s the will of rail entrepreneurs generally prevailed, but as California's economy grew and became more complex, other economic interests became more powerful. Even as rail managers industriously expanded and strengthened California's rail facilities and services in the decade preceding 1910, business and development interests in the state weakened them through regulation and competition.

Under such forces the political hegemony of the national rail corporations rapidly crumbled in California after 1910, and their economic hegemony in passenger travel crumbled almost as fast. By 1920 not only did electric railways and steamships threaten their once profitable passenger business, but a comprehensive state highway system paralleled the major rail routes within the state. Rapidly increasing numbers of motorists drove over concrete highways between major cities and small towns alike, leaving behind slower and more indirect trains. Primitive bus competition also appeared in the closing days of the dirt road era. Offering several trips per day over most of the new state highways, interurban jitneys gave travelers still another choice.

Railroad managers faced a new era in which their passenger and even freight trains were no longer essential. Various interests in the regions they served wanted cheap and plentiful transportation, which almost all agreed spurred rapid regional economic growth, but they cared little about the health of the transportation companies providing it. Such interests created a situation where, if one transportation company or technology disappeared, two or three others easily could step in, using subsidized infrastructure. To adapt the passenger train to the new era, railroad managers had to change their emphasis from building capacity sufficient for demand to finding a role acceptable to California's business interests for at least some of their vast collection of passenger train services.

2
Management and Its Ability to Change, 1910–1920

The ability of railroad passenger managers to react to the hostile new order turned on the management structures and cultures of which they were a part. These had developed over the preceding half century through trial and error. Before the railroads appeared in the 1830s, large business organizations did not exist. The business historians Thomas C. Cochran and Alfred D. Chandler, Jr., credit railroad entrepreneurs for innovating the hierarchical, multidivisional management organization roughly between 1840 and 1890. Staffed by salaried professional managers rather than proprietors, the organizations grew in response to unprecedented requirements for coordination brought about by the railroad systems' complicated technology, vast size, and geographic scope.[1]

The structures of such large bureaucracies and the attitudes of their managers colored the way in which managers interpreted their changing business environment. As railroad managers learned how to organize and improve railroad technology, they formed attitudes about the environment in which they worked. In the late nineteenth century, technological improvement meant bigger and more massive machines. After the introduction of steel rails, which could support much heavier trains, managers learned that they could decrease unit costs by building larger cars, filling them more fully, coupling them onto longer trains, and pulling them with ever larger locomotives. Managers took pride in the progress they made through these means. Perpetuating such progress over the geographic scope of the railroad through standardized organizational procedures became one of the central objectives of the organization. The business historian Glenn Porter calls the cohesiveness surrounding this attitude an engineering culture and shows how it developed among the managers of the Pennsylvania Railroad before the 1890s.[2]

As this culture developed, a gulf opened between railroad managers and those who used their services. Managers feared that meddling in railroad decisions by groups outside of the railroad organizations would lead to dire financial consequences. They thus steadfastly resisted efforts by passengers, shippers, and developers to influence transportation decisions that affected the lives of users. In the eyes of railroad managers these groups were ignorant, shortsighted, and self-interested. Railroad managers were knowledgeable, farsighted, and altruistic, and only they were in a position to make decisions that would result in the greatest good for the greatest number while ensuring the continued growth and health of the railroad industry.

Managers saw railroads as crucial to society and felt an obligation to transfer wealth from society's more successful parts to its less successful ones. Known as cross subsidization, this practice was not imposed on the railroads by regulatory authorities, as believed by present-day policy analysts, but came from within the railroad organizations as a consequence of their paternalistic culture.

Not surprisingly, such an attitude aroused extreme resentment. As American society became more interdependent and specialized, various parts of it increasingly attacked the railroad position. Railroad managers responded by adding a new dimension to their culture—what business historian Maury Klein describes as a siege or "us versus them" mentality.[3]

Railroad management paternalism and its siege mentality affected the way management interpreted the changing environment and formed new passenger policies between 1910 and 1920. So did management's view that passenger service promoted the main business of railroading, which was freight movement. The structure itself also led to decisions that proved financially disastrous by the 1930s.

Management structures for the Southern Pacific and the Santa Fe typified those of most large railroad corporations and changed little from the 1890s through the 1930s. Both were huge bureaucracies. In 1921, for example, the Southern Pacific boasted that its headquarters building in San Francisco daily handled about 60,000 pieces of mail, as much as did Sacramento, the state capital. Telegrams and telephone calls to the headquarters averaged 20,000 per day.[4]

As is typical of large railroads, the Southern Pacific and the Santa Fe organized their bureaucracies into three major line functions of operations, accounting, and traffic. Vice presidents headed these departments and reported to a president, who in turn reported to a board of directors. The board represented not only stockholders but also banking interests who financed the heavy debt typical of railroads. It also represented management, with the president and one or more vice presidents sitting on it. Committees of the board usually established important policy; for the Southern Pacific the executive committee and the finance committee were important.[5]

To develop and analyze positions, Southern Pacific's president relied not only upon his principal line officers but also upon several staff assistants and organizations. Because of fights with users, regulatory bodies, and politicians, the legal department dominated staff functions and by the early 1920s occupied fully half the executive floor.[6]

Other staff functions provided technical and planning information. The chief engineer evaluated the costs of constructing and operating new alignments and also chaired the technical research committee, which alone or with suppliers developed such passenger products as the all-steel passenger car, air-conditioning systems, and streamlined trains. In this committee, the chief engineer drew upon the resources of the electrical engineer, the vice president and general manager of the Southern Pacific Land Company, the general superintendent of motive power, the mechanical engineer, and the engineer of tests.[7]

In addition to these staff offices, individuals assisted the president by preparing analyses of the consequences of courses of action that the president was considering. For example, during the 1930s presidential assistant Marion J. Wise estimated the cost and revenue consequences of proposed new passenger trains.[8]

The president relied most heavily on the vice president of operations, who directed the largest and most prestigious part of the organization. Operations included not only the movement of trains and the operation of tracks and terminals, but also their maintenance and betterment. The operations vice president managed these activities through superintendents, each of whom directed the affairs of the railroad within a specified territory, called a division. Each superintendent in turn directed an operating, traffic, and accounting staff. Traffic and accounting personnel within each division reported both to their division superintendents and to traffic and accounting officers in headquarters.[9]

Officers in headquarters coordinated the affairs of these far-flung empires with the aid of several types of information that flowed from the division level. One was cost accounting. In *The Visible Hand* Alfred D. Chandler documents the evolution of cost accounting, which he holds as essential for the success of the business bureaucracy. Through cost accounting, top executives measured and controlled efficiency in the multidivisional and professionally managed firm. Railroad managers developed the technique in the period between 1850 and 1880, after which it spread to other industries.[10] Harold Livesay asserts that cost accounting, and hence cost rather than price control, determined the success of big businesses such as Carnegie Steel: "By adhering constantly to his principle of knowing costs and reducing them at every turn, Carnegie drove his firm to the top, beat back his competitors as swiftly as they emerged, and set a pattern of bureaucratic management that American industry copied widely." [11]

From early in its history the railroad industry posted labor and material expenses into various accounts for each of its operating divisions. Separate accounts existed for such categories as maintaining locomotives, operating signals, and replacing rails on mainline tracks. From 1907 railroads kept accounts in accordance to the ICC-promulgated uniform system of accounts.[12]

Chandler shows how Albert Fink used accounts to develop operating statistics for assessing the performance of subordinates. Fink, a civil engineer and general manager of the Louisville & Nashville during the 1870s, studied his railroad's cost behavior and came to rely on statistics such as the cost per train mile for different divisions to assess the relative efficiency of division superintendents. Fink also developed statistics such as the cost per locomotive mile and fuel consumed per locomotive mile, observing that longer trains cost more to operate per mile, but that the cost per ton mile of goods carried in longer trains was less.[13]

Southern Pacific cost accounting and operational control practices followed this general pattern during the first part of the twentieth century. A 1908 report by two operating officers of the Pennsylvania Railroad describes the statistics in use on the combined Southern Pacific–Union Pacific system. The report notes that the use of statistics led Julius Kruttschnitt, director of maintenance and operation of the system, to operate longer, heavier trains. According to division managers, the most useful statistics were the gross and net tons per mile, average tons per train, and freight locomotive mileage. There were also costs per locomotive mile and per gross ton mile, and costs per ton handled in freight stations for agents, clerks, and station labor.[14] A 1914 Southern Pacific management training course inculcated trainees with the message that longer and heavier freight trains saved money and taught them what statistics to look for to achieve such objectives. These were similar to those in the 1908 report.[15]

Other crucial information included trends in costs and revenues. Railroads incurred costs and brought in revenue on a daily basis at hundreds of dispersed locations. The accounting department kept running tabs on these, allowing management to continually monitor the critical operating ratio: operating costs divided by revenues. The operating ratio told management whether the company was financially healthy and substituted for return on investment, used for this purpose in most other businesses. As Chandler describes, railroads could not calculate return on investment because railroad managements did not engage in depreciation accounting and therefore lacked an understanding of their net investment in equipment and facilities. Instead, the trend in the operating ratio informed them of the value of recent investments. If the operating ratio went down after major investments, or if it held steady while traffic surged upward, the investments were earning a healthy return. The operating ratio also told management whether sufficient reserves would be left to service debt, pay leases and dividends, pay for the future betterment of plant, and provide profits.[16] During the first decade of the twentieth century, Southern Pacific's operating ratio hovered in the mid-50s, which was considered adequate.

Southern Pacific's accounting department also provided management with the gross revenues earned by every train. Usually it divided these by the number of miles that the train operated to provide a statistic of gross revenue per train mile. With this number management could compare trends in gross earnings between different trains. Unfortunately, during the first two decades of the twentieth century management had no idea of how much it cost to operate a train, except for the cost of the train crew and of fuel. These two categories amounted to about 10 percent of the cost of running the railroad. Thus, while management could compare trends in gross earnings for individual trains, it could not compare trends in net earnings, a shortcoming that proved crippling to the evolution of management strategy in the ensuing years.

Railroad management structures divided passenger responsibility among several officers. The only officer who (supposedly) oversaw all aspects of passenger management was the president, who rarely had time for this task. Most responsibility fell to the superintendent of transportation and to the manager of passenger traffic.[17]

Such divisions of responsibility typified both the Southern Pacific and the Santa Fe. On both roads, the general manager of the operating department made major passenger operating decisions. These included what trains to run; where, when, and how fast to run them; and what equipment to use. Assisting the general manager, the superintendent of transportation specialized in matching forecasts and desires from the traffic department with the capabilities of the operating department. Informed by routine reports of train earnings emanating from the accounting office, the superintendent prepared the passenger schedules and sought operational means for reducing costs or enhancing the marketability of services. Equipment designs and planning work came from the executive offices.[18]

The manager of passenger traffic oversaw solicitation and forecasting of passenger traffic, represented the company in passenger matters with other railroads and with the public, and prepared tariffs consistent with regulatory requirements. Several sources of information allowed him to feel and interpret the pulse of passenger traffic. He could compare passenger earnings for particular trains and for the entire railroad with the growing population of the Southern Pacific territory to determine whether passenger traffic was increasing with the area. From ticket receipts he could determine between what points the greatest volume of passengers rode. Ticket agents and passenger agents who rode trains could convey more personal impressions of traffic trends and make observations about what passengers liked and disliked about Southern Pacific services. The passenger traffic manager also employed agents to ride and make reports on competing services. He participated actively in the association of western traffic officers. Finally, as a member of the most prestigious social clubs of San Francisco and Los Angeles, he obtained firsthand opinions of what elite groups thought about Southern Pacific services and about alternative methods of travel. Gradual trends in preferences manifested themselves through these indicators, as did public reaction to major service changes.[19]

In general the passenger traffic manager reported to the vice president of traffic, who also oversaw freight traffic. This was true of the Santa Fe through the entire period of this study, and it was true of the Southern Pacific until the late 1920s.[20] In 1929 the Southern Pacific promoted Felix S. McGinnis, passenger traffic manager of the Pacific System, to a new position—vice president of passenger traffic for the entire company, including rail operations in Texas and Louisiana and the company's steamship operations.[21]

Railroad passenger management also included dealings with the Pullman Company, which contracted with most of the nation's railroads to build and operate sleeping cars. Contracts varied from road to road but generally incorporated remuneration to the Pullman Company for the break-even cost of building and operating its cars. Included were the capital and operating costs of the Pullman manufacturing and maintenance plants. From around the turn of the century until the early 1920s the Pullman Company used a figure of about $7,500 per car per year as the amount necessary to make itself financially whole. If room fees that sleeping car passengers on each railroad paid the Pullman Company exceeded this amount, Pullman shared the excess with the railroad. If room fees fell short, the company required the railroad to pay it an additional amount, which usually amounted to one to two cents per car mile. If confronted with situations where they would have to pay more than this amount because of light traffic, railroads typically would not operate sleeping car service.[22]

Under this arrangement railroads with rapidly expanding long distance traffic built up substantial sleeping car fleets. By the early 1920s the Southern Pacific and the Santa Fe contracted for the third and fourth largest fleets of Pullman cars in the United States, and each year the Pullman Company returned to each of them excess revenues, which in 1923 amounted to about $3,500 per car.[23]

Such a structure and information system produced a relatively straightforward management method. Traffic officers solicited as much freight and passenger business as possible. They also predicted traffic growth based on population and income growth. Division operating officers organized trains to move the traffic as efficiently as possible. If traffic rose, they operated more and longer trains. If it fell, they cut back the number of trains but tried to refrain from reducing their lengths. Track and shop maintenance forces repaired any damage that train operations caused. The movement of more tonnage caused more damage, necessitating the hiring of additional maintenance forces. If tonnage fell, less maintenance was needed and forces were laid off. Division officers and those in headquarters monitored the flows of trains and prepared plans for additional tracks or larger terminals to alleviate congested bottlenecks. They also devised capital programs to lower operating costs, usually by lowering grades, installing larger rails, and designing larger cars and bigger and more powerful locomotives. Operating longer and heavier trains was the goal. If traffic was falling, they discontinued trains whose gross earnings fell below crew and fuel costs. In short, traffic officers created traffic, and a myriad of operating and maintenance officers almost semiautomatically reacted under the general theme of moving traffic as efficiently as possible.

All of these activities incurred expenses and earned revenues, whose relationship the accounting department closely watched. If the operating ratio (expenses divided by gross revenues) looked healthy, the executive office routinely approved requests from the divisions to expand the physical plant to alleviate congestion or improve efficiency. On the other hand, a ratio creeping upward signaled a need for rate increases, and if these failed, the executive office cut off investments. If the ratio became dangerously high, the executive office ordered cutbacks in all but the most immediately needed operating and maintenance expenses, regardless of the dictates of moving traffic.

In the decade following 1910 such railroad management methods came under increasing criticism because they treated revenues and costs as independent phenomena. Management attempted to get as much gross revenue as possible, and it attempted to move traffic at the lowest possible cost. Although this practice often yielded profitable results, it could lead to unprofitable situations. Traffic bringing in high gross revenues might incur even greater costs. Profits would be higher if management did not carry such traffic. On the other hand, when management cut back expenses during times of recession, it might unknowingly eliminate the means for bringing in revenues. For example, a recession might prompt management to institute severe reductions in equipment maintenance, leading to service deterioration and the subsequent loss of profitable traffic. Both types of abuses could occur because management ignored the relationship between costs and revenues for different types of traffic.

Such criticisms arose as railroads became increasingly less profitable after 1907, even as traffic continued to rise. Up to this time railroad managements made dramatic improvements in railroad productivity. The economic historian Albert Fishlow demonstrates that between 1839 and 1910 American railroad productivity advanced at the average rate of 3.5 percent per year, considerably faster than the 1.3 percent rate of productivity growth for the economy as a whole. According to Fishlow, such growth resulted from ever longer trains composed of ever larger cars more heavily loaded and pulled by ever larger and more efficient locomotives. The development of cheap steel rails, more than any other technological innovation, spurred this development.[24]

By 1910 the railroad strategy of operating longer and heavier trains produced diminishing returns, slowing railroad productivity growth to an annual average of about 2.7 percent. At the same time, productivity growth for the nation accelerated to more than 3 percent. Railroad productivity improvements no longer could compensate for increasing prices of materials needed to operate the railroad, and operating ratios of railroads across the country moved ominously upward. Three times between 1910 and 1917 the nation's railroads sought blanket rate increases, but each time the Interstate Commerce Commission denied them. The huge investments that most of the nation's railroads made between 1897 and 1910 were not producing the desired results. As Albro Martin documents, railroad managers after 1910 found it increasingly difficult to obtain enough capital to keep ahead of traffic growth.[25]

While the railroads argued that the Interstate Commerce Commission's failure to grant rate increases had gotten them into such desperate financial straits, critics replied that railroads got themselves into the situation through cost ignorance that caused them to carry substantial volumes of traffic at below cost. This criticism took note of a growing body of evidence showing that management's paradigm of railroad economics was false. As described in the previous chapter, management believed that most costs of running a railroad were constant. Managers believed that if they got traffic at rates slightly more than those compensating them for fuel and crew costs, they increased their profits. By 1910 knowledge centered in the Interstate Commerce Commission showed this notion to be false: if traffic moved at rates close to what managers thought the out-of-pocket costs were, such traffic in fact increased total railroad costs more than it contributed to revenue. If railroads carried a large amount of this type of traffic, they were forced to raise general rates to remain solvent.

Such evidence began accumulating as early as the 1870s, when Albert Fink studied the variation of individual cost accounts on different divisions of the Louisville & Nashville. Watching how the accounts changed as traffic fluctuated, he concluded that more than 60 percent of total costs varied with traffic. Another southern railway manager, T. M. R. Talcott, corroborated these findings in the 1890s.[26] In 1901 he wrote that management must understand the costs of moving different types of traffic if it was to defend itself against cross subsidy complaints:

> There is a strong and abiding impression in some quarters that railway companies charge high rates on local freight traffic to make up for losses on competitive traffic; and how are we to say that such is not the case if we do not know the cost of doing either local or competitive business? Railways will never be able to make proper defence against this and other charges until they can show with some degree of accuracy what each and every class of business does cost them.[27]

Unfortunately, Talcott's work, like Fink's before him, showed that the railroads probably did lose money on competitive traffic because the true costs of moving this traffic were far higher than management thought. Later that decade the future head of the ICC economics section came to the same conclusion. Having recently obtained his Ph.D. in economics from the University of Wisconsin, Max O. Lorenz in 1907 published findings in the *Quarterly Journal of Economics* showing that as traffic grew on railroads, the accounts typically thought of as being fixed grew as fast as or faster than traffic. Sometimes they grew even faster than accounts that were supposed to be variable.[28] Almost a decade later Lorenz presented fresh research showing that for mainline traffic densities, almost 100 percent of costs were variable. This means that if one took the total fixed and operating costs for running a railroad for one year and divided them by the total number of ton miles (with passenger miles converted to a ton mile equivalent) operated that year, the resulting cost per ton mile would accurately reflect how much the railroad's total annual cost would increase if it carried one more ton one more mile.[29]

Such knowledge led the ICC staff to conclude that many types of railroad traffic lost money. As special counsel to the ICC, Louis D. Brandeis reflected this view when he argued against general rate increases in 1914:

A most surprising difference exists in respect to cost accounting between railroading and manufacturing. Leading American manufacturers know accurately to-day the cost of every one of the numerous articles made and sold by them. Railroads which make and sell a most varied transportation service do not know the cost of any of the services which they furnish. Only a few of the railroads undertake to separate even the cost of freight and passenger service in the aggregate; and among these few there is nothing approaching a consensus of opinion as to the proper basis for such separation. . . . In manufacturing accurate cost accounting was found to be a condition precedent to high operating efficiency; and it was found even more essential as a means of insuring the concern against engaging in unremunerative business. What was thus found to be true in manufacturing is equally true in railroading. Cost of service should not, perhaps, determine the reasonableness of a rate; but it is clear that without knowledge of the cost of a particular service it is impossible for railroad officials to protect the company's revenues against unremunerative rates. Carriers' legitimate revenues can not be conserved unless the rate maker has a reasonably accurate knowledge whether a particular service is rendered at a profit or at a loss. In the absence of such knowledge, the traffic manager's success or failure is tested by the tonnage moved instead of profit earned. No adequate explanation can be found for the multitudinous instances of unremunerative rates and practices prevailing on our railroads hereinafter referred to, except lack of knowledge on the part of managers of the disastrous financial result of these rates and practices.[30]

Such beliefs led Brandeis to proselytize against cross subsidization— the practice of the railroad using profits from one area to cover losses in another. Since at least 1910 the ICC endorsed the principle that each type of service should be self-supporting in all respects. In several cases rail carriers sought rate increases for noncompensatory services. They would not provide the commission with cost data. However, the cases were such that the railroads obviously were incurring higher costs providing one type of service compared to another having similar rates. In such cases the commission granted rate increases for the apparently higher cost services. Such willingness in the absence of hard cost data suggests that if the railroads had systematic cost data, the commission would have allowed widespread rate increases for unremunerative services.[31]

Railroad management typically rejected ICC pressure to end cross subsidies by pointing out that ICC directives ran counter to the railroads' social obligations. The Pennsylvania Railroad's George Stuart Patterson set the tone when he replied to Brandeis on behalf of the eastern railroads. Patterson stated that railroad management methods reflected the value of service theory of making rates and that to upset this theory with another based on cost of service would upset American society. He added that it was the duty of American railroads to protect less fortunate areas and users with cross subsidies. If the railroads did not do this, many markets would fail, as would railroads with long, indirect routes. He concluded that the effect of railroads ending cross subsidies would be revolutionary, and neither the public nor the railroads would stand for it.[32] Today many criticize regulation for having fostered cross subsidies against the will of efficiency-minded railroads. In reality quite the opposite was true during the Progressive era.

Management revealed another reason for not wanting to identify the costs of particular classes of service. It thought that such knowledge in the hands of politicians or shippers would further weaken its control over transportation policy. The Interstate Commerce Commission commented on this fear in 1915 when it forced the railroads to estimate the costs of running passenger service: "The possible misuse of information collected was also urged as a reason for not developing the subject of railway cost accounting. It was argued [by the carriers] that to give cost accounting information to the public would be the same as giving dangerous instruments to children."[33] This comment also reflects the paternalistic attitude of railroad managers toward the groups who used their services.

Southern Pacific's management methods followed the generalizations drawn from national experience. The company generally did not try to find the costs of moving different types of traffic and instead relied on the operating ratio as an indicator of the success or failure of investments and operating practices. Such methods adequately served management when it monopolized transportation and engaged in geographic rate discrimination. Falling corporate profits could be corrected merely by a general rate increase. However, after about 1910 such methods proved increasingly inadequate. Tightening rate regulation and increasing competition circumscribed management's ability to raise general rates. In the new environment management needed to know the profitability of each type of traffic that it carried and to either lower costs or raise rates for categories of traffic that were unprofitable. In the new environment, management's blindness to the profitability of its various types of traffic proved to be an ever greater liability that contributed to an unsatisfactory bottom line.

The company's operating ratio told management the grim story, although it provided little guidance about what was causing the problem. As documented in table 5, during the first years of the century the Southern Pacific's operating ratio generally was in the low to mid-50s, which was considered adequate. Investments that the Harriman regime made between 1901 and 1910 enabled the company to accommodate an astonishing growth in traffic with no loss in profit margins, as indicated by generally stable operating ratios during those years. Because overall company operating profits were the product of unit profits multiplied by volume, surging volume between 1900 and 1910 brought surging profits.

After 1910 the results looked much less favorable. Management continued to make large investments, but freight and passenger traffic remained relatively flat, while the operating ratio rose from 53 in 1910 to 60 in 1915. Management saw declining profit margins on each unit of traffic, represented by the increasing operating ratio, multiplied by stagnant sales, represented by traffic volume. Apparently the massive investments made after 1910 were going to waste.

The situation failed to improve in 1916 and 1917. Because the war in Europe began to stimulate U.S. industry, traffic rose rapidly in both of those years, but the operating ratio also climbed to 63 in 1916 and dropped just slightly to 62 in 1917. These trends indicated to managers and investors alike that the Southern Pacific was not an attractive investment.

By 1914 suspicion began to focus on passenger traffic as one culprit in the worsening financial picture of the nation's railroads. Brandeis and the ICC staff suspected that railroad passenger service constituted the most blatant example of cross subsidies. While railroad executives admitted that passenger service lost money, Brandeis believed that it lost much more than they thought. To shed light on this issue, as well as to take the first step in finding the cost of other services that railroads provided, the ICC in 1915 ordered the railroads to separate costs between freight and passenger service.[34] According to the order, railroad accountants were to divide expenses in each railroad account into solely related freight expenses, solely related passenger expenses, apportioned freight expenses, apportioned passenger expenses, and unapportioned expenses. In the account for operating signals, for example, the cost of operating signals in passenger terminals was entered into the solely related passenger category, while the cost of operating signals on the mainline was divided between the apportioned passenger and apportioned freight categories, generally in accordance to the relative passenger and freight ton miles passing the signals. The total cost of a railroad's passenger operation was the sum of the solely related and apportioned parts of each expense account.[35]

Railroad managers resisted commission directives to separate costs because they could see no benefit from the effort. They devised different methods for apportioning costs and argued that because there was no theoretical justification for choosing one method over another, cost separation studies produced arbitrary results. Commission statisticians countered by demonstrating that for practical purposes all of the railroad methods yielded the same results. The statisticians also argued that expense accounts jointly shared by freight and passenger service were not fixed expenses, as most railroad managers believed. The statisticians knew very well that if either passenger or freight service increased, so did the expenses in the particular joint expense account. For these reasons the ICC kept and refined the formula for separating freight and passenger expenses, and some railroad managers gradually came to accept it as providing a rough indicator of how much total passenger service drew upon company resources.[36]

The first separation of expenses occurred in 1916 and is summarized in table 2 for the Eastern, Western, and Southern districts of the United States. For the nation as a whole, the separation showed operating ratios of 72 and 74 for freight and passenger service respectively. Knowledgeable railroad industry critics generally conceded in the early 1920s that the railroads were not earning an adequate rate of return for several years prior to World War I.[37] Martin shows that 1916 was a year typical of this period. Thus, an operating ratio of 74 indicates unprofitable passenger service in 1916. Passenger service grossed enough to cover its operating costs but not enough to provide an adequate return on investment. Because the passenger operating ratio stood at the even more unsatisfactory level of 77 for the Western District, in which the Southern Pacific and the Santa Fe were the largest companies, it is likely that passenger service for both of these railroads was unprofitable in 1916. This condition represented a considerable deterioration from the profitable operating ratios of 55 and 58 for Southern Pacific local and long distance passenger trains respectively in 1911, as estimated in the notes for tables 1 and 2 and as discussed in the previous chapter.

Part of the turnaround in passenger fortunes came from rapidly falling demand. Trends in the gross earnings per train mile for different trains could not be located, but statistics reported to the California Railroad Commission suggest what the revenue per train mile for individual trains told management. One message was the collapse in demand for many (but not all) local trains. Total traffic using intrastate trains remained fairly static over the period, but usage per person declined steadily after 1913. During this time, Americans were getting richer, as measured in gross national product per capita. Passenger traffic managers knew this in a general sense, and they expected local passenger traffic to increase with rising income. Yet we see in figure 2.1 that the percentage of income that Californians spent on intrastate trains declined by 70 percent between 1911 and 1917, much faster than the decline in spending by the average American for all passenger service. It also declined much faster than Californians' spending

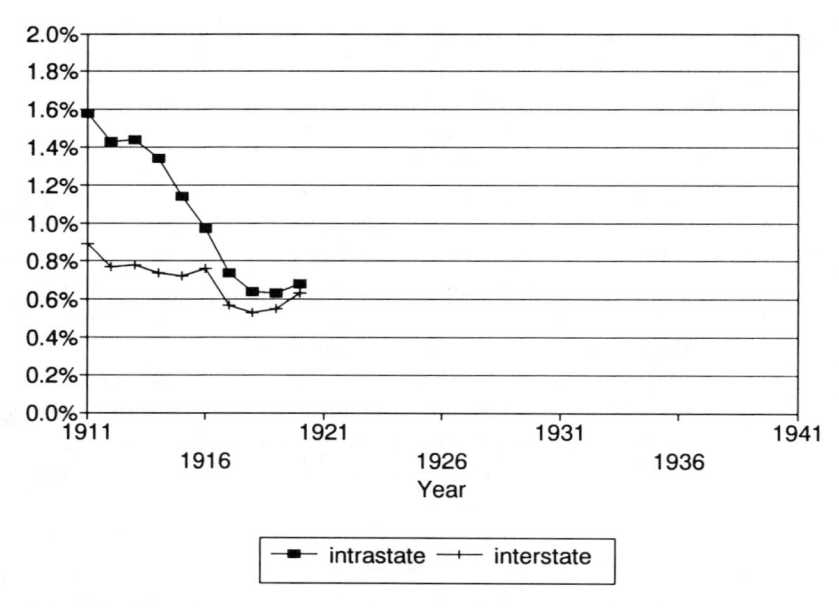

2.1 California passenger revenues as a percentage of California income, 1911–1920. Source: Table 20

on interstate trains. There could be no doubt in the minds of passenger traffic officers that many local passenger services were rapidly becoming less important in the lives of Californians.

Because the intrastate figures in table 6 are averages, they mask differences in demand for different types of intrastate trains. They reflect the results of trains as diverse as Pullman limiteds operating between Los Angeles and San Francisco, intercity locals running between large cities such as San Francisco and Sacramento, and rural locals such as those shuttling between Exeter and Coalinga in the San Joaquin Valley. Although revenue per train mile figures could not be found for such diverse trains, by looking at trends in electric interurban train usage, shown in table 7, we can infer what they told management. These figures suggest that the more rurally oriented the rail service, the earlier and more severe was the traffic decline.[38] The most rurally oriented of these services, the Visalia Electric, carried sizable passenger volumes after it opened in 1908, but despite rapid population growth in its service territory, patronage dropped rapidly after 1914.[39] The Tidewater Southern, connecting the larger towns of Modesto and Stockton, carried traffic more intercity in nature. Traffic grew faster than the rapidly growing population that it served until 1917, after which traffic started dropping. Finally, the Oakland, Antioch & Eastern and its successors connected San Francisco and Sacramento with service that was faster than Southern Pacific's until 1930, and it catered mostly to intercity travelers between large urban areas. Its traffic grew until the nationwide fare increase of August 1920, after which it shrank less drastically than the traffic of the other lines.[40]

These figures suggest that management saw demand collapse for its once lucrative rural passenger train services beginning about 1912. However, demand held up much more for trains linking large urban centers, such as Sacramento and San Francisco. Demand also likely held up for the Pullman and day trains linking Los Angeles and San Francisco, although even for these trains rapid growth likely tapered off.

The latter can be inferred by the fact that demand for some of the interstate trains serving California also started declining before World War I. Demand for Southern Pacific interstate trains kept up with population growth (see table 6), but not with income (figure 2.1). Economic cycles also influenced it. As shown in table 6, a two-year recession in 1914–15 broke a generally positive trend in long distance train usage between 1911 and 1917 for the Southern Pacific.

Another reason for the poor financial showing of passenger service was the fact that management used it partly as a ploy to smooth over relations with the public. For most American railroads throughout most of their history, management viewed passenger service as a by-product of a physical plant whose primary function was to move freight.[41] Even at its peak around 1916, American passenger service accounted for only a quarter of gross railroad revenues, although in more urban regions, such as the Northeast, the Great Lakes industrial areas, and California, the percentage was higher. Because of the Southern Pacific's heavy local traffic in California, passenger revenues accounted for 36 percent of its operating revenues in 1916.[42]

The by-product status of passenger service suggests that management could have viewed it as something other than a source of profits if it chose to do so. Statements by railroad executives suggest such was the case. After several months of observing American railroad practices and interviewing the industry's top managers in 1900, London *Times* reporter Edwin Pratt concluded that railroad managers stimulated passenger service as a means for promoting freight traffic:

> Railway officials in America have an axiom that a man "ships" his merchandise by the route he travels, so that, if they can only secure his patronage as a traveler, which in itself may not be much, they will count on carrying his merchandise or agricultural products, which may amount to a great deal. . . . The leading

trains . . . become little more than traveling advertisements, which are talked about, make the line better known, but are not run at any direct profit.[43]

Pratt added that management operated the great majority of passenger trains for the average person riding short distances and generally neglected these, an argument also made by the intellectual Walter E. Weyl.[44] The *Railway Age Gazette* editorialized in 1914 that Pullman services, luxury trains, and the great marble temples serving as passenger terminals cost the industry dearly.[45] John A. Droege, a superintendent for one of the nation's important passenger haulers, echoed these views two years later when he wrote: "There are many reasons why the passenger business of American railroads does not pay; they nearly all come down to the simple fact that the American carriers, as far as passenger traffic is concerned, have ever made service their watchword instead of profits." Droege went on to list the luxury services that railroads provided for elite groups at little or no added cost. In addition to palace-like city terminals, these included "observation cars, buffet smoking cars, and the provision of libraries, baths, stenographers, valets, maids, and barbers, either free or for a nominal charge." [46]

Few if any railroad executives argued that the railroads should curtail such wasteful passenger practices. Rather, they wanted more revenues to finance them. Had they viewed passenger service as a profit-making enterprise, they would have looked to passengers, particularly those who benefited from luxuries and the great marble palaces, as the source of extra revenues. Only in a few states in the West outside of California did the railroads seek minor passenger rate increases, and these were to bring local rates up to long distance rates.[47] To finance these practices, as well as many others, the nation's railroads wanted general freight rate increases.[48] Thus, even the passenger services that the public demanded lost money in 1916, and they did so because the railroads did not run them in a businesslike—i.e., profit-oriented—manner.

Southern Pacific's passenger decisions after 1910 reflected such objectives. Generally where the public, particularly members of the elite public, continued to use passenger trains, the company continued investing in the services, whether or not the trains earned a profit. Where the public stopped using trains, the company stopped investing in the services.

These practices perhaps grew out of efforts the company made after 1910 to heal the rift with California's elites. Until his death in 1909, Edward H. Harriman served as president of the combined Union Pacific and Southern Pacific system. Harriman directed the affairs of the colossus from his offices in New York. Robert S. Lovett followed as president in 1910, but he quickly implemented a policy of decentralization. In 1911, following the disastrous California elections, Lovett relinquished the presidency of both roads to separate presidents, who managed their respective companies from offices within the territories served. Lovett chose William Sproule, an affable Irishman with excellent public-speaking abilities, to manage the Southern Pacific from San Francisco.[49] After assuming the job, Sproule participated in the city's social circles and carried the message throughout the state that the railroad was an institution whose well-being was essential for California.[50] Other Southern Pacific executives also stressed the theme that if the public wanted continued service, it had an obligation to give its servant the sustenance necessary for good health.[51] A nurtured, regulated California monopoly was preferable to competition from out-of-state corporations.

Danny McGanny credited Sproule with winning California's elites to the railroad's side during its fights with the Justice Department over control of the Central Pacific. McGanny was in a position to know the company's lore. He hired on as an office boy in the San Francisco headquarters before World War I and rose to become the railroad's vice president of research during the 1960s. He was particularly proud of the fact that even the newly reorganized railroad commission came to the Southern Pacific's support. Stuart Daggett's writings confirm this and also stress that the normally anti-railroad San Francisco *Chronicle* changed its editorial tone before World War I. By the early 1920s, if not before, the weight of California opinion supported the Southern Pacific.[52]

Under Sproule, it appears that the railroad entered into a social contract with the state's leading interests. Part of the railroad's obligation in return for support in the Central Pacific fight was to provide a comprehensive transportation service to the state. Its decisions on passenger service suggest that Southern Pacific management viewed heavily used passenger services as essential to its social contract, even if they were unprofitable. However, if the public stopped using passenger services, the company would discontinue them.

By 1914 Southern Pacific management realized that passenger traffic growth no longer kept pace with the mushrooming population. It attributed part of the slow growth to temporary conditions, including the economic slump of 1914 as well as the deferment of long distance travel to 1915, when San Francisco would host the Pan Pacific Exposition. More ominously, it noted a new condition that only could be expected to worsen: growing use of the private automobile, which particularly affected rural local trains.[53] By 1916 management added the state highway policy to the list of causes. In that year of economic recovery, long distance passenger traffic rebounded, but rural local traffic continued to decline. The company reprinted a story from the Redding *Courier Free Press* entitled "What is to Become of Railroads Paralleled by State Highways?" The writer argued that highways should be built to serve stations in order to build up rail traffic, but instead they were being built parallel to mainlines and were designed to siphon traffic away from trains. The reporter observed that empty trains ran along mainlines paralleled by new state highways over which traveled hundreds of automobiles carrying freight and passengers.[54]

Southern Pacific executives undoubtedly were among the first buyers and users of autos, as were their social contacts in San Francisco's elite clubs. From such a perspective they likely viewed the impact of autos and highways on local trains fatalistically. If passengers stopped using trains because they owned autos and advocated roads, so be it. As early as 1915 the company's timetables advertised that passengers could take their autos with them on the company's Sacramento River steamers. By 1917 a company brochure promoting travel to San Francisco gave more details about getting around the Bay Area by automobile than it did about local trains.[55]

In 1915 the company ceased expanding rural local trains and stopped investing in them as well. Its opening in 1915 of a large and beautiful passenger station in Visalia marked the end of such investments. Most of the trains themselves continued to operate with increasingly outmoded wooden cars.

Thereafter the company sought means to reduce operating costs. It experimented in the application of motor vehicle technology in an effort to cut operating costs where traffic was light. By 1914 it had implemented McKeen gas-mechanical cars on several runs over the Sierra and on its old mainline into San Francisco, as well as on the Los Banos route in the San Joaquin Valley. It also installed automatic ticket machines in the Ferry building to expedite exposition traffic. To make coach travel more attractive in the San Joaquin Valley at a low cost, the company in 1917 equipped some trains with small lunch trolleys that served passengers from the aisles, much like today's airline service. It also improved food and beverage service on its *El Dorado* operating between San Francisco and Sacramento.[56]

The company treated its electric operations more favorably, although its heavy investments in suburban electric train operations apparently never earned a return. The financial performance of the electric lines stood out, because the company organized them as autonomous sections of the railroad or as subsidiary companies, effectively segregating their financial performance from the rest of the system. In 1914 the Pacific Electric Railway carried huge and increasing numbers of passengers in the rapidly growing Los Angeles metropolitan area, and although revenues covered expenses, not enough was left to pay bond interest. Electric operations in the San Francisco area performed even more poorly. After about 1917 the Peninsular Railway no longer covered operating expenses, although the economic historians George Hilton and John Due attributed part of the problem with this system to absentee management. Work rules contributed to financial problems for the company's East Bay electric operations, which operated under steam railroad work rules rather than the less restrictive streetcar work rules governing the Pacific Electric. Southern Pacific's $10 million investment made between 1909 and 1912 to improve these lines failed to earn even operating costs in 1914, let alone a return on investment. I have no evidence on the profitability of Southern Pacific's rural electric services in Oregon, but in view of the results in the Bay Area, it is almost certain that they, too, lost heavily.[57]

Although the electric operations lost money, their ridership grew rapidly into the 1920s. As we have seen, the company attempted to increase the revenues of its East Bay electric services by fare hikes and decrease their costs by work rule changes, but when politics foiled both efforts, the company faithfully continued operations. It continued investing in both its Oregon and its Los Angeles suburban operations until the early and mid-1920s, when ridership began to decline.

Long distance trains presented still a different situation. Although their usage increased, they lost money by 1914, according to Southern Pacific board chairman Julius Kruttschnitt. Kruttschnitt testified that Pullman services cost more than the railroad received in compensation. Yet everybody believed that Pullman trains were necessary, and the Southern Pacific kept expanding them.[58] Between 1910 and 1917 it replaced their wooden coaches, dining cars, and observation cars with new steel cars. This was partly in response to the Pullman Company's retiring most of its wooden sleeping cars in favor of the steel cars. The policy also reflected the fact that California's elites rode such trains and would continue doing so, even if they owned autos. Unfortunately, the heavy steel trains, which increased the tare weight per passenger by more than 40 percent, contributed to the worsening economic performance of passenger service. They cost much more than the wooden-bodied trains they replaced, and the weight liability came not only in the cars but in the locomotives. To pull the heavy steel trains, the railroads ordered much larger and costlier locomotives. Through the 1920s locomotive weight increased as the heavy trains were speeded up. By the end of the decade locomotives generally weighed half as much as the rest of the train. Trains almost always were accelerating or braking, and as average speeds for passenger trains increased, the liability of the heavy steel equipment became ever greater in fuel consumption and in wear and tear on the locomotives and track. These factors undoubtedly contributed to the trains' declining economic performance by 1914 and likely plagued the railroads even more in later years as they converted ever greater proportions of their service to the heavy steel equipment while also speeding up service.[59]

General investments in Southern Pacific infrastructure declined after

1913. In that year Sproule threatened to cease investments if earnings were not permitted to increase.[60] They were not, and with the Justice Department threatening to strip the Central Pacific from the company, the company curtailed many of its planned investments in 1913, including double tracking the main route between Sacramento and Ogden, building a new line between California and Oregon, and improving the line over Tehachapi Pass.[61]

Santa Fe management generally adopted the same approaches toward its passenger operations as did the Southern Pacific before 1918. Between 1911 and 1916 the Santa Fe expanded its intra-California passenger service by 45 percent, measured in train miles, even though in 1914 Santa Fe president E. P. Ripley claimed all passenger service lost money:

> You may say of the traveling public that the freight business is paying a portion of their expenses right now, for there is not a railroad in this country, at least no railroad west of the Allegheny Mountains, whose passenger business and mail business, judged by any proper standard of the ratio of expenses to income, is compensatory.[62]

The company also re-equipped its mainline passenger trains between Los Angeles and Chicago with steel cars, and it increased the amount of service offered by these trains. Between 1911 and 1917 their California service grew by 26 percent, and in 1917 it grew by another 2 percent.[63]

Although both types of Santa Fe passenger trains lost money, the company expanded them until 1916, and after 1916 it continued to expand its interstate trains. However, in 1917 the company abruptly changed its strategy for intra-California services by cutting train mileage 7 percent. At that time these trains provided heavy local service in the San Joaquin Valley, on various main and branch lines in the Los Angeles basin, and between Los Angeles and San Diego. It can be inferred by this action that the importance of at least some of the trains suddenly diminished in the eyes of company managers.

Had the United States not entered World War I, California's rail passenger managers probably would have done little more for several years. As it was, the country's entry into the conflict in April 1917 precipitated a crisis for American railroads that drastically changed the nature of passenger service in California and forced rail managers to inject a greater dose of economic considerations into their passenger decision making.

After the country entered the war, rapidly rising freight traffic paralyzed eastern ports and the rail yards serving them. The paralysis spread as eastbound freight trains backed up along mainlines feeding into the eastern seaboard. Soon choked yards and stranded trains tied up so many cars that shippers across the country could not obtain empty cars. To unsnarl the mess, the nation's rail leaders formed coordinating councils. When their efforts failed, the government stepped in.[64]

In a December 1917 executive order, President Woodrow Wilson established a new federal controlling agency, the United States Railroad Administration (USRA). Wilson appointed Secretary of Commerce William McAdoo as director general of railroads and charged him with the task of getting freight where it was needed for the war effort. While the operation of the nation's trains remained under the control of most of the same managers who had previously operated them, these managers now looked to McAdoo for leadership. Decisions were made by councils of railroad executives and labor officials in consultation with McAdoo. In a move that neither users nor the Interstate Commerce Commission anticipated when they encouraged federal control, Wilson, and later Congress, left them out of the decision-making process.[65]

McAdoo ordered that each railroad eliminate unessential passenger service. He also prohibited competitive passenger service between railroads. Where competition existed, one railroad would emerge as the dominant carrier. To the extent feasible, railroads also would jointly use passenger terminals and city ticket offices, closing those made redundant by such consolidation. Finally, McAdoo ordered railroads to curtail the use of observation and dining cars and to cut out the operation of second and third sections of trains to the extent feasible.[66]

In California the USRA designated the Southern Pacific/Union Pacific Overland Route as the primary passenger service between San Francisco and Chicago. It chose the Santa Fe as the primary carrier between Los Angeles and Chicago. It evidently chose the Southern Pacific as the dominant carrier for most intra-California traffic.[67]

California's railroads quickly responded. The Santa Fe abandoned its efforts to develop local train service in California, while the Southern Pacific showed its intent to keep providing comprehensive passenger rail service in the state. On New Year's Day 1918, Santa Fe president E. P. Ripley ordered the demise of the *Saint* and the *Angel*. Only seven years earlier he had inaugurated these overnight luxury sleeping car trains between Los Angeles and San Francisco to compete with the Southern Pacific *Lark* and *Sunset Limited*. Although the Santa Fe ran its contenders as fast as possible, speed could not overcome the Santa Fe's inferior route between Los Angeles and San Francisco. The *Saint* and *Angel*'s seventeen-hour schedule paled in comparison to the *Lark*'s fourteen hours. Except for the exposition year of 1915 and the war-inflated year of 1917, the two trains typically carried about forty to fifty passengers each.[68] They expired on January 6,

1918. Six months later the Santa Fe eliminated more than half of its intra-California train mileage. Its Los Angeles to San Diego line emerged as its only strong service in the state. The Santa Fe also virtually eliminated service between San Francisco and Chicago. While the Southern Pacific also cut back its mainline and local trains in California, it continued to operate more complete service, with several trains per day on most of its routes. The exception was in the Los Angeles basin, where it slashed most of its remaining local train service. However, its subsidiary Pacific Electric Railway served these areas.[69]

War-related policy of the USRA favored the Southern Pacific by eliminating most coastal shipping competition during the duration. The War Department requisitioned the *Harvard* and the *Yale* as well as other fast passenger ships in the San Francisco to Portland trade. Remaining coastal steamers came under the jurisdiction of the USRA, which raised their rates. Coastal steamer companies had already raised their rates by 63 percent in 1917 to compensate for higher costs. In 1918 the USRA increased coastal steamer rates by another 25 percent, bringing rates to 108 percent higher than in 1916.[70] As is seen in table 6, these actions, together with the end of Santa Fe competition, swelled the volume of Southern Pacific passenger traffic in California, while the Santa Fe's intrastate passenger presence dropped precipitously. However, the Santa Fe emerged from the conflict with heavily developed passenger service between Los Angeles and Chicago.

Federal control also increased both the costs and fares for passenger service. In 1918 McAdoo granted skilled railroad workers 30 percent wage increases to keep them from leaving railroad shops and trains for more lucrative manufacturing jobs. Coming on top of a 1916 law that reduced the railroad worker day from ten to eight hours, this increase pushed daily wages to 62.5 percent above those in 1916. McAdoo raised both freight and passenger rates about 40 percent in partial compensation. Passenger fares, which had hovered around 2.2 cents per mile for the previous twenty years, rose to 3 cents per mile in 1918. McAdoo also slapped a surcharge on the rent for Pullman rooms. Railroads rather than the Pullman Company kept this amount. The surcharge was intended both to depress Pullman usage and to compensate railroads for a service that railroad managers believed was becoming increasingly unprofitable.[71]

Users protested the rate increases, to little avail. While their protests prompted McAdoo to rescind the Pullman surcharge, they had no effect on the other freight and passenger rate increases.[72] Because they were excluded from decisions affecting what they considered to be their transportation system, shippers turned against government control.

When the war ended in November 1918 McAdoo recommended that Congress extend government control for another five years. Labor interests and some others advocated outright nationalization. Users, on the other hand, demanded a return to the pre-war situation when their voices dominated decisions of the Interstate Commerce Commission. Railroad managers vehemently opposed nationalization but would submit again to the ICC if it were made more responsible to the needs of the railroad industry. A compromise between railroad users and managers prevailed. Congress returned the nation's railroads to private operation with reformed regulatory oversight in March 1920.[73]

Before they did so the USRA and labor agreed on new national work rules and cost increases that were to affect the postwar viability of passenger service. Many view these agreements as a deleterious consequence of government control; a more accurate interpretation is that they were the price railroad management paid to return to private control. Upon deciphering the will of Congress in January 1919, McAdoo resigned as director general in favor of Walker D. Hines, a lawyer and board chairman of the Santa Fe who allegedly was contemptuous of labor and shipper interests. He subsequently signed national agreements with the railroad brotherhoods on the eve of private control in order to quell labor unrest. Labor's mood turned ugly upon learning of Congress's intent to return the roads to private control. It appears that managers needed a labor force with a better attitude and gave labor large concessions in an attempt to get it.[74]

Whatever the reasons, the agreements left the nation's railroads headed for a $1.2 billion operating deficit. Higher rates were needed, but Hines refused to further anger users. Instead, he slashed the 1919 maintenance program and passed the onus of rate increases on to the new Interstate Commerce Commission. When the USRA returned the railroads to private control in March 1920, deferred maintenance and the need for higher rates for both freight and passenger service topped the agendas of railroad managers. The ICC would have to deal with these issues.[75]

During the 1910s Southern Pacific and Santa Fe managers interpreted the changing context for passenger service through managerial hierarchies that typified those of the industry. These structures separated the analysis of costs and revenues into separate functions and led to large-scale cross subsidization within the industry. Cross subsidization also supported the growing awareness among railroad managers of their status as servants to their users, which included protecting less efficient markets from the more efficient.

As it became aware of the falseness of the traditional railroad cost paradigm, the ICC increasingly criticized such railroad management methods. It advocated a more efficient approach based on cost analysis and cost-based rates. Its efforts resulted in the separation of costs between freight and passenger service, which from that point on pressured railroad managements to make passenger service self-sustaining. The USRA further pushed railroad managements to consider passenger service in a business sense.

Under these circumstances passenger service changed its character in California. As the dominant carrier in the state, the Southern Pacific sought to provide comprehensive passenger service wherever its tracks ran, even if it lost money. While rural local trains were rapidly becoming unimportant to Californians, the Santa Fe's departure from the market gave the Southern Pacific incentive to continue providing such service, if on a reduced basis. Although they lost large amounts of money, Southern Pacific's electric operations were well used, and the company kept investing in them. This also was true for its long distance trains. The Santa Fe, on the other hand, greatly reduced the amount of its intrastate service while it increasingly concentrated its passenger efforts on trains running from Los Angeles to Chicago. As the 1920s dawned all of these passenger services as a whole were losing money.

3
Troubles during Prosperity, 1920–1929

The return of American railroads to private control on 1 March 1920 gave rail managements an opportunity to revise their passenger strategies. At the end of federal control rail passenger service lost money, and freight service lost even more, but new regulatory legislation promised railroad managements a fairer deal. Although highway construction continued at an even more rapid pace than before World War I, rail management had more latitude to alter and price passenger service. It hoped it would find a better way to serve the public with passenger trains and make adequate profits at the same time.

By the end of the 1920s, management was failing. Despite a decade of prosperity and favorable regulatory policy, railroad passenger service lost more money in 1929 than it did in 1920. Its share of the passenger market plummeted as well. Growing automobile ownership and improved highways during the 1920s explain much of the loss of market share during the decade, but despite some successes, railroad management failures in pricing, investments, and cost control played significant roles. An analysis of the passenger management practices of the Southern Pacific and Santa Fe in the context of national legislation, management thought, and traffic trends illuminates national problems with American passenger service during the 1920s.

The ICC's order to separate freight and passenger expenses in 1916 revealed that passenger service lost money for the nation's railroads as a whole. The passenger operating ratio of 74 meant that operating expenses consumed 74 percent of operating revenues, leaving an insufficient operating surplus to pay interest on debt and other fixed expenses and return an adequate profit (see table 2).

With an operating ratio of 86 in 1920, passenger service was showing even larger losses when Congress returned the nation's railroads to private control. The losses, resulting from hefty labor settlements in 1918 and 1919, would have been even greater if not for passenger efficiencies introduced during federal control. Because the freight operating ratio stood at the even higher level of 98, railroad managers could not cross subsidize passenger losses with freight profits, even if they wanted to do so. Only two options for restoring financial viability to passenger service faced them. They could reduce costs, or they could raise fares.[1]

Although the ICC generally prevented managers from raising rates before World War I, under the new rules of the Transportation Act of 1920 the ICC would not stand in the way of managers who wanted to follow this course, at least up to a point. In the 1920 act Congress directed the ICC to take the financial health of the railroads into account as well as the needs of shippers. The legislation defined a financially healthy railroad as one earning a 5.75 percent return on investment.[2]

Through the act Congress also encouraged the railroads to improve operating efficiency by entering into pooling agreements. In such an agreement competing railroads could coordinate their facilities and services between large cities and share the pooled revenues among themselves. The Interstate Commerce Act of 1887 had outlawed this practice, but the United States Railroad Administration (USRA) in effect followed it during government control, and Congress wanted efficiencies introduced by the USRA to continue under private control. Consequently, the act of 1920 nullified the anti-pooling provisions of the act of 1887.[3]

The 1920 act also promoted improved railroad efficiency by discouraging cross subsidies. It encouraged private railroads to provide only those services and facilities for which users were willing to pay. In the Hoch-Smith Resolution of 1925 Congress rescinded part of its prohibition against cross subsidies by specifying that other freight shippers cross subsidize grain movements, but before World War II it never altered its directive that freight and passenger services were to be self-supporting. The worsening deficits of passenger service after 1920, financed by ever larger cross subsidies from freight service, resulted from causes other than regulatory policy.[4]

Different classes of passenger service were also supposed to be financially supported by their users. If railroads spent more money to move a passenger one mile in a sleeping car than in a coach, regulatory policy encouraged the railroad to charge more for the use of the sleeping car.

In deciding what strategy to follow, railroad managers had to consider how sensitive passenger demand was to fare increases. As they did before World War I, managers in 1920 thought that the demand for passenger service was inelastic. This meant that the public considered passenger fares to be such a small part of their daily expenses that they would not mind paying higher fares. Managers were confident that they could raise fares without causing traffic to decline by much.

At the same time, managers considered competitive pressures between railroads. In competing for freight traffic, railroad companies used their passenger service to project their corporate identities and win business. Pooling agreements masked corporate identity. For this reason, managers intended to restore competitive luxury passenger trains complete with dining and observation cars. They also intended to resume the use of separate terminals and ticket offices. This meant that passenger costs would increase, further compelling fare increases.[5]

For all of these reasons railroad managers leaned toward the option of passenger fare increases when they retook control of the nation's railroads in 1920. Rather than improving on passenger efficiencies introduced by the USRA, or even maintaining such efficiencies, they intended to increase passenger costs even further and make the passengers pay for the increased costs. Although passengers never asked for such expensive items as ostentatious city terminals and duplicate luxury services, the ICC gave its blessing to fare increases with the hope that passengers would finance such unproductive debt and expenses.

After gaining ICC approval, the nation's railroads in August 1920 increased the one-way fare from $0.030 per passenger mile to $0.036, while they reimposed the Pullman surcharge that the USRA had briefly applied during World War I. The surcharge amounted to about a half cent a passenger mile and went to the railroads. The Pullman Company continued to collect room fees. The railroads also increased freight rates by 40 percent, although under strong pressure from shippers the ICC rolled back half of this increase two years later.[6]

Railroad management's position on the Pullman surcharge indicated its growing opposition to the idea of cross subsidies. Management claimed that Pullman cars cost more to haul than coaches because the lower capacity of Pullman cars meant that railroads had to operate longer or more trains to carry the same number of passengers. As the railroads argued in the early 1920s, and as the urban historian Carl Condit demonstrates in his studies of railroad terminals in Cincinnati and New York, more or longer trains cost the railroads dearly. First, running more trains increased fuel, wage, and maintenance costs. Second, to handle the increasing numbers of all-Pullman limiteds, terminals needed lengthened and additional tracks, more complex interconnections between tracks, and more elaborate servicing facilities. Pullman cars also caused much greater than average switching expenses and necessitated costly and cumbersome reservation systems. A substantial part of the costs of the great, burdensome city terminals, as well as many intermediate stations, arose from serving Pullman trains, although only a tiny fraction of the passengers using the terminals were Pullman passengers.[7] Appealing to Brandeis's arguments of 1914, the railroads argued for more compensation from each Pullman passenger. E. L. Bevington, chairman of the Transcontinental Passenger Association, testified on behalf of the Western Carriers on 5 September 1923:

> The carriers submit that this additional cost [of Pullman cars] should not be borne by them; neither should it be shifted to coach passengers nor reflected in the additional revenue which must be derived from freight traffic. In making an additional charge for transportation in sleeping and parlor cars, the carriers are merely applying the principle which has frequently been upheld by this commission and by the Supreme Court of the United States that each service furnished by the carrier should stand upon its own bottom and pay its own way.[8]

The ICC not only accepted this reasoning, it upheld it in 1924 after two years of hearings in which commercial traveler associations complained of the hardship of the surcharge. The ICC did this even though the railroads stubbornly refused to provide estimates of costs for moving Pullman and coach passengers.[9] In granting these fare increases and in subsequent reviews of them in 1922 and 1923, the ICC agreed with the railroads' argument that every source of passenger revenue had to be protected. The railroads could not afford fare experimentation.[10]

At first the fare increase appeared to have no impact on ridership. The huge passenger flows of early 1920 continued unabated, and passenger revenues swelled. This happy situation continued until the recession of 1921, during which passenger revenues rapidly fell nationally as well as in California.

The drop in revenues that began in 1921 reflected more than a temporary downturn in the economy. It reflected the intensification of economic and competitive trends that had set in after 1910. As the economy continued to specialize and expand, competitive enterprises catering to its transportation demands continued to proliferate.

During the 1920s the production of consumer durables came to dominate American industry and alter American life. Auto manufacturing led the way, becoming by the middle 1920s the nation's largest industry.[11] There were few individual habits the auto, its manufacturers, and its sellers did not alter in the process. Among the most radically changed were those of intercity travel.[12]

The auto not only expanded the volume of intercity travel, it cut into the passenger train market as well. In 1920 average Americans used autos

50 miles per year for intercity travel, while they used intercity trains 450 miles per year. Just ten years later the average American drove 1,691 miles per year in intercity travel but rode only 219 miles per year on the train. By this time the American passenger train failed to earn its operating expenses, according to Interstate Commerce Commission statistics.[13]

California exaggerated such trends because of its extraordinary population growth and rapid motorization. Having reached 2.4 million people in 1910, the state's population climbed to 3.6 million by 1920. During the next ten years, another 2.1 million people moved to the state. They settled largely in the suburban communities of Los Angeles County and to a lesser extent in the suburban counties of the Bay Area.[14] At the same time, auto ownership in the state rose from 150 cars per 1,000 population in 1920 to 340 cars per 1,000 by 1930 (see table 3). Auto-oriented newcomers increasingly ignored rail service in deciding where to live and work, and the state's development interests considered it increasingly irrelevant.

Such economic and population growth, combined with rapid motorization, rapidly congested the state's new highway system. These factors altered the emphasis in road construction in the early 1920s. Attention shifted to improving the concrete roads that already existed. For some time rural and urban interests debated methods for determining road improvement priorities. The original statewide standard of four-inch-thick, fifteen-foot-wide concrete pavement was clearly inadequate. The thin pavement quickly shattered under the weight of the primitive trucks of the time, while the narrow width could not accommodate any but the lightest traffic. The highway commission debated whether it should adopt a revised uniform standard for all of the state's highways or vary its standards according to actual traffic conditions. The issue has never been resolved, but by the early 1920s traffic volume became an increasingly potent weapon in political fights over standards and the allocation of road funds.[15] Generally the highway commission adopted higher standards for roads with greater traffic.

Traffic counts became the informational method used for determining road improvement priorities. In 1920 the highway commission conducted its first count, and it made a second in 1922. Traffic crossing the 103 counting stations increased by 43 percent in this two-year period. Thereafter the highway commission conducted counts annually. In 1926 state highway traffic was 300 percent greater than in 1920.[16] The next year the highway commission began using such trends to project road needs for the future: "From the general increase noted yearly in the traffic, the Maintenance Department has prepared a chart setting forth the expected increase up to the year 1940. As all California state highways are now being constructed to take care of future traffic, as well as that of the present, the traffic count in this way has become a valuable aid to the Construction Department."[17]

Through the 1920s the state and counties spent $512 million on road construction. Adjusted for inflation, the pace of road construction outraced the state's mushrooming population. Year by year motoring Californians encountered larger and more numerous construction and improvement projects. As in the teens, county expenditures generally exceeded those of the state, but not by much, and by the end of the decade the ever thinner lead in county expenditures evaporated. This change reflected increasing priority for the improvement of trunk roads (see table 4).

With the aid of federal funds and state gas taxes, the highway commission extended, straightened, widened, and thickened the more heavily traveled trunk roads throughout the 1920s. Multiple-lane roads appeared in the suburban Los Angeles and San Francisco areas and began extending outward along main routes into rural areas. At the same time, county highway commissions built thousands of miles of additional concrete highways. There was also a push to connect California with the outside world by paved highways. The first links across the Sierra to Reno and across the Imperial Valley to Yuma opened shortly after 1925; the link to Oregon opened soon after.[18]

In the late 1920s, the highway commission unveiled a new type of mountain highway. Its curves had minimum radii of one thousand feet, and it was designed to be driven continuously at the legal speed limit of forty miles per hour. The commission planned this type of road for all of the major mountain passes and grades along those parts of the system linking the state's large cities, many of which suffered terrible congestion by the middle 1920s. The first application of this radically new idea would replace the original Ridge Route between Los Angeles and Bakersfield. By 1930 the new route was under construction.[19]

As the 1920s progressed the highway commission more zealously articulated its ideology of providing the state with free roads, and by the end of the decade it decided that private road initiatives clashed with its mission. Private toll-financed companies built and operated several roads and bridges in the state, including the spectacular Carquinez Straits Bridge between Vallejo and Crockett on the San Francisco–Sacramento route. Built by the American Toll Bridge Company, this was by far the most ambitious highway bridge in the state, but in the early 1920s several private toll bridge companies sought franchises to build a much grander project to link San Francisco and Oakland with what would be the world's greatest bridge. After years of hearings that showed the feasibility of the bridge, but which failed to authorize private companies to build it, the highway commission adopted a policy in 1928 calling for the elimination of all private toll facilities in California. It sought state legislation to establish a toll bridge authority to assume the task of building the San Francisco–Oakland Bay bridge and to eventually take over private toll roads and bridges in the state. The legislation passed in 1929, and although the California Supreme Court did not uphold its legality until 1931, the California Toll Bridge Authority was formed and began work in 1929. It opened the Bay Bridge to autos in 1936 and to interurban trains in 1939, and by 1941 it took over the remaining private road facilities in California.[20]

As if such ubiquitous road construction projects combined with state attacks on the involvement of private enterprise with transportation infrastructure were not enough to dispirit California's railroad management, the reorganization of the intercity bus industry began competing with trains by the early 1920s. The regional monopolies that emerged at the end of World War I continued to expand through mergers. As the companies grew, they lengthened and strengthened trunk routes between major metropolitan areas and increasingly abandoned other services. By 1926 two statewide systems and one regional system dominated the intercity bus industry in California. Under the direction of Charles Wren, Pickwick Stages operated the largest intercity bus system in the United States. Routes covered much of California and extended north to Portland and east as well. Buck Travis directed Pickwick's tough and nearly as large rival, the California Transit Company. A third company, Motor Transit, held suburban rights in the greater Los Angeles area, including the towns of San Bernardino, Riverside, and Santa Ana.

Under this arrangement the California Railroad Commission allowed little competition among bus carriers for local traffic. Where two or more carriers used the same highway, only one held rights for local traffic.[21] However, bus lines competed with trains.

Wren and Travis expanded their bus operations rapidly after 1926. Both organized holding companies to take over operating properties in other parts of the country and forge national systems. In 1927, Travis formed the American Motor Transportation Company, which included his California Transit Company and other smaller operators that he purchased. In 1928, under the trade name of Pioneer Yelloway Stages, American Motor Transportation started service between San Francisco and New York, the first transcontinental bus service in the United States.[22]

Steamships also made a comeback. In 1921 Los Angeles interests organized the Los Angeles Steamship Company and returned the *Harvard* and the *Yale* to the West Coast for five-day-a-week service between San

Diego, Los Angeles, and San Francisco. Compared to 1917, the refurbished ships featured almost twice as much space per passenger and a faster eighteen-hour schedule for the San Pedro to San Francisco part of the run. Through the 1920s these ships carried on average 1,400 to 2,100 passengers per week between the three coastal cities, although summer traffic greatly exceeded the average.[23] The one-way fare of $18 (including berth and meals) between Los Angeles and San Francisco matched the Southern Pacific coach fare and considerably undercut the sleeping car fare. Fast passenger steamships also returned to service between San Francisco, Portland, and Seattle and continued to beat Southern Pacific passenger trains during the early 1920s.[24]

Competitive pressures during the 1920s devastated Southern Pacific and Santa Fe passenger revenues, which fell 55 and 45 percent respectively between 1920 and 1929. Conventional wisdom holds that most of the ridership loss resulted from short haul coach riders deserting trains for automobiles, while long distance sleeping car travel remained robust. This view is supported by the fact that the average trip length of Santa Fe passengers increased from 139 miles in 1920 to 292 miles in 1929. Santa Fe historian Keith Bryant attributes the increase to the drying up of branch line and local coach traffic. On the surface, national statistics support this interpretation. Table 8 shows a remarkable 67 percent collapse in national coach traffic during the 1920s, which observers at the time attributed to the same cause as Bryant.[25]

Other evidence suggests a more complex explanation for the decline in Southern Pacific and Santa Fe passenger revenues. Table 8 also shows that the average distance traveled by intercity coach passengers remained about the same in the United States through the 1920s, revealing that long distance coach passengers left the rails just as rapidly as did short distance coach passengers. At the beginning of the 1920s many coach passengers rode very long distances. For example, in 1921 the Santa Fe gained about a third of its Chicago–Los Angeles passenger revenue from coach passengers riding the full 2,000-mile distance between those cities.[26] These figures suggest that in addition to coach passengers deserting rural local trains, such as those in the San Joaquin Valley, many transcontinental coach passengers left the rails as well. At the same time, the Pullman market softened remarkably during the 1920s. Many businesspeople who rode Pullman cars on runs as short as 90 miles in the early 1920s switched to speeded-up day trains or to automobiles by the end of the decade, reflected in table 8 by a 25 percent decline in the number of Pullman users and an increase in the average distance that each Pullman passenger traveled from 367 miles in 1920 to 486 miles in 1929. Many long distance tourists also stopped using Pullman cars in the mid-1920s, as discussed later in this chapter. So, while the Santa Fe lost 55 percent of its 1920 intra-California revenue by 1929 and the Southern Pacific lost 41 percent, both railroads also lost substantial interstate passenger revenue. Despite the dramatic population growth in southern California, the two railroads' revenues earned from interstate passengers in California dropped by 24 and 27 percent respectively during that period. Because interstate traffic fell while population increased, the percentage of California income spent on interstate train travel fell by more than half during the 1920s, as shown in figure 3.1.[27]

While certain long distance markets declined during the 1920s, some short distance markets remained relatively stable. The heaviest noncommuter rail passenger haulers in the United States—the Pennsylvania Railroad, the New York Central, and the New York, New Haven & Hartford—served numerous short haul markets in the East. These companies experienced passenger revenue losses of 5, 8, and 12 percent respectively between 1920 and 1929. In 1933 far more noncommuter passengers traveled between New York and Philadelphia, only 91 miles apart, than between any other pair of cities in the United States. In that year, when Southern Pacific and Santa Fe passenger revenues stood respectively at only 14 and 18 percent of their 1920 levels, the most heavily traveled noncommuter rail route in the West was that between San Francisco and Sacramento, only 92 miles apart.[28]

These considerations suggest that during the 1920s not so much the distance between cities as the nature of the service area and the traveler determined the competitiveness of passenger trains. Rail travel increasingly involved people traveling between big cities, whether far apart or close together, and it increasingly involved people traveling on business. Not short distance riders but price-sensitive travelers left the rails in droves during the 1920s, particularly in rural areas. Railroads such as the Southern Pacific and the Santa Fe, who gained substantial revenue from rurally oriented and price-sensitive passengers at the zenith of the passenger train era circa 1910, suffered greatly during the 1920s. Their remaining market increasingly centered on businesspeople traveling between the few large cities in their respective territories.

The Southern Pacific and Santa Fe managements reacted to the local traffic trends in California differently, primarily because the companies played different roles in the state's economy. As the regulated transportation monopoly in much of California, the Southern Pacific assumed responsibilities that the Santa Fe did not. Its managers felt obligated to provide some unprofitable passenger services; Santa Fe managers felt such obligations to a much lesser extent and consequently acted more decisively and in a more businesslike manner.

As a regulated monopoly, Southern Pacific needed to provide complete

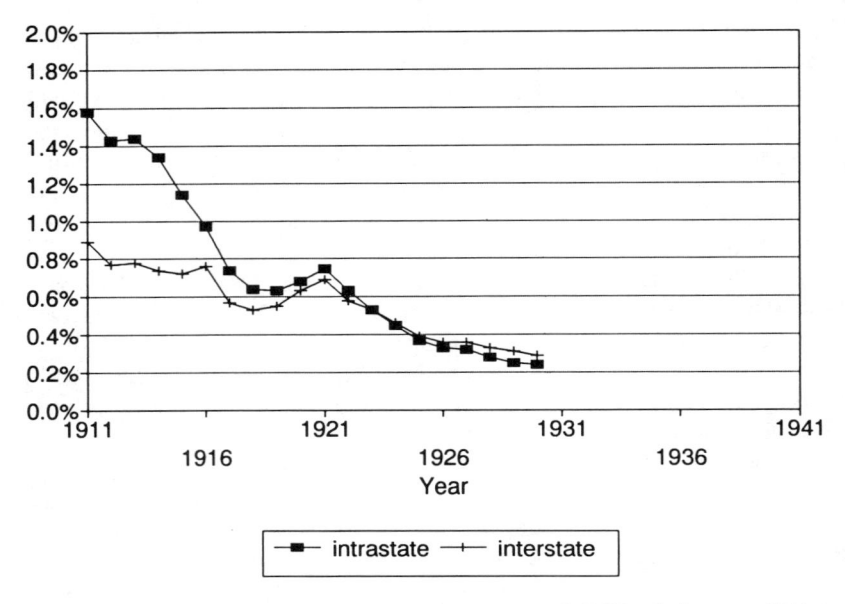

3.1 California passenger revenues as a percentage of California income, 1911–1930. Source: Table 20

passenger transportation service. This meant coverage to populated areas, service at the most demanded times, and sufficient space so as never to leave a passenger behind, even during peak demand times. Criticisms about wasteful passenger service and dictums not to cross subsidize tempered such considerations.

Examination of Southern Pacific's passenger decisions suggests that it compromised between the conflicting goals by trimming rural local services as traffic dwindled and expanding its mainline train services. Southern Pacific strategy differed from the Santa Fe's in that it did not cut back its local trains to what the Santa Fe called the irreducible minimum (a daily gas-electric car), but instead converted them to bus services offering several trips each day when traffic became embarrassingly light.

By comparing the pattern of train service that the Southern Pacific operated in central California at various times between 1915 and 1930, one can see the broad outline of the company's passenger strategy. Figures 3.2, 3.3, and 3.4 taken together and compared to figure 1.1 in chapter 1 show the pattern of change in Southern Pacific passenger service during the 1920s. The company reduced rural local train service and expanded the number of through trains between San Francisco and Los Angeles. During the 1920s train mileage additions roughly matched train mileage reductions. The total number of passenger train miles remained roughly constant until 1928 (see table 11).

In the early 1920s the company attempted to protect the demand for all of its passenger train services by politically denouncing intercity buses. Southern Pacific *Bulletins* between 1921 and 1923 contain numerous editorials by top company officers attacking unfair bus competition. They demanded that the state prohibit profit-making companies from using public roads, which they said the state should preserve only for private motorists. Letters to the editor from train and shop employees working in centers of local train operation echoed these points. In 1922 train and shop workers employed in Vallejo demonstrated against buses. Sixty-one train and shop employees based in that town operated and maintained a network of local passenger trains that fanned out to Santa Rosa, Calistoga, and Fairfield. Spokespeople for the employees stressed that their payroll of $131,000 helped support Vallejo's economy. They argued that buses were destroying this base, forcing the elimination of twenty employees.[29]

In later years Buck Travis, the California bus entrepreneur, bitterly referred to this period when he claimed that the Southern Pacific attempted to use its influence in Sacramento to legislate buses off state roads. Fighting back through the Motor Carriers Association, the bus interests eventually won and continued their mergers and restructuring of service into long intercity trunk routes.[30]

Even as it sought legislation against buses, the Southern Pacific Company discontinued local trains. Cases on the discontinuances suggest that management sought to eliminate some local trains when revenues no longer covered out-of-pocket costs. Railroads defined these as the direct costs of running passenger trains, which were a small fraction of average costs. In 1923 the average cost of operating a Southern Pacific passenger train was about $2.50 per train mile, according to Interstate Commerce Commission statistics. This figure is the ICC-defined fully allocated cost for passenger service for 1923 divided by the number of passenger train miles operated that year. It indicates all operating expenses that the Southern Pacific directly or indirectly attributed to passenger service, but the company believed that if it reduced passenger service by one mile, it would save only a small part of these expenses. The company kept a summary sheet of each passenger train on each division that showed the train weight behind the locomotive and revenues and costs that the company thought were directly attributable to the train operation. These included engine crew, train crew, and fuel expenses and totaled between $0.33 and $0.50 per train mile. For example, for a particular day in 1923 the *Lark,* Southern Pacific's crack overnight limited between Los Angeles and San Francisco, weighed 710 tons, cost $0.39 per mile to operate, and brought in $4.82 per mile in gross

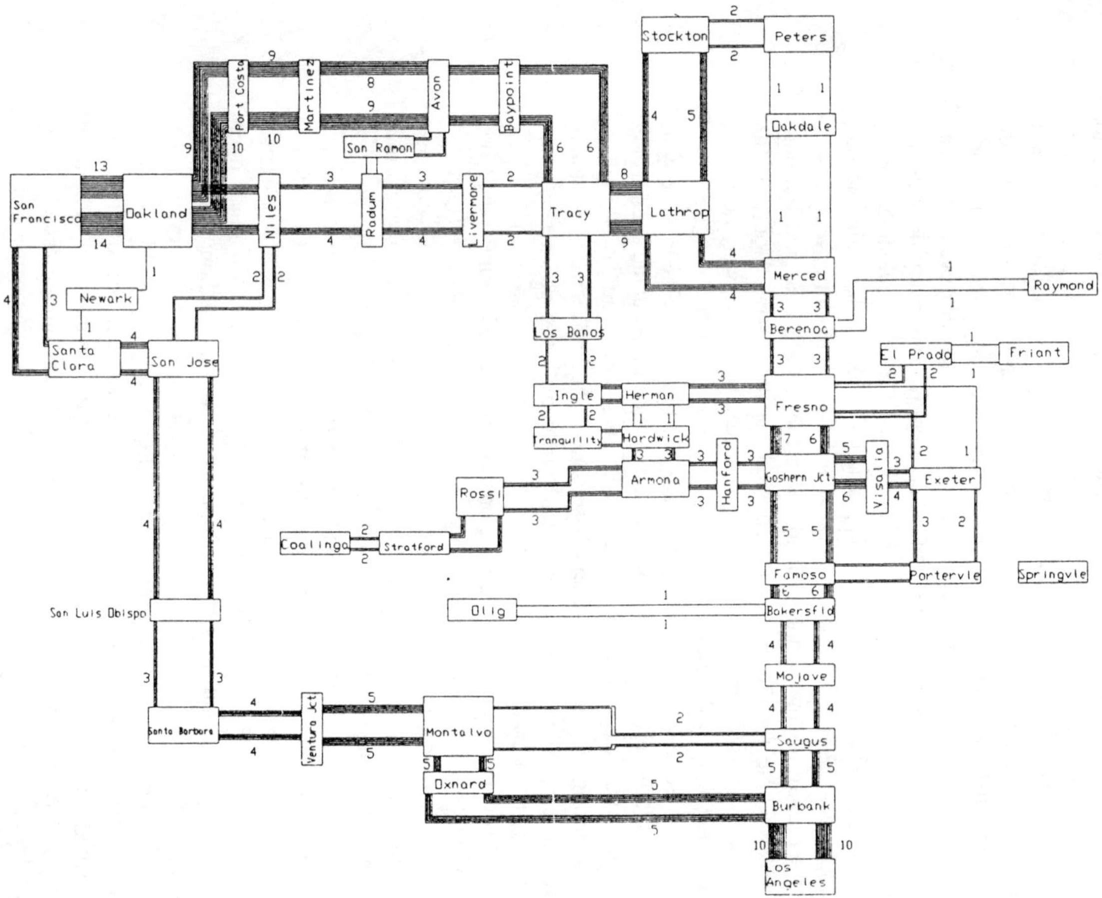

3.2 Southern Pacific passenger train services in central California, ca. 1920. Source: SFC, exhibit 626

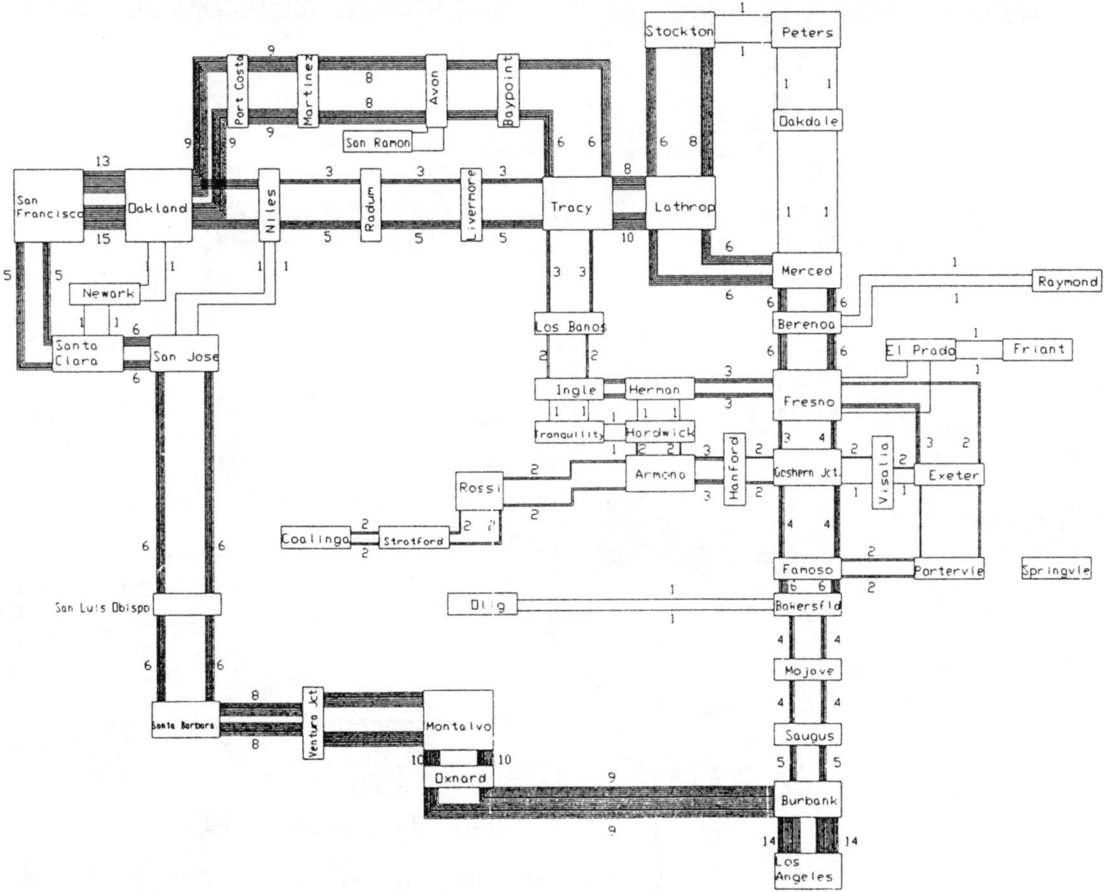

3.3 Southern Pacific passenger train services in central California, ca. 1925. Source: SFC, exhibit 626

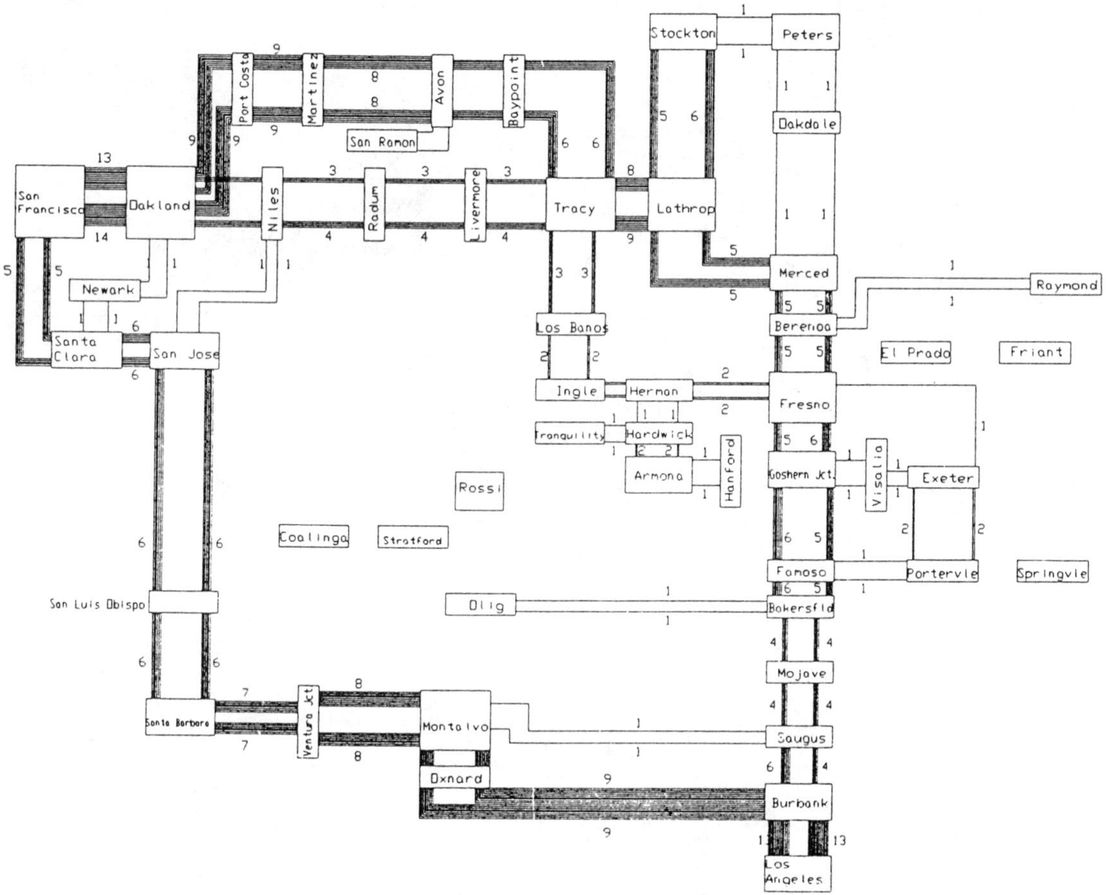

3.4 Southern Pacific passenger train services in central California, ca. 1930. Source: SFC, exhibit 626

revenue. On the other hand, No. 24, the San Francisco to San Luis Obispo local, weighed 156 tons, cost $0.33 per mile to operate, and brought in $0.67 per mile in gross revenue. Company records showed virtually no difference between the cost of running a heavy train compared to a light one, and in both cases costs were less than one-fifth the ICC-defined average cost for running a typical Southern Pacific train.[31]

In the mid-1920s Southern Pacific ceased keeping such records of passenger train performance, but on an ad hoc basis it estimated out-of-pocket passenger costs when it considered abandoning a train with low gross earnings or running a new train. So did the Santa Fe. An examination of such figures shows that out-of-pocket costs, as defined by management, steadily rose through the 1920s, reaching about $1.00 a train mile for steam trains by the end of the decade. During this time the figure included more expense accounts that management came to believe were variable, such as passenger car and locomotive maintenance, train supplies, and engine house expenses, as well as a small amount for track maintenance.[32]

Trains that management abandoned typically grossed less than $0.50 per train mile, sometimes half that, suggesting average traffic of less than ten passengers and a handful of mail and express. I could find no record of controversy surrounding such abandonments. The railroad commission routinely approved and reported them, generally without comment.

Because of its desire to maintain the Southern Pacific image as a comprehensive transportation system, management refused to reduce branch line passenger service in many areas below several schedules per day. As traffic on rural trains continued to decline, management sought ways to operate them more cheaply. In 1927 it decided that the best strategy was to replace such trains with Southern Pacific buses, which management figured would cost much less to operate and look more modern. Coordinated with through trains, buses would meet the company's objective of providing comprehensive transportation service. No potential railroad competitor could accuse it of shirking its duty and abandoning the field.

Lee D. Jones, Southern Pacific's superintendent of transportation in the mid-1920s, scheduled the company's passenger trains. In 1936 he testified that by the mid-1920s most rural local passengers had abandoned trains for automobiles. What local business remained for public carriers used buses, which offered more frequent service on the parallel highways. Only long distance passengers used the rural local trains to begin or end their trips, and according to Jones, Southern Pacific management thought such passengers were too few to justify the local trains. On the other hand, while Southern Pacific management believed the railroad commission would let it abandon any local train it chose to discontinue, it feared that by doing so it would lose what it called presence in the state. It is difficult to determine what Jones meant by "presence," but he probably meant that influential groups in various communities in the state would think less of the railroad if it eliminated its remaining networks of local trains. There was also the consideration that the railroad commission or the Interstate Commerce Commission might become more inclined to allow competing railroads to expand their operations in California if the Southern Pacific ceased to provide comprehensive passenger service. In the mid-1920s the Southern Pacific vigorously fought initiatives by the Great Northern Railway to build into northern California and the Western Pacific to extend routes deep into the San Joaquin Valley. To maintain presence, according to Jones, Southern Pacific management decided not to eliminate all local train service but to replace remaining rural local trains with company-owned buses.[33]

Before entering the bus business, Southern Pacific president William Sproule pulled several of his officers together into an ad hoc committee to study bus operations throughout the United States. The committee reported to Executive Vice President Paul Shoup, who headed several of Southern Pacific's electric railway subsidiaries and who in 1929 replaced Sproule as company president.[34]

The committee's attention soon focused on a bus operation begun by the New York, New Haven & Hartford Railroad. During the first two decades of the century the New Haven built up a huge debt in order to finance its monopolization of surface transportation in southern New England. In the mid-1920s passengers began deserting many of the rural local services for which the company had paid so dearly a few years earlier. The company then attempted to cut costs by substituting buses for many of its local trains. To operate its buses it formed the New England Transportation Company, a wholly owned subsidiary, in 1925.[35]

Finding itself in circumstances not dissimilar to the New Haven's, Southern Pacific management in the spring of 1927 formed the Southern Pacific Motor Transport Company (SPMT), a bus subsidiary modeled after the New Haven effort. Appointed superintendent of the new bus operation, Jones immediately began drawing up bus schedules to replace entire systems of branch line trains centered in Santa Cruz and Vallejo as well as many trains in the Sacramento and San Joaquin valleys. The Southern Pacific organized another bus subsidiary, Oregon Motor Stages, to replace remaining steam trains and the entire electric rail operation centered in Portland. Far more rural than suburban in character, Southern Pacific's Portland electric operation had lost much of its traffic, unlike the company's East Bay electric operations or its Pacific Electric subsidiary in Los Angeles.[36]

To implement its plans in California, SPMT needed certificates of convenience and necessity, which it sought to purchase from established bus operators. Because of the low traffic density of the territories that SPMT intended to serve, most of the existing bus lines still were provided by owner-operators or small-scale companies. SPMT generally succeeded in buying the rights from the established operators, but in the Santa Cruz area an owner refused to sell. SPMT then applied to the railroad commission for a bus certificate allowing it to operate bus service that would compete with the established operator.[37]

Through the Motor Carriers Association Travis and Wren bitterly fought this seemingly unimportant application. Both entrepreneurs built their bus empires with confidence that the railroad commission never issued certificates where service already existed. Neither wanted a powerful railroad to break this precedent. If the Southern Pacific won the Santa Cruz case, it could quickly establish trunk bus lines along its own mainlines throughout California. This would put Southern Pacific buses in head-to-head competition with both Pickwick and California Transit. In 1928 the Southern Pacific had the financial resources to put either bus company out of business, if it so chose, and given the Southern Pacific's efforts to legislate buses off the roads in the early 1920s, neither Travis nor Wren trusted the company's motives.[38]

Despite Travis and Wren's arguments, the Southern Pacific won its case in October 1928. It quickly discontinued trains and implemented its bus operations in California and Oregon. Generally the new buses operated more frequently than the trains they replaced, but they lost money, and traffic continued to decline. Because of this and because of the fears aroused in Travis and Wren, the stage was set for the formation of Pacific Greyhound Lines, discussed in the next chapter.[39]

As the 1920s unfolded, Southern Pacific management realized that declining passenger train profitability stemmed not only from branch line trains but from mainline trains. Earnings per train mile were slipping on popular trains. In 1923, for example, the company began a daily luxury coach train on a fast twelve-hour daytime schedule between San Francisco and Los Angeles. Called the *Daylight,* the new train appealed to the public, and by 1925 it grossed an average of $4.71 per train mile. Whether caused by growing auto use or a price war between Pickwick and California Transit for through Los Angeles to San Francisco business, usage of the *Daylight* declined after 1925. By 1928 the train grossed only $3.87 per train mile.[40]

The company reacted to declining earnings of important trains in several ways. One was to discount fares. The high 3.6 cent fare that the ICC approved for national application in 1920 applied to one-way fares. If railroad managements wanted to lower fares in specific markets, they could alter round trip and excursion fares without petitioning the ICC for approval. This they increasingly did in the latter half of the 1920s.

Where a railroad monopolized rail service, as the Southern Pacific did between Los Angeles and San Francisco, management could act more freely than where competition existed. In the latter case custom compelled it to convince the competing road of the wisdom of the fare change, and then the competing road would also implement it. California railroads observed such niceties since before 1906, when John J. Byrne, the Santa Fe's assistant passenger traffic manager in Los Angeles, outlined the basic arrangement before a gathering of railroad traffic officers.[41] The traffic association served as the forum for deliberations between traffic officers of different railroads over fares, although in at least some cases individual traffic officers of two roads would work together outside of the association.

The passenger traffic manager generally was management's expert on fares. After 1925 Felix S. McGinnis held this position on the Southern Pacific's Pacific Lines. A Los Angeles native, McGinnis started with the Southern Pacific as an office boy in 1900 and rose through the upper managerial ranks during the reign of President William Sproule in the early 1920s. Following Sproule's example, McGinnis cultivated ties with the most prestigious social clubs in the area where he resided. In the early 1920s this was still Los Angeles, but after moving to San Francisco in 1925, McGinnis did likewise in that city. In 1929 the company promoted him to vice president of passenger traffic, a new post that extended his duties to overseeing passenger traffic of all properties owned by the Southern Pacific Company. Prominent in San Francisco and Los Angeles social circles, he represented the company and divined the tastes of both the traveling public and the social elite of the state.[42]

In 1936 McGinnis testified that the public's willingness to pay railroad fares varied for different types of traffic and between different pairs of cities. In general McGinnis believed that a fare existed in each market above which traffic would not flow and below which further fare reductions would stimulate little additional traffic. Rail passenger traffic managers of the period often stated this theory. They called fares above this level "traffic-rejecting fares," and in general they sought to keep fares just below this level. If they succeeded, they obtained the most possible gross revenue for a particular service.[43]

McGinnis believed that the official fare established in 1920 had been implemented as a wartime measure to suppress demand and was from the outset a traffic-rejecting fare.[44] In the late 1920s he sought to selectively overturn it as revenues per train mile sagged on many previously popular trains. He did this by increasingly discounting round trips and weekend

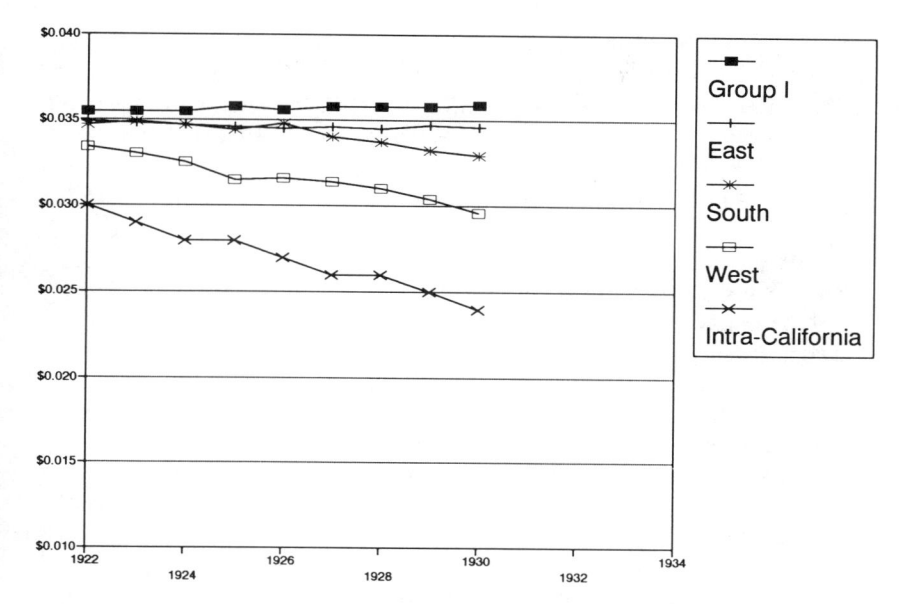

3.5 Passenger fare yields in U.S. regions, 1922–1930. Group 1 includes the Pennsylvania Railroad, the New York Central, and the New Haven. Source: Table 24

excursion fares and often was gratified by at least a temporary recovery of gross earnings.[45] The company also began discounting long distance coach and tourist sleeping car fares on numerous trains affected by long distance bus competition. Southern Pacific even lowered the basic one-way fare on the *Daylight* in 1929, which restored its earnings to $4.60 per train mile, albeit at the cost of carrying many more passengers, which meant higher operating costs and lower surpluses compared to 1925.[46]

Fare discounts lowered the revenue that each passenger mile brought in for the Southern Pacific. The revenue per passenger mile declined most severely for travel within California, but it declined generally for the system, as it did for all western and southern railroads. Only in the Northeast did revenue yields hold up. This phenomenon, shown in figure 3.5, reflected the lessening value that the public placed on rail service. In the Northeast the public continued to ride high-priced trains, most likely because northeastern trains operated at almost double the speed of those in the West and consequently were of higher value to business travelers.

Lowered bus and train fares combined with faster train schedules spelled the end for passenger coastal steamship service along the West Coast. While the steamship companies succeeded in holding on to traffic by meeting lowered rail coach fares at the end of the 1920s, the reduced revenues failed to cover costs. Deficits rapidly accelerated as steamships met further rail and bus fares reductions in the early 1930s. After one of the two Los Angeles Steamship Company ships ran aground in 1931, making daily service impossible, the steamship service ceased to compete significantly in the California market. A bitter West Coast maritime strike in 1934 sealed its fate.[47]

While Southern Pacific management discounted fares on long distance trains, it also speeded the trains up in response to auto competition. Under USRA control, the *Overland Limited* ran between San Francisco and Chicago in seventy-two hours. In late 1920 Southern Pacific cut the schedule to sixty-eight hours, but it made no further schedule improvements until 1926. Thereafter, the company cut additional time from the schedule almost every year. By May 1930 the *Overland* completed the run in fifty-seven hours.[48]

Almost certainly the automobile played a role in these speedups. Paved roads connected California to the East about 1926, and long distance auto touring was not only feasible but popular. Warren Bellasco shows that after 1925 autos accounted for much more travel to western national parks than did trains. Richard Overton reports that the Burlington complained about reduced earnings from its trains to the Rockies in 1927 because of auto competition. Taken in the context of Bellasco's and Overton's observations, the fact that significant speedups on the *Overland Limited* did not occur between 1920 and 1926, and were then followed by a series of improvements, suggests that management made the improvements at least in part in response to automobile competition.[49]

Competition between cities on the West Coast also influenced Southern Pacific's decisions on speed and appointments of its transcontinental trains. The railroad and business historian Maury Klein points out that railroad managements strived to equalize service between Chicago and the large cities on the West Coast in order not to anger jealous business elites in the various cities. Prior to World War I the railroads agreed among themselves to provide equal but not excessively extravagant service on these routes, and the agreements generally held until the mid-1920s, when the Santa Fe broke ranks. Most likely driven by auto competition, the Santa Fe then began speeding up its trains and improving their amenities. Union Pacific responded on its own route to Los Angeles, obligating it to make similar improvements to the *Overland* service that it jointly operated with Southern Pacific to San Francisco.[50]

Under the threat of auto competition, Southern Pacific management speeded up most of its passenger trains modestly between 1925 and 1930, as shown in table 12. Investments in improved locomotive designs at the end of the 1920s helped management to realize the speedups. Modern passenger locomotives of the 4-6-4 varieties introduced by the New York Central about 1927 showed that steam engines could efficiently cruise in the sixty to seventy mile per hour range, in contrast to about forty miles per hour for the 4-6-2 locomotives they replaced. Southern Pacific ordered larger but slower 4-8-2s to replace its 4-6-2s on important passenger trains; like the New York Central engines, they allowed for the operation of longer trains at faster speeds more economically than previously was possible.[51]

Two investments in track and signal improvements also allowed significantly higher Southern Pacific train speeds in the 1920s. In the San Francisco suburban district Southern Pacific spent approximately $4 million during the early 1920s to expedite its growing but unprofitable commuter traffic. This sum provided for a more complex track structure, additional interlockings, and a replacement block signal system between San Francisco and San Jose, allowing the company to operate more suburban and long distance passenger trains into San Francisco at higher speeds.[52]

In 1928 the company also began work to replace its train ferries across the Carquinez Straits with a large bridge costing $12 million. Completed in 1930, the bridge unplugged a major bottleneck for both freight and passenger trains. After it opened, passenger trains completed the run between San Francisco and Sacramento one-half hour faster.[53]

Southern Pacific could have increased speeds substantially more between San Francisco and Los Angeles had it invested in shortening the San Joaquin Line linking these major markets. While auto competition was drying up rural rail traffic in the state, heavy freight and passenger traffic flows continued between Los Angeles and San Francisco, which constituted one of the Southern Pacific's largest passenger and freight markets in the 1920s. If the company was to continue thriving in these markets, it needed a better rail route linking the two metropolitan regions. Year by year improvements to the state highway system, particularly in mountain passes, accentuated the tremendous circuity of both the Coast and the San Joaquin lines and lessened their competitiveness. The 1916 opening of the original Ridge Route cut the highway distance between San Francisco and Los Angeles to 425 miles, compared to the San Joaquin Line's approximate 480 miles and the Coast Line's approximate 470 miles. Curve straightenings and widenings during the 1920s improved driving conditions considerably.

Southern Pacific management invested relatively little money to make its rail routes between San Francisco and Los Angeles more competitive with such highway improvements. Outside of the San Francisco suburban project and improvements in the Los Angeles terminal district, the company between 1916 and 1935 invested only $7.7 million chargeable to capital in the Coast Line and $8.3 million in the San Joaquin Line.[54] Most of the Coast Line work centered on a $6 million project begun in the late 1920s to re-signal and otherwise increase the capacity and speed of the Coast Line between San Jose and Watsonville Junction. Approximately $3.3 million of this amount paid for a line change and new passenger terminal in San Jose to take tracks off city streets. The remainder increased the capacity and reduced the curvature between San Jose and Watsonville Junction, where increasing perishable traffic and inbound and outbound passenger trains caused ever growing congestion.[55]

The San Joaquin Line improvement may have hindered rather than helped the competitiveness of the state's rail system. Its timing suggests that the company made it primarily to thwart a Santa Fe proposal for entering the Los Angeles to San Francisco market. In 1922 the Santa Fe not only surveyed a 128-mile line between Los Angeles and Bakersfield, which California Division of Highways engineers followed six years later with their new superhighway, but it went so far as to purchase land for right of way in the vicinity of Tejon Pass. This line would have created a Los Angeles to San Francisco route forty miles shorter than the Southern Pacific's Coast Line and likely would have resulted in increased passenger and freight traffic between northern and southern California.[56]

I have not discovered Santa Fe management's thinking on this proposal, which I estimate would have cost between $50 and $60 million.[57] Perhaps the management decided that it could better spend resources on improvements to the route between Los Angeles and Chicago. Perhaps the state highway program dissuaded it. Perhaps the proposal merely was a ploy to force Southern Pacific to improve its route over Tehachapi Pass, which the Santa Fe used to reach the San Joaquin Valley from eastern points. In any event, Southern Pacific in 1923 offered the Santa Fe a renewed lease for the use of its Tehachapi Pass tracks and announced that it would build a second track on the congested route at a cost of $10 million. The work cost less than this because the Southern Pacific later substituted improved signaling for some of the double track. As a result, for the sum of $8.8 million the Southern Pacific defended its most important market from the Santa Fe, while at no cost the Santa Fe gained improved access between the East and the San Joaquin Valley. However, the rail infrastructure between southern and northern California remained sadly underdeveloped.

Instead of investing more in its main California trunk lines, the Southern Pacific made significant politically motivated investments intended to prevent possible competition. In 1923 the company announced that as a result of winning its battle to keep the Central Pacific, it would invest $50 million in new track. Many of these projects, including the Natron Cut-Off (a new, more direct line between California and Oregon), double tracking the mainline east from Sacramento over the Sierra, and double tracking the line over Tehachapi Pass between Bakersfield and Mojave, were part of the 1913 capital budget. Other projects included a new passenger depot at Sacramento and new terminal facilities and mainlines in central Los Angeles, designed to take mainline freight trains off city streets. Shortly afterward the company announced that it would build a mainline connecting the Central Pacific and points in Oregon. It also announced that it would build a new mainline through Phoenix. Finally, it announced that it would build a large $12 million bridge to replace the train ferry across the Carquinez Straits on the mainline between Oakland and Sacramento.[58]

Some of these projects, such as the Natron Cut-Off, the double tracking of the Overland Route, and the Carquinez Straits bridge, improved heavily traveled routes. They undoubtedly increased the operating efficiency and competitiveness of the company. Others, such as the connecting line to Oregon and the line through Phoenix, promised but light traffic or operating economies. The Southern Pacific evidently agreed to build the former in exchange for political support for its continued control of the Central Pacific, and evidently agreed to the latter in exchange for support of its ICC petition to take over the El Paso & Southwestern. The EP&SW operated to Tucson from eastern connections in Texas and New Mexico. In the early 1920s the EP&SW threatened to extend its line to Los Angeles via Phoenix, a feasible proposition if backed by either of its eastern connections. The company went so far as to buy terminal property in Los Angeles—the site of the present-day Los Angeles Union Passenger Terminal. By purchasing the company in 1924, Southern Pacific ended this threat at the price of building about 150 miles of new mainline that added little to revenue or did little to reduce costs.[59]

Southern Pacific's investment in passenger cars also was of questionable economic merit. When management realized the magnitude and irreversibility of the loss of rural traffic about 1915, it limited further investment in steel cars to either accommodate rising traffic or to increase luxury. In the early 1920s only the Peninsula suburban service experienced rising traffic, and the company purchased about seventy high capacity steel coaches for this service, even though it lost money. Much of the elite of San Francisco (including many Southern Pacific executives) used this service. Most of the remaining car orders during the 1920s improved luxury trains. Probably the largest of such orders occurred in 1926 when the company outfitted the *Overland Limited* with eight sets of cars at a cost of $3 million. The *Bulletin* described the new trains as "aristocrats of western transportation."[60] In addition to these train sets, the company during the

1920s ordered large numbers of new dining, observation, and chair cars for its other luxury trains.[61] Although they heavily lost money, dining cars seemed particularly important to management for the marketability of its leading trains. During the 1920s the *Bulletin,* in nine major articles, commented more on them than on any other aspect of the Southern Pacific's passenger service. The company's ninety-seven dining cars constituted the largest such fleet in the United States during the early 1920s.[62]

Southern Pacific directed other investments to improving productivity by the traditional method of operating longer freight trains composed of bigger cars, each of which was more heavily loaded. During the 1920s the company bought larger and more efficient locomotives that could pull longer trains. It bought larger freight cars to make up the trains, and it sought to load them more fully. It also laid heavier rail to hold the heavier trains. The *Bulletin* boasted throughout the 1920s of continuing freight productivity improvements resulting from such measures.

Unfortunately these measures taken together yielded a disappointing bottom line. Although Southern Pacific's operating ratio improved from the unsatisfactory level of 76 in 1920 to the marginally acceptable level of 71 in 1923, the important statistic failed to further improve significantly for the rest of the decade. At the same time traffic grew by 28 percent (see table 5). These statistics told management that despite growing traffic and heavy investments, the company remained only marginally profitable. Southern Pacific historian Don Hofsommer reports that at the end of the 1920s the company's board, noting record gross earnings but a disappointing 3.98 percent return on investment, questioned management about the wisdom of its investments.[63]

Many other U.S. railroad managements faced equally disappointing results. The Harvard economist William Cunningham reports that railroad productivity improvement in the 1920s came from a continuation of the trend of operating longer, larger, and heavier trains, but such investments no longer earned a competitive return.[64] Albert Fishlow reports that between 1909 and 1953 railroad productivity advanced at an average of 2.7 percent per year, but this rate was slower than the rate of productivity growth for the American economy.[65]

By the end of the decade, Southern Pacific's passenger service performed considerably more poorly than its freight service, although it showed signs of improvement. The operating ratio declined to 84 in 1929 from 88 in 1927. Gross revenues increased to $53 million in 1929, from $52 million in 1927. Intrastate passenger riding declined by only 10 percent, interstate riding held steady, and mail and express revenue increased. Apparently the conversion of little-used rural local trains to buses improved passenger service's financial performance.[66] The conversion lost little revenue, while it saved substantial expenses. The closure of entire operating centers in locations such as Vallejo, Santa Cruz, and Portland saved much more than the reduction in train and car miles would suggest. These results outshined those for the nation's railroads, whose passenger ratio climbed slightly from about 97 in 1927 to about 98 in 1929.[67] Perhaps for this reason, McGinnis saw 1929 as the year by which Southern Pacific's rail demand and services had adjusted to the automobile.[68]

Much less information is available on the Santa Fe's passenger strategy during this period. What there is shows that the Santa Fe's status as a challenger to the Southern Pacific for intrastate traffic left its management unburdened by the self-imposed service obligations that saddled Southern Pacific management. As a consequence, Santa Fe management responded more freely to changing market signals, although its conception of passenger service as a marketing ploy for freight service moderated its responses.

In 1920 the Santa Fe restored some of the service that it deleted in 1918, increasing its intrastate train mileage from 1.7 million train miles per year in 1919 to 2.0 million per year in 1921. This number remained far below the 1916 peak of 3.3 million train miles, but management decided not to restore more service because of traffic losses to the automobile during the period of federal control.[69] Instead, it concentrated on its Los Angeles to Chicago trains, increasing their mileage operated within California from 1.3 million miles in 1916 to 1.6 million miles in 1921.[70]

Management considered restoring the *Saint* and *Angel*, the pre-war overnight trains between Los Angeles and San Francisco, but decided not to do so. The road's Los Angeles traffic managers had recommended restoration in order to reestablish the Santa Fe corporate identity in the lucrative freight market between Los Angeles and San Francisco. They argued there was little cost in this strategy. Before the war the trains usually covered their direct costs and likely would do so again, or so the Los Angeles management thought. After considering the rampant highway construction then occurring in California, Santa Fe's Chicago executives vetoed the idea.[71]

Traffic results quickly convinced Santa Fe officials of their wisdom in not emphasizing local trains. In 1920 the Santa Fe carried 104 million intrastate passenger miles in California, up from 89 million in 1919. In 1921 the number plummeted to 69 million despite the modest added service.[72]

Rather than restoring more intrastate trains, the Santa Fe took advantage of pooling provisions in the Transportation Act of 1920. In 1921 the Santa Fe asked the Southern Pacific for an agreement to carry Santa Fe passengers on Southern Pacific trains locally within California, to which the Southern Pacific consented.[73]

Santa Fe management also relied on the automobile for taking care of the local travel needs of its transcontinental rail passengers. In 1921 the company ran newspaper ads in the Chicago papers exhorting midwesterners to take their cars with them when they traveled west on the *California Limited*. The ads proclaimed that a just-passed bond issue would finance several thousand miles of additional roads. Once in California the midwestern traveler could drive the length of the state in all seasons on unsurpassed roads and avoid local trains altogether. These ads so upset the Southern Pacific's passenger agent in Chicago, Frank E. Batters, that he clipped an ad from the 10 October 1921 Chicago *Tribune* and scrawled a note to his superior in California across the top: "Black [Santa Fe's passenger traffic manager] don't seem to care much for his or our local business in California. Santa Fe all the way both ways including freight."[74] In the eyes of McGinnis in the mid-1930s, this ad symbolized the Santa Fe's passenger policy after 1921 of concentrating on its Los Angeles to Chicago trains. Except for trains between Los Angeles and San Diego, the Santa Fe operated other trains in California only as token services intended to preserve its corporate identity.[75]

The company's investment program reflected this orientation. The rural passenger market, which had been the objective of the Santa Fe's service expansion strategy prior to 1916, was dead. To break into the state's lucrative market between Los Angeles and San Francisco, the Santa Fe needed a direct track between Los Angeles and the San Joaquin Valley. After considering building such a line, it decided to instead place all of its limited resources into upgrading its mainline and services between Los Angeles and Chicago. Buck Travis commented on this in 1936:

> Succeeding the close of the United States Railroad Administration, when the railroads were returned to private enterprise, the management of the Santa Fe Railway decided to build its main line across the country, this requiring all the energies the Santa Fe could bring to bear upon this project for several years; as a consequence, the Santa Fe could not give much attention then to the re-establishment of the Los Angeles-San Francisco service, all of the Santa Fe resources being applied to build up the main line.[76]

Along with building up the mainline, Santa Fe invested in new equipment and faster schedules for its limited trains between Los Angeles and Chicago. In 1921 trains operating between the two cities accumulated 1.6 million miles within California. By 1929 this figure increased to 2 million miles. Management added the extra fare *Chief* to the Chicago–Los Angeles route in 1926. To regain tourist traffic, it discounted coach and tourist sleeper fares and expanded Chicago–Los Angeles tourist service on its *Scout*, *Navajo*, and *Grand Canyon Limited* at the end of the decade.[77]

The Santa Fe's local traffic generally reflected management's priorities. After holding at about 70 million passenger miles per year through 1924, traffic within California steadily declined to 43 million passenger miles in 1930. Most of this remaining traffic rode on trains between Los Angeles and San Diego, and it continued at this level because Santa Fe management, like the Southern Pacific's, began discounting fares heavily.[78]

While not as disheartening, trends in the Santa Fe's long distance traffic could not have comforted management. Despite the phenomenal growth of Los Angeles, improvements to the Santa Fe service between Los Angeles and Chicago failed to increase usage on this route. Interstate traffic declined from 184 million passenger miles within California in 1920 to 135 million in 1921. Although interstate traffic partially rebounded to 154 million passenger miles in 1924, thereafter it slid every year to a low in 1928, and then slightly rebounded to 133 million passenger miles in 1929.[79]

U.S. railroad passenger service began the 1920s in a deficit position and ended the decade in worse financial shape. In 1920 revenues more than covered operating expenses, but not by enough to fully pay for fixed expenses. Nine years later revenues barely covered operating expenses, leaving nothing left over for fixed expenses. During the same period the passenger train's share of intercity travel declined precipitously. What had been a general form of transportation in 1920 changed into primarily a specialized means of business travel by 1929. In the latter year the Southern Pacific's passenger service fared somewhat better than the national average, but in general terms both it and the Santa Fe mirrored the national trend.

The primary problem with passenger service at the beginning of the 1920s was its high cost of operation. Rather than addressing this problem, most railroad managements raised fares to absurdly high levels. Since about 1910 railroad management had argued that if only it had the freedom to raise rates, its financial problems would be solved. Dismissing critics such as Brandeis, who argued that many railroad financial problems derived from inefficient practices, management was not about to change course in 1920 by concentrating on efficiency while ignoring the opportunity to raise rates. Despite abundant evidence beginning in 1921 that the nonbusiness public would not pay such high fares, managements left fares at the high levels for most of the decade. Both the Southern Pacific and the Santa Fe managements followed this path. Only at the end of the decade did they begin to concede that fares had been too high since 1920 for all types of train services (except commuter service), and then they cautiously began fare reduction experiments.

Managements then found that although lowered fares increased gross revenues, they also increased costs by almost as much. Moving the added passengers brought in by the lowered fares cost money. Compared to buses or autos, moving passengers by rail, at least the way the U.S. railroads did it, was a costly business. Management did little to address this problem during the 1920s. What actions it did take involved the operation of trains that the public no longer used. One of the few U.S. railroads to take advantage of pooling provisions in the Transportation Act of 1920, the Santa Fe avoided the costs of reinstating many rural local trains in 1921 by making agreements with the Southern Pacific to transport local passengers. Of the trains that it did reinstate, it wasted no time in taking them off again once usage declined. On the other hand, the Southern Pacific felt compelled to operate a comprehensive passenger network long after traffic would no longer support it. Ultimately the railroad turned to buses as a cost-saving measure for rural local services.

Neither railroad addressed the high cost of moving passengers in their mainline limited trains. To the contrary, they continued investing heavily in the same massive, uneconomic steel equipment that remained virtually unchanged from the previous decade. This equipment proved to be an ever greater liability as automobile competition forced reluctant railroad managements to increase passenger train speeds. Only toward the end of the decade did the Southern Pacific and Santa Fe managements make some technological advance when they began ordering locomotives that could move the heavy trains somewhat more efficiently at higher speeds.

Both managements also failed to address the increasing obsolescence of their main rail routes in California. Dramatic advancements made in California's highway system each year cut into the earning power of the circuitous rail routes linking the lucrative freight and passenger market between northern and southern California. Perhaps because public sentiment in California during the 1920s scorned private investment in transportation infrastructure, both railroad managements invested elsewhere. Rather than making its services more competitive in California, Southern Pacific management invested in a scatter-gun array of productive and nonproductive projects intended to stifle competition from potential railroad threats on the approaches to California. It also resorted to politics in an unsuccessful effort to stifle bus competition. Santa Fe management channeled its investments into a more focused and productive program of improving its mainline between Los Angeles and Chicago. Consequently, rail routes serving perhaps the most heavily traveled corridors in the West failed to improve significantly during the 1920s, even though, as argued later, the rail market would have supported such improvements.

Fig. 1 Southern Pacific San Joaquin Valley local, ca. 1910. Few of these local trains were photographed, except when in distress. This train is on the line between Visalia and Exeter, jointly used by the Southern Pacific and the Visalia Electric. Courtesy of the Tulare County Museum.

Fig. 2 Southern Pacific San Joaquin Valley local, ca. 1910, in the vicinity of Visalia. The locomotive was running backward, suggesting that this train shuttled back and forth, perhaps several times daily, between valley points. Courtesy of the Tulare County Museum.

Fig. 3 Southern Pacific limited sleeping car train departing Oakland, ca. 1910. The relatively light locomotive, a 4-4-2 Atlantic, could make good time with the wooden cars. Courtesy of the California State Railroad Museum.

Fig. 4 The *Sunset Limited* rolls up the peninsula toward San Francisco after traveling more than 2,500 miles from New Orleans. This train, ca. 1925, is typical of limiteds from about 1915 well into the 1930s. The heavier steel cars required larger 4-6-2 locomotives, and when they were speeded up in the late 1920s, even larger 4-8-2 locomotives. Courtesy of the California State Railroad Museum.

Fig. 5 George Tatterson's Ripon–Manteca–Stockton stage in Stockton, 1910. This was one of the first interurban jitneys (later known as intercity buses) in the United States. SFC, exhibit 327. Courtesy of William A. Myers.

Fig. 6 Promoting good roads, Wheatland tract, north of Sacramento, 1914. Automobiles were adopted first in rural areas and greatly reduced the demand for local trains. Influenced by automobile technology, the Southern Pacific introduced gasoline-mechanical McKeen rail cars before 1914 to cut costs on several local trains, including the one shown here. Courtesy of the California Department of Transportation.

Fig. 7 California Transit Company intercity bus, Oakland, 1921. SFC, exhibit 327. Courtesy of William A. Myers.

Fig. 8 The new three-lane Ridge Route, 1933. For the first time motorists could drive across mountain barriers at the legal speed limit of 40 miles per hour without having to slow for curves. Courtesy of the California Department of Transportation.

Fig. 9 New road alignments, San Diego County, 1925. The highway commission started a road-straightening program in the early 1920s. As projects were completed, driving speeds approached train speeds on parallel railroads. From *California Highways and Public Works*, January 1925. Courtesy of the California Department of Transportation.

Figs. 10 & 11 The standard Greyhound bus of 1935 (top) and the Greyhound Superbus that began replacing it in 1936. SFC, exhibit 327. Courtesy of William A. Myers.

Fig. 12   The Southern Pacific *Daylight* climbing Cuesta Grade, ca. 1940. The streamlined *Daylight* offered luxurious accommodations and cut more than an hour from the schedule between Los Angeles and San Francisco. Tortuous mountain crossings and an indirect route prevented it from saving even more time. Southern Pacific Company photo by A. W. Rommel. Courtesy of William A. Myers.

Fig. 13   A Santa Fe *Golden Gate* streaks along U.S. 50 as it leaves the Bay Area, 1947. Unlike the conservative Southern Pacific, the Santa Fe fully embraced diesel power, which helped improve the financial performance of its passenger trains at the end of the 1930s. Courtesy of Fred Matthews, Jr.

Fig. 14 The *Daylight* races trucks on U.S. 101, 1937. The new train compared favorably to state highway alignments dating from the 1920s—at least in relatively flat country. Courtesy of the California Department of Transportation.

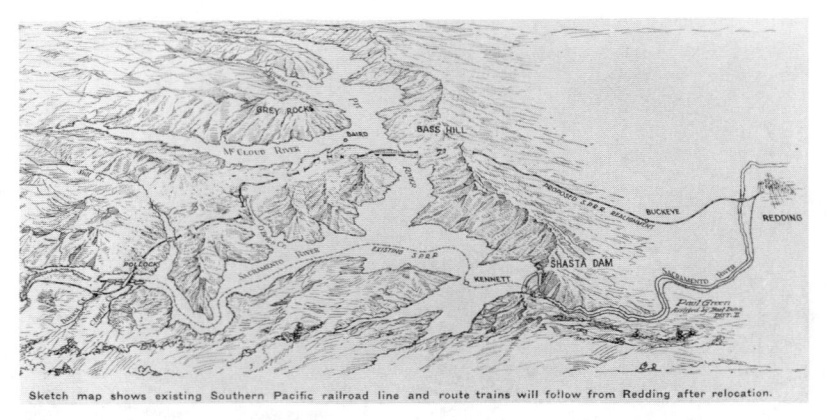

Fig. 15 Because of the construction of Shasta Dam, the Bureau of Reclamation built a thirty-two-mile modern mountain railroad for the Southern Pacific in the late 1930s. Similar projects on the main rail routes linking California's population centers might have made a difference in the fate of the state's rail industry. Courtesy of the California Department of Transportation.

Fig. 16 New highway construction, Cuesta Grade, 1937. Even as the Southern Pacific broke in its new streamliner, the California Highway Commission feverishly continued to improve roads over mountain passes. Courtesy of the California Department of Transportation.

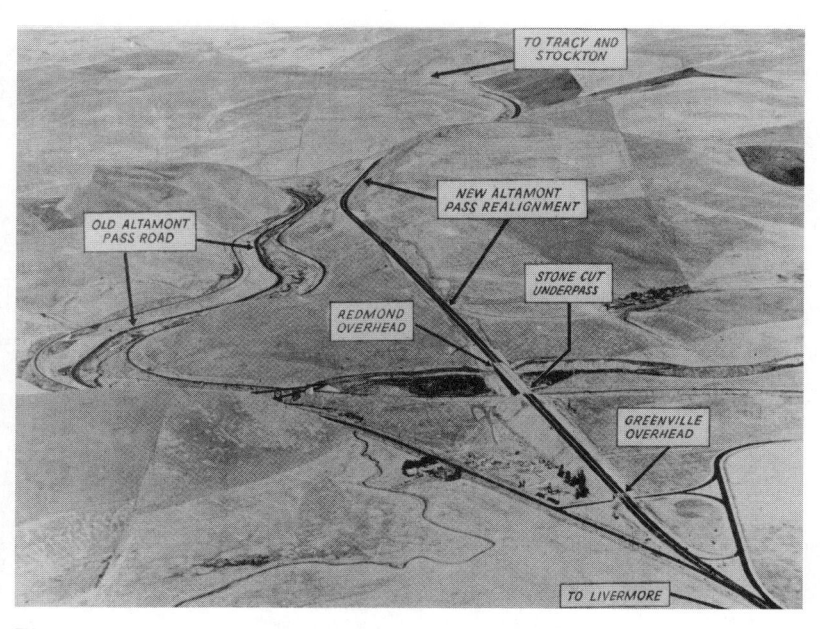

Fig. 17 The new high-speed, four-lane Altamont Pass highway between Stockton and San Francisco, 1938. This coastal mountain crossing opened the same year that the Santa Fe inaugurated the *Golden Gate* on a much longer and slower route out of the Bay Area. Note the obsolete highway paralleling mainlines of the Southern Pacific and Western Pacific. Courtesy of the California Department of Transportation.

4
Pacific Greyhound Lines and the Southern Pacific, 1929–1936

Southern Pacific's entry into the bus business upset the two largest entrepreneurs in California's bus industry, Pickwick's Charles Wren and California Transit's Buck Travis. Both had built their respective empires knowing that the California Railroad Commission would prohibit other bus operators from competing with them. Their confidence was shattered in 1928 when the railroad commission granted the Southern Pacific Company a certificate of convenience and necessity to establish bus service in competition with an established bus operator running out of Santa Cruz. After the so-called Santa Cruz decision, Wren and Travis feared that at any time the financially strong railroad might turn its attention from insignificant branch line bus operations to the lucrative trunk routes in the state. The California Railroad Commission showed that it would allow the Southern Pacific to run buses wherever it ran trains, despite the presence of established bus operators.

Travis's reaction to these fears led to the formation of Pacific Greyhound Lines in 1929. California and Chicago bus interests as well as the Southern Pacific Company shared in the ownership and management of what immediately became the largest operating bus company in the United States. Despite the Depression, Pacific Greyhound Lines earned enormous profits by the mid-1930s.

Pacific Greyhound Lines is important to the analysis of rail passenger management efficiency in California for several reasons. First, the bus company figured as an element of Southern Pacific strategy for adjusting to the automobile during the 1930s. Second, collusion between Pacific Greyhound Lines and the Southern Pacific Company provoked the Santa Fe Railway into a great offensive that dramatically altered rail and bus service in California during the latter half of the 1930s. Last, an understanding of how the bus company did business is useful in evaluating both the efficacy of rail management methods and policies and the conspiracy explanation for rail passenger service decline.

These areas of concern are so closely intertwined that I treat them together. In this chapter I examine the formation of Pacific Greyhound Lines, its management structure and methods, and competition and cooperation between it and the Southern Pacific. I explain why I believe the conspiracy explanation is invalid, and I put forth an explanation for the bus company's success. In the following chapters I examine rail strategies during the same period and evaluate why they failed while the bus company succeeded.

Shaken by the Santa Cruz decision, Travis in 1928 offered to sell all of his bus interests to a Chicago holding company called the Motor Transit Corporation. Two of Motor Transit's principle owners, Carl E. Wickman and Glenn Traer, had approached Travis a year earlier with a proposal to buy California Transit. Having pioneered intercity bus service in Minnesota beginning about 1914, Wickman and Traer gradually accumulated capital and organized Motor Transit in 1925 as a holding company to purchase and control bus operating companies in the Midwest. By 1927 they were ready to expand to the West Coast, which prompted their offer to Travis. During the negotiations Travis and his associate, Fred Ackerman, visited Motor Transit's operations in Chicago and learned about the holding company concept. It impressed them so much that they rejected Motor Transit's offer and set up a rival holding company to compete with Motor Transit head to head. They called their new company the American Motor Transportation Company.[1]

These events happened as Southern Pacific was preparing its bus plans. As Travis began to appreciate their potential later in 1927, he regretted his decision not to accept the Motor Transit offer. He reopened negotiations with Wickman and Traer and in October 1928 reached agreement. Travis and Ackerman turned over all of their bus interests to Motor Transit. In exchange they received sizable stock interests in Motor Transit, seats on the company's board of directors, and membership on its executive committee. About this time Motor Transit's board renamed the company the Greyhound Corporation.[2]

Almost at the same time as Travis reached agreement with what soon became the Greyhound Corporation, the California Railroad Commission decided in favor of the Southern Pacific in the Santa Cruz bus case.[3] As a representative of the Greyhound Corporation, Travis then approached Southern Pacific's management with a proposal. He pointed out that the railroad's bus operation was losing money and that neither Greyhound's

California Transit nor the Southern Pacific would benefit from bus competition. It would be far better to have just one bus company in California in which all of the major players would have a stake. Obviously, Pickwick Stages would have to be brought in. So would the Santa Fe Railway. Travis then proposed a grand bus merger between all of the major bus routes in Southern Pacific (Pacific Lines) territory. Primarily these would include California Transit and Pickwick Stages routes, but also all Southern Pacific Motor Transport routes and those of most remaining smaller bus operators in California and Oregon. A new operating company would run these routes, and the major players who contributed to the company would own and control it jointly. It appeared that the owners would be the Greyhound Corporation, the Pickwick Corporation, the Southern Pacific Company, and perhaps the Santa Fe Railway. Because Southern Pacific did not yet operate much bus service, it was to mostly contribute desperately needed cash to the new enterprise. The railroad also promised to refrain from operating its own buses. If the Santa Fe entered, it would have to contribute even more cash, because it operated no buses at all.[4]

All major parties except the Santa Fe Railway formally agreed to this proposal on 1 January 1929. The Santa Fe informed the Southern Pacific that it had no interest in local passenger transportation and could see no value in contributing to the bus monopoly.[5] The remaining three partners formed a New Jersey holding company in early 1929 to hold the securities and certificates for the routes that would become the new bus system. By mid-1930 Pacific Greyhound Lines became an operating reality. The Greyhound Corporation, the Pickwick Corporation, and the Southern Pacific Company each owned one-third of the company and appointed one-third of its directors.[6]

California's great bus merger of 1929 absorbed most of the state's significant intercity bus operations, except for the large Los Angeles suburban bus operation known as Motor Transit (not to be confused with the Chicago holding company). The merger agreement left Motor Transit as a separate company under the joint control of Pacific Greyhound Lines and the Pacific Electric Railway. With two-thirds ownership, the Pacific Electric controlled its former bus rival.[7]

Pacific Greyhound Lines management consisted largely of former Southern Pacific employees. Its president, T. B. Wilson, previously served as vice president of Southern Pacific Motor Transport and before that as supervisor of transportation for the Southern Pacific Company.[8] Southern Pacific's superintendent of transportation, Lee D. Jones, who helped design Southern Pacific Motor Transport, forfeited twenty-two years of Southern Pacific service and seniority to become Pacific Greyhound's general manager. T. Finkbohner, formerly a transportation supervisor for the Southern Pacific Company in Exeter, forfeited nineteen years of employment to become superintendent of transportation for Pacific Greyhound.[9] C. E. Quigley, who succeeded Fred W. Ackerman as general auditor shortly after Pacific Greyhound's formation, came from the Southern Pacific.[10] M. C. Frailey, Pacific Greyhound's assistant auditor, previously audited Southern Pacific's electric railroad subsidiaries.[11] Several other less important positions in the management were filled by ex-Southern Pacific employees.[12]

The new organization left Travis with minor managerial control over Pacific Greyhound Lines. Wickman provided overall supervision as chairman of Pacific Greyhound's board of directors and moved to California to carry out his responsibilities. Although he also served as president of the Greyhound Corporation, he considered Pacific Greyhound important enough to warrant his personal attention. Under Wickman, Pickwick's Charles Wren served as chairman of Pacific Greyhound's executive committee. He also continued to direct the Pickwick Corporation, which owned a bus manufacturing company and other bus operations outside of Pacific Greyhound's territory. Travis and Ackerman had to content themselves with more passive board roles. Both sat on the Greyhound Corporation's executive committee, and Travis also sat on Pacific Greyhound's board.[13]

Pacific Greyhound's first full year of operation in 1931 coincided with the rapidly deepening Depression, and the company barely survived. Its gross revenues covered little more than its operating costs; none of the three owning corporations could offer much support. The Pickwick Corporation went bankrupt and was dissolved in 1932, while the Greyhound Corporation and the Southern Pacific Company teetered on the edge of bankruptcy. Loans from the General Motors Corporation saved the Greyhound Corporation. The Southern Pacific Company managed to stay afloat with its own resources.[14]

Such trying conditions precipitated what appears to have been a Travis-led coup that took control of Pacific Greyhound in 1932–33. The California bus company's poor financial performance caused Travis to fear for his investment. In Travis's eyes, earnings needed to increase substantially. Pickwick's failure gave him an opportunity to better manage his assets. In 1932 the Greyhound Corporation bought Pickwick's share in Pacific Greyhound and resold some of the share to the Southern Pacific. By 1936 the Greyhound Corporation owned 61 percent of Pacific Greyhound and appointed six members to the board, including Ackerman, Travis, and W. G. Filer, all original investors in California Transit. Southern Pacific owned 39 percent and appointed three members to Pacific Greyhound's board.[15] At the request of the Greyhound Corporation, Travis replaced Wren as chairman of

Pacific Greyhound's executive committee in 1932; in 1933, again at the request of the Greyhound Corporation, Travis replaced Wilson as president.[16] Wickman moved back to Chicago. Travis brought his California Transit colleagues, accountant Fred Ackerman and lawyer Earl Bagby, with him into Pacific Greyhound's top management.[17] However, the ex-Southern Pacific bureaucracy below the president remained mostly intact.

Travis turned his attention toward increasing the cost-consciousness of his managers. The early Pacific Greyhound management could design and operate a service that satisfied the public's needs, but it could not operate the service at a low enough cost. Travis believed that this trait derived from railroads, and to get the most out of his ex-railroad managers, he had to alter their consciousness. To illustrate this point, Travis argued that the Pacific Electric mismanaged Motor Transit in Los Angeles, endangering Pacific Greyhound's investment in that enterprise. There was little that Travis could do about this except sell Pacific Greyhound's interest to the Pacific Electric, which he did. In Pacific Greyhound he had greater control. Rather than fire the Southern Pacific management team, he remolded it to fit his own image. This came out in the *Santa Fe Case* under cross examination by Santa Fe counsel Allan Matthew:

> Q. [Matthew] But I have understood you to argue quite insistently that men of railroad experience are not very well fitted to conduct a bus operation?
> A. [Travis] It has so proven—and we had to change the spots on the gentlemen and they came over, before they fitted into our transportation scheme.
> Q. Then you made a mistake in taking them over in the first instance, is that right?
> A. Well, I wouldn't say that; they have all developed and helped work it out to its present successful issue.[18]

The Fred Ackerman protege, Cloyd Kimball, who later served as president of Eastern Greyhound Lines and vice president of the Greyhound Corporation, offered additional reasons why Travis kept the Southern Pacific team. Most of the pioneering bus entrepreneurs lacked the organizational discipline to manage an enterprise as large as Pacific Greyhound. Of the companies that merged to form Pacific Greyhound, only Southern Pacific Motor Transport had a formal management structure. By importing virtually intact this small professional bureaucracy, the original owning corporations were able to obtain the professional management needed for their operating company. Although the original Wickman/Wren/Wilson executive team failed, the iron-fisted executive team of Travis/Ackerman succeeded to mold the bureaucracy into its own image. Kimball believed that some of the ex-Southern Pacific managers became among the best bus men in the industry.[19]

One of the ex-Southern Pacific men, Pacific Greyhound general manager Lee D. Jones, testified in 1936 that economical operation derived from an attitude of cost consciousness that emanated from top management:

> The economy of the operation is affected a great deal by the executive direction to department heads and in turn by department heads to the personnel. . . . Hardly a day passes but what the president of the company brings the subject of economy to our attention in one way or another, and inasmuch as he supervises all but routine expenditures and he even supervises them in their original establishment, our personnel is certainly kept on its toes in relation to every avenue through which money may be expended. If I knew of any method whereby the purposes of my department might be accomplished with lesser expenditure, it would certainly be my business to reduce its costs, and if I did not I am sure the president of the company would discover my own inefficiency within a short time.[20]

This attitude pushed company superintendent T. Finkbohner to obtain the maximum use of drivers and buses. The number of miles that a driver drove in a day determined his or her pay, subject to a minimum regardless of miles. Finkbohner, another ex-Southern Pacific manager, strove to assign enough miles to drivers each day that they earned their pay in miles driven and not in sitting around. He calculated the "average normal cost" for driver pay and tried not to exceed this amount when assigning drivers. Finkbohner also sought to get maximum mileage out of a bus. At terminals, drivers usually laid over, but Finkbohner strove to turn buses "in an hour or 30 minutes or 15 minutes at times."[21] A bus sitting several hours in a terminal was unproductive capital and a waste to the company.

To promote cost and efficiency analysis, Pacific Greyhound's accounting department kept various operating statistics. It prepared irregular summaries and, after 1937, regular monthly reports of the number of bus miles operated on each route, the number of passengers boarded, the number of passenger miles carried, the number of seat miles provided, and the revenue earned.[22] The accounting department also prepared statements on the average cost of operating a bus each mile and divided this cost into a variable and fixed component. For 1935, the 20.5 cent average operating cost was made up of 14.9 cents of direct cost and 5.6 cents of overhead expense.[23] The accounting department further prepared statistics of the gross revenue per bus mile for each trip operated on each route.[24]

Such information assisted the superintendent in making schedule changes. He had extra buses placed at key points on the system, so that when more passengers appeared than could sit on a scheduled bus, his subordinates could place the additional buses into service. If managers noted a persistent pattern of the so-called extra sections being placed into service, they added an additional run to the schedule that might be slightly ahead of or behind the popular bus. Alternatively, it might leave at the same time but run as an express, while the original schedule remained as a local. This process resulted in both expresses and locals serving the major trunk routes by the mid-1930s.[25]

When revenues fell below costs for particular runs, Travis testified, the company initiated special studies to determine the reason and possible remedies. The study might precipitate a rewriting of the schedule to eliminate certain trips, or it could result in the abandonment of an entire route.[26] However, the company guarded against cost-cutting moves that might reduce gross revenues even more. Company culture called for offering a full schedule of services throughout the day and year, even if every run did not pay, or if the entire schedule did not pay for part of the year.[27] As Jones explained:

> It has been the policy of Pacific Greyhound Lines since its organization, to give a frequency of service throughout the year, even though the revenue shows a serious decrease during the winter months. This policy was maintained during the depression years and caused us to operate in the red for the first 4 months of each year during the depression and left the officials in the position of holding the sack, in the event the later months did not increase revenue to offset the poorer months. Fortunately we were able to do so.[28]

Pacific Greyhound also practiced Southern Pacific's policy of accommodating all traffic that showed up. Even if an extra bus scheduled to alleviate an overload carried only two or three passengers, the average filled seats (load factor) of the two buses taken together exceeded 50 percent.[29]

Such close monitoring of Pacific Greyhound's service increased the number of passengers on buses, despite the company's concern for meeting certain service standards even if all schedules were not profitable. Between 1931 and 1935 management increased the number of passengers on board each bus by 60 percent. In the latter year Pacific Greyhound maintained an average systemwide load factor of about 55 percent in its unreserved seat buses. Its trunk routes between southern and central California along the coast and through the San Joaquin Valley enjoyed load factors between 55 and 60 percent during the mid-1930s.[30]

These practices paid off and enabled profits to increase even as demand, measured by how much the public was willing to pay for service, fell. During 1931, Pacific Greyhound's first full year of operation, it netted only $.016 for every mile that a bus traveled, as shown in table 13. By 1935 this figure increased almost fivefold to $.080. During this time passenger fares fell substantially. In 1929 the company collected 3.1 cents from each passenger traveling one mile. This figure fell to 2 cents in 1933, and by 1936 it fell further to 1.8 cents.[31]

The widening profit margin reflected Pacific Greyhound management's obsession with effectiveness and efficiency. Management's careful monitoring of load factors increased the number of passengers on buses as the fare yield fell. Consequently, the revenue per bus mile did not fall by much. Management's close control of efficiency significantly lowered the cost per bus mile. Research by the transportation geographer Gordon J. Fielding highlights these two indicators as among the most important in analyzing a transit company's operations. For Pacific Greyhound Lines, both were moving in the right direction, indicating superior management.[32]

The large 1935 profit margin of $0.08 per bus mile, coupled with an ever increasing volume of bus miles, produced large profits. These amounted to about a 30 percent return on the company's tangible assets of $5,616,721 in terminals, garages, and four hundred buses.[33] When it became apparent that the California Railroad Commission would hold investigations into the possibility that excessive profits derived from Pacific Greyhound's monopoly status, the company further lowered fares. Ridership and gross revenues increased substantially, but so did expenses, and net revenues remained about the same.[34]

The development of new bus technology figured in lowered bus costs as well as greater appeal to the public. The Depression, falling rail fares, and the automobile constrained the potential gross revenue that bus operators could squeeze out of each bus mile they operated. If they were going to continue to reap high profits, they had to lower the cost of operating buses. They needed a new, more efficient bus.

Public tastes also demanded a more modern vehicle. In 1930 people would ride anything, according to T. L. Vaughn, superintendent of the Southern Division of the Southern Kansas Stage Lines. Vaughn observed that by 1936 new streamlined trains and automobiles made the public more particular. The typical intercity bus of the period seemed increasingly dated and uncomfortable.[35]

In 1934 executives from the Greyhound Corporation entered into talks with General Motors to design a new bus. The two companies appointed a committee of the maintenance heads from the various Greyhound subsidiaries and Dwight Austin, the late Pickwick Corporation's highly talented bus designer, whom General Motors had just employed. As the committee developed innovations, it tried them out on production-run buses built by the GM subsidiary company, Yellow Coach. After 1934 the Greyhound Corporation ordered buses for its subsidiaries almost exclusively from Yellow Coach. By 1935 Yellow Coach assembled a prototype modern bus, which Greyhound called the Superbus.[36]

The ancestor to the present-day highway coach, the Superbus incorporated numerous changes to prevailing design. It carried more passengers in far greater comfort, it provided a large amount of space for baggage and express freight, it revolutionized the appearance of buses, it weighed much less, it was more powerful, and it cost less to operate than earlier buses. For all of these advantages, it cost little more to buy. At approximately $13,600 per unit, the Superbus compared very favorably to the $11,400 unit price for Pacific Greyhound's last order of old-style Yellow Coaches in 1936.[37]

When production of the Superbus started, General Motors had spent approximately $600,000 on the project, according to Travis's recollection, and would not accept an order of fewer than three hundred of the new buses.[38] Perhaps not coincidentally, the Greyhound Corporation was of sufficient size to place such an order and did so in July 1935. By the fall of 1936 fifty of the first-order Superbuses entered Pacific Greyhound service. The public received them so enthusiastically, according to Travis, that the Greyhound Corporation placed an order for 505 more of the units, with a hundred of them scheduled to enter Pacific Greyhound service in the fall of 1937.[39]

The history of the Superbus casts doubt on one part of Bradford Snell's conspiracy theory. Snell charged that General Motors interests forced the Greyhound Corporation to purchase buses exclusively from Yellow Coach, the General Motors subsidiary, since 1926. Pacific Greyhound's program of purchasing buses shows that this statement is not entirely accurate. Pacific Greyhound's predecessor companies bequeathed the new organization a diverse collection of buses, a large proportion of which required replacement, according to Travis.[40] From January 1929 through 1933 Pacific Greyhound bought 195 new buses, only 72 of which were purchased from Yellow Coach.[41] Because of the Superbus program, and perhaps because the Greyhound Corporation controlled Pacific Greyhound for the first time, Pacific Greyhound purchased exclusively from Yellow Coach beginning in 1934. That year it bought 38 Yellow Coaches, followed by 53 in 1935 and 68 in 1936, 50 of which were Superbuses.[42]

Pacific Greyhound's increasing profit margin on each passenger explains only part of the company's large profits. Its rapidly increasing number of passengers explains the other part. Even before the Depression reached its lowest point in 1933, Pacific Greyhound's passenger traffic trend shifted upward. Based upon the average one-way fare per passenger during various years, Pacific Greyhound carried about 203 million passenger miles in 1931, 168 million in 1932, 210 million in 1933, 285 million in 1934, 345

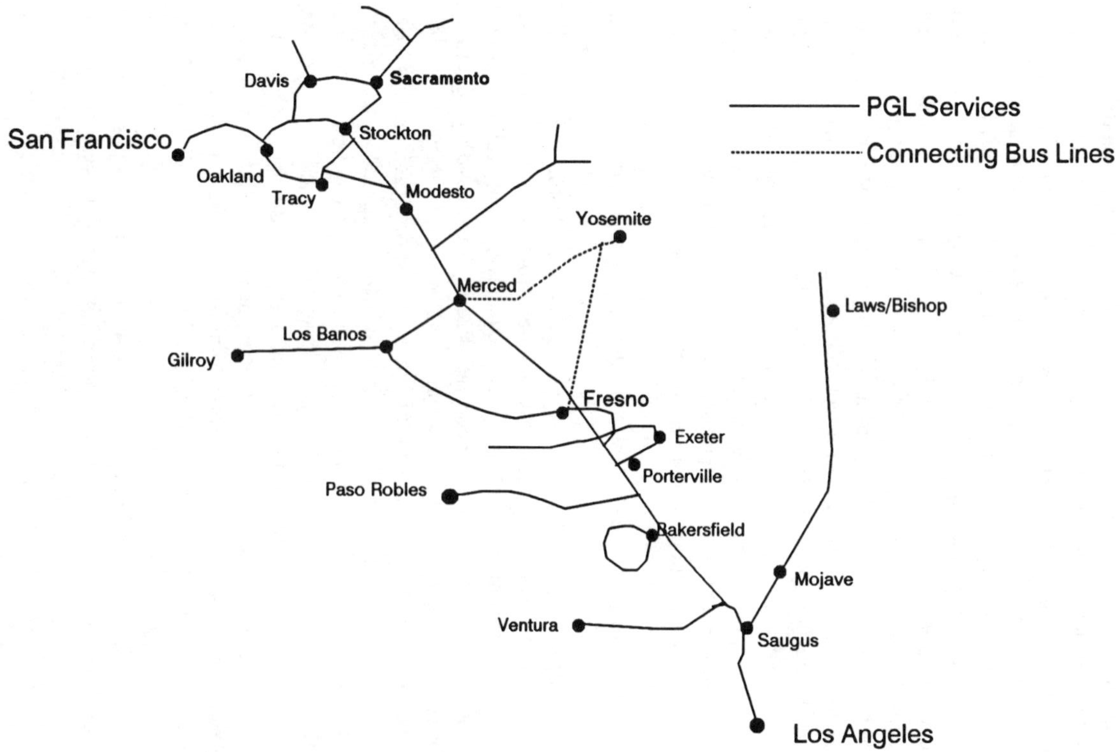

4.1 Pacific Greyhound Lines, routes in central California, 1931

million in 1935, and 455 million in 1936. Because the average one-way fare exceeded the average yield per passenger mile, these patronage figures are probably low, but they indicate the general upward trend in traffic.[43]

If one could show that such substantial traffic growth resulted from bus and rail managements colluding to divert train passengers to buses, the conspiracy argument would carry more force. However, the evidence fails to support this contention. Generally, bus passengers did not come from trains. By examining the effects of Pacific Greyhound's service and fare policies on Pacific Greyhound's and Southern Pacific's traffic growth, we can infer three conclusions. First, many bus passengers came from stops not served by trains. Although Pacific Greyhound earned its largest profits on bus routes that directly paralleled Southern Pacific and Santa Fe passenger trains, the trains usually attracted the lion's share of traffic between pairs of stops that the two modes had in common. This occurred even where the train was slower and less frequent. Second, the bus catered to nonbusiness travelers, even where bus service was faster and more frequent than train service. Both points suggest a third conclusion that buses and trains drew many of their passengers from different markets.

The results of Pacific Greyhound's service improvements lead to these conclusions. As Pacific Greyhound gradually lowered fares, speeded up buses, and ran more of them, traffic grew rapidly, but not at the expense of train traffic, which also grew rapidly. Train riders were affluent; bus riders most likely were not. Both classes of riders traveled more as the economy and their respective transportation services improved.

By the mid-1930s Pacific Greyhound's greatest profits came from its San Joaquin Valley and Coast routes, as shown in table 14. The company substantially improved these services since 1931, while at the same time it trimmed back branch line services. Maps 4.1 and 4.2 show the increasing concentration on trunk line operations as the 1930s progressed, and table 15 shows the rapidly falling use of the company's small-town agencies. By 1936 the rather extensive network of branch line services that in 1931 generally followed the routes of earlier Southern Pacific local train services disappeared from the Greyhound corporate fold. In most cases some bus services still operated over those routes under the banners of assorted local owners, but the fact that Pacific Greyhound discarded them indicates low patronage and poor financial performance. The one branch line route still operating in the valley, that between Selma, Dinuba, and Visalia, grossed only 7.5 cents per bus mile.[44]

Improvements to the state highway system facilitated faster bus service on the trunk routes. In 1929 the pace of highway funding and construction picked up and remained at a high level through the deepening Depression.

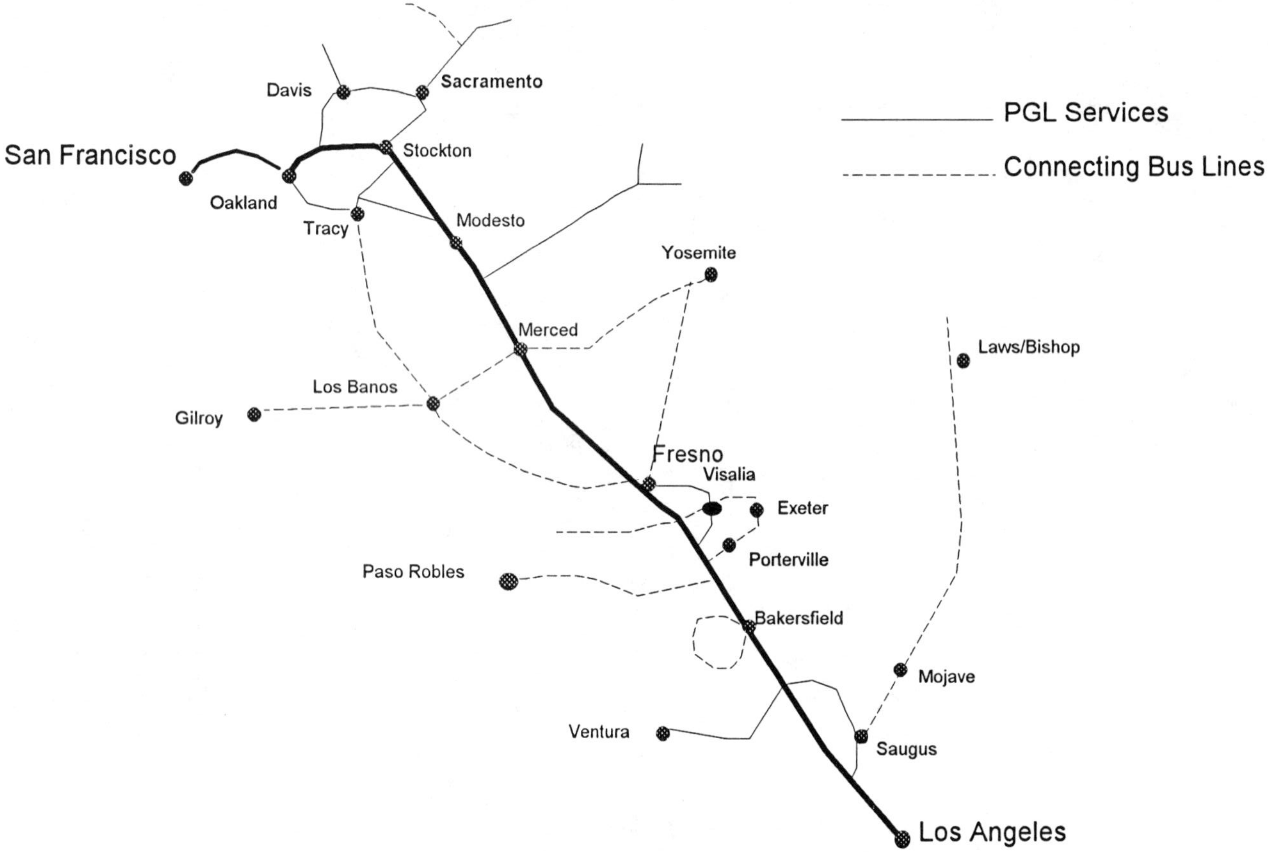

4.2 Pacific Greyhound Lines, routes in central California, 1936

Increasingly the federal government contributed funds to state road departments to help put people to work, and state departments paid increasing attention to urban road improvements, which hard-pressed municipal authorities could not fund. As the Depression continued, California state and highway construction per capita ran about 30 percent ahead of the level in the 1920s (see table 4). Combined with slower but substantial population growth during the 1930s of about 2 percent a year, this effort resulted in major highway improvements during the decade.

The new high-speed highway over the Ridge Route between Los Angeles and Bakersfield opened in late 1933. The $2.9 million project cut fourteen miles from the old route and lowered the summit by about seven hundred feet. By 1934, after it and two other large projects opened on this route, motorists could drive the 111-mile mountain road between Los Angeles and Bakersfield in less than three hours, an hour faster than in the previous year.[45] Pacific Greyhound expresses covered the route in about three and a half hours, while Southern Pacific passenger trains still required six to seven hours. The lower summit also greatly increased the competitiveness of high-volume truck traffic between southern and central California.[46]

Other improvements quickly followed. By the late 1930s, the California Highway Commission completed construction of high-speed roads over all of the passes and grades on the shortest highways linking the state's major population centers. It constructed those leading into the Bay Area from the San Joaquin Valley as four-lane divided highways.[47] In 1935 the highway commission widened the Los Angeles–Bakersfield route to three lanes, and by 1941 it completed four-lane divided stretches along several sections of U.S. 99 in the San Joaquin Valley. In 1938, after the completion of five contracts, 220 miles of unbroken three- and four-lane highway connected Santa Barbara and San Diego. Grade-separated junctions, the first constructed in Manzanita in Marin County in 1930, became commonplace by the end of the decade. Urban freeways also began appearing.[48]

The opening of these links during the 1930s speeded up auto and bus travel and also improved its reliability. Previously, motorists could drive many of the old mountain passes relatively quickly in light traffic, but most traffic conditions caused maddening delays. A theoretically possible ten-minute drive up Cuesta Grade on the Coast Route north of San Luis Obispo usually took forty-five minutes, for example. The new four-lane semi-divided road that opened there in 1938 reduced the time to five minutes under most traffic conditions.[49]

With the new Ridge Route opening and improvements leading into the Bay Area via Altamont Pass, U.S. 99 through the San Joaquin Valley replaced U.S. 101 along the coast as the main traffic artery linking San Francisco and Los Angeles. By 1936 motorists typically allowed ten hours to complete the 411-mile drive between those points.[50] Since 1931 Pacific Greyhound offered twelve-hour service between San Francisco and Los Angeles via the Coast Route, U.S. 101. In 1936 it also began offering twelve-hour and twenty-minute express bus service between those cities via U.S. 99, while its many locals covered the valley run in fourteen hours.[51]

Pacific Greyhound buses ran every two hours along U.S. 99 on the route between Los Angeles and San Francisco and also every two hours on the route between Los Angeles and Sacramento. Other buses ran only partway up and down the valley. All of these buses in both directions averaged twenty-one buses per day along U.S. 99. Pacific Greyhound operated another seventeen per day along U.S. 101 on the Coast Route.[52]

In comparison, Southern Pacific operated much less frequent service of comparable speed. Along its 470-mile Coast Line it provided one day train, the *Daylight,* which required twelve and a half hours to complete the Los Angeles to San Francisco run in the early 1930s. The railroad cut this time to eleven hours in 1936. It also operated two overnight trains, the *Lark* and the *Sunset Limited,* and an additional local train. On the 484-mile San Joaquin Valley route, the railroad operated a through day train and two through overnight trains, in addition to several locals. The *San Joaquin* day train required fourteen hours and twenty-five minutes for the San Francisco to Los Angeles run, slower than Pacific Greyhound's local buses.[53]

Pacific Greyhound pegged its fare policy to railroad fares. For short distance traffic it charged higher fares than trains on the grounds that its more frequent service made buses more attractive. For long distance traffic it charged lower fares on the grounds that the greater discomfort of the bus made lower fares necessary. As railroad managers lowered passenger fares to retain traffic, Pacific Greyhound felt compelled to do likewise.[54]

The fares that passengers actually paid to ride trains and buses in 1933 generally reflected this policy. Table 16 summarizes such information for all U.S. western and eastern seaboard points where at least fifty passengers per year used either bus or rail services in 1933.[55] It shows that the rate per mile that passengers actually paid to ride buses in the West approximately equalled the rate they paid to ride trains for markets up to four hundred miles in length. In important California rail markets, bus fares usually were higher, as shown in table 17.

Tables 16 and 17 disprove the contention that collusion between bus and rail managers diverted passengers from mainline trains on the West Coast. If this were true, bus fares would have undercut rail fares in important markets. Table 17 shows that this failed to happen. While West Coast bus fares generally approximated those on the East Coast, West Coast rail fares were far lower than East Coast rail fares and usually equal or lower than bus fares.

Table 17 also illustrates that in the early 1930s Pacific Greyhound Lines set much higher fares in markets where it had no bus competition. While the California Railroad Commission prohibited bus competition within California, it had no jurisdiction on interstate bus service. Cut-rate bus carriers operated into California from Arizona and Oregon, compelling Pacific Greyhound to lower rates on those routes.

Bus and rail traffic patterns in the mid-1930s also counter the collusion hypothesis. In the important markets where trains and buses competed head to head, more passengers used trains, as shown in tables 9, 10, and 17. This occurred even where buses were faster and more frequent than trains, such as between San Francisco and Stockton. It also occurred on the East Coast, where train fares substantially exceeded bus fares. Pacific Greyhound's heavy and growing traffic evidently came to a large extent from the many stops along the trunk highways that trains did not serve.

The latter point is corroborated by surveys that Pacific Greyhound Lines made of its passengers in the San Joaquin Valley. During the summer of 1936 the typical valley bus carried eighteen passengers, one of whom was making a short hop of less than fifty miles. Another two to three were making longer trips of between fifty-one and one hundred miles. Approximately four passengers were riding one hundred to two hundred miles, while another two to three were riding between two hundred and three hundred miles. Between four and five passengers rode through between Los Angeles and San Francisco, while the remaining two to three passengers were on one leg of a longer, most likely interstate trip.[56] Pacific Greyhound's market strength came from the company's ability to knit together multitudes of individual markets with a relatively small number of bus routes. No individual market offered much traffic, but all markets taken together provided a large traffic volume.

Because it interconnected many diverse markets, Pacific Greyhound Lines successfully competed with illegal owner-operator bus competition. So-called wildcat sedans operated between the Los Angeles and San Francisco areas since at least 1920, serving traveling salespeople, employment agencies, and transients.[57] The railroad commission had insufficient staff to stop these operations and generally did not try to, instead concentrating on the much more numerous wildcat truckers. In early 1936, between thirty-five and forty eight-passenger sedans operated between second-class hotels in San Francisco, Oakland, Los Angeles, and Hollywood. The sedans also served employment agencies and circulated through industrial districts such as Vernon, located about four miles south of downtown Los Angeles. They solicited passengers on the street and through hotel clerks, who cooperated for a 20 percent commission on each five-dollar ticket. Clerks worked together via phone to match passenger loads with available vehicles. Employment agencies also used the sedans to send clients to jobs filled in the opposite metropolitan area. On average about twenty-four sedans operated each day, most traveling overnight via the Valley Route. They carried between 60 to 150 passengers per day, compared to Pacific Greyhound's roughly 300 to 400 and Southern Pacific's roughly 500 to 600 point-to-point daily passengers. When Pacific Greyhound lowered its fare to $6.25 in mid-1936, the sedan operators lowered theirs to $4.00 and stayed in business at the lower fare until Pacific Greyhound and Santa Fe Trailways jointly forced the railroad commission to put them out of business in 1942.[58]

The sedans clearly contributed to public welfare by serving specialized markets that Pacific Greyhound would not serve, either in ultra-low fares or in door-to-door pick-up and delivery. However, despite the fact that they could have operated anywhere in the state that they wanted, the sedan operators chose to serve only one, rather limited market. In contrast, the regulated monopoly offered a comprehensive service in California and to eastern and northern points at relatively low fares, including (after mid-1936) a $6.25 fare between Los Angeles and San Francisco, while making a 30 percent return on investment. While the sedans carried roughly 15 million annual passenger miles at a small profit, Pacific Greyhound carried more than 450 million annual passenger miles at a large profit.

Owner-operators could not match Pacific Greyhound's performance, because the market provided no mechanism by which they could coordinate their operations so as to interconnect a large number of origins and destinations. Each operator could serve a unique point-to-point market. Theoretically this meant that owner-operators could serve the public with a multitude of services tailored to a multitude of individual demands. In reality, by the 1930s auto competition had left such a thin market for the bus that only the huge metropolitan areas of Los Angeles and San Francisco offered enough traffic to make the operation of point-to-point wildcat sedans profitable.

The comparison between Pacific Greyhound Lines and the wildcat sedan operators illustrates that the bus giant's strength derived in large measure from its size. Its buses, operating frequently along main highways, could stop on demand, making them attractive to passengers riding short distances as well as long distances. Trains stopped much less frequently, so they served fewer markets. This fact alone suggests that the bus and rail markets grew largely independently of each other, and that the bus company did not steal its passengers from trains.

Evidence from the period also suggests that buses and trains appealed to different classes of people in the markets where they directly competed. This is illustrated by the fact that trains sometimes carried more passengers than buses even when they were slower and less frequent. Jones's and Travis's testimony in the *Santa Fe Case* supported this hypothesis, while Southern Pacific vice president of passenger traffic Felix S. McGinnis offered insight into the two types of travelers. Replying to questioning by Santa Fe's Allan Matthew, Jones stated that buses and trains tapped different markets:

> [Jones] There is a class of people, Mr. Matthew, that use the rail to-day, always have and probably always will. We have never been able to have them use the bus.
> Q. [Matthew] Referring to the so-called Pullman passengers?
> A. No, I am not.
> Q. Day coach passengers?
> A. Day coach passengers.[59]

Travis shared Jones's view of different rail and bus markets:

> Not all people are bus travelers. Regardless of service or rates, there are certain classes who will not use the bus lines. There is a large group of people who might be called non-travelers who, if they travel at all, do so infrequently, if only a short distance, and then by private car. There is another class which invariably uses the airplane, the steamships and the railroads, both coach and Pullman service. The greatest number of travelers at the present time are those who use their private cars.[60]

McGinnis characterized rail passengers as urban and affluent. Rural folk, the uneducated, and the poor did not ride trains, even when fares were very low. For these reasons, McGinnis stated, rail usage per capita in California in 1935 exceeded that in the South by 60 percent, even though California's automobile ownership rate stood at 309 autos per 1,000 population, compared to 114 per 1,000 in the South.[61] These views echoed those of F. W. Conner, assistant passenger traffic manager of the Pennsylvania Railroad, who testified that "high-class" commercial traffic constituted the largest component of his and other eastern roads' passenger traffic, accounting for $32 million out of the Pennsylvania's $48 million gross passenger revenues for 1933.[62]

These statements show that trains and buses appealed to different types of people and that trains carried well-off people. By implication, buses carried the less well-off. Jones stated that Pacific Greyhound made little attempt to attract motorists to its services and cited the failure of a major attempt when it did try. In mid-1936 Pacific Greyhound introduced scrip books costing ten dollars and good for seven hundred miles of travel over a six-month period. The fare rate was 1.4 cents a mile. Officers in the company believed that this rate and the elimination of the necessity to purchase tickets would attract traveling salespeople, who customarily made short hops on ad hoc itineraries. Pacific Greyhound's marketing people approached commercial firms, particularly wholesalers, but failed to interest them in the ticket books. Jones commented:

> We are constantly told that no matter if we made our fares one-half cent a mile they would still prefer the use of the private car for their business, explaining that it is not conceivable that any common carrier service can be made to equal the necessary flexibility for travel by the commercial man. . . . The commercial man is on the road to get business for his firm and to sell its commodities, and the saving in transportation does not justify any slowing down of the speed in making of sales.[63]

Over a three-month period, from August to October of 1936, Pacific Greyhound sold only 180 of these books.[64] The experiment strengthened Pacific Greyhound's conviction that it could not divert passengers from the private automobile.

Thus, a pattern well known in the 1950s was already established by the mid-1930s. Trains carried the affluent, and buses did not. While some passengers would shift from trains to buses or vice versa, depending upon who offered the better service and fares, a large number of passengers would not. This would have made it difficult for colluding rail and bus managers to shift passengers from trains to buses.

Pacific Greyhound's major fare reduction in 1936 provided further evidence that the rail and bus markets remained largely independent of each other. As the economy improved after 1933, Pacific Greyhound Lines earned excessive profits in the eyes of the railroad commission. In 1936 the commission launched a preliminary investigation of Pacific Greyhound's return on investment; by quickly and substantially reducing its rates, Pacific Greyhound management cut the investigation short. The bus company based its new fares on a rate of 1.5 cents per mile of highway distance for distances in excess of four hundred miles, and higher rates not exceeding 2 cents per mile for shorter distances.[65] Because Travis based the new fares on the highway distance rather than the rail distance, bus fares dropped up to 30 percent below rail fares in the many markets where the road distance was shorter. McGinnis and Southern Pacific president Angus McDonald informally objected to the proposal, but Travis countered that the adjustments had to be made because of popular opinion. The railroad chose not to formally protest the fare reductions, but it also chose not to match them.[66]

Pacific Greyhound's fare decrease of 1 July 1936 proved highly successful for the bus company, while it affected the Southern Pacific hardly at all. Before the fare reduction, gross revenue earned by the Pacific Greyhound San Joaquin Valley trunk route increased 11 percent over the same period a year earlier. During the six months following the fare decrease, the route's gross earnings jumped 32.2 percent over the corresponding period in the previous year.[67] The fare decrease apparently spurred additional riding and additional revenue, revealing an elastic market.

The increased bus traffic largely did not come from trains. In the first half of 1936 the Southern Pacific Company earned 15 percent more passenger revenue than in the comparable period a year earlier. In the six months following Pacific Greyhound's fare increase, Southern Pacific passenger trains earned 13 percent more revenue than during the same period in 1935.[68] While bus fares fell from $8.00 to $6.25 in the important San Francisco–Los Angeles market, all but one Coast Line and San Joaquin Line passenger trains connecting San Francisco and Los Angeles experienced double digit revenue growth before and after the bus fare decrease. The exception was the slow San Joaquin Valley day train.[69] During the first six months of 1936 its passenger revenue increased 16 percent over the corresponding period in 1935, but revenues declined by 2 percent in the next six months compared to 1935.[70]

Except for the San Joaquin day train, the figures support the contention that the bus appealed to a different market than the train, and that both markets grew in the mid-1930s. This behavior and the relative popularity of the train in those markets where the bus and train directly competed strongly argue against the conspiracy theory of passenger train decline. Pacific Greyhound's high profits can be explained by the bus company's obsession with efficiency and by the fact that its trunk lines served many more points than did the rail lines.

Examination of the three types of formal agreements between the Southern Pacific Company and Pacific Greyhound Lines also fails to support the conspiracy theory. One type of agreement allowed one carrier to help the other in emergencies, at specified rates. Pacific Greyhound sometimes routed its passengers on Southern Pacific passenger trains at a rate of two cents a passenger mile. Occasionally, when snow blocked mountain passes, Pacific Greyhound chartered Southern Pacific trains at $1.50 per train mile to continue bus passengers on their way. Far more frequently the Southern Pacific called on Pacific Greyhound Lines for help. Several times monthly it chartered Pacific Greyhound buses to take train passengers around wrecks, line washouts, landslides, and general flooding that often blocked the passage of trains. This type of agreement helped rather than hurt rail passengers, because it reduced their delays. Prior to Pacific Greyhound Lines' assistance, passengers had to sit out line closures or endure backtracking and detours of hundreds of miles over other railroads.[71]

In another type of agreement the Southern Pacific Company guaranteed Pacific Greyhound Lines a profit of two cents a bus mile to operate buses in addition to the bus company's regular service. Southern Pacific used such supplemental bus services to substitute for discontinued trains, replace ferries once the highway commission opened new bridges, or provide continued service to a town bypassed because of a line relocation, as in the case of Benicia. While this arrangement potentially could divert train passengers to buses, in practice it diverted few passengers.[72] Table 18 shows the trains that the Southern Pacific replaced with buses between 1927 and the mid-1930s. I have not found traffic figures for most of these trains, but they connected small towns with each other or a nearby city, or they connected with long distance trains. These are the types of markets that began evaporating after 1910. In the case of trains serving the vicinities of Santa Cruz and Salinas, where traffic figures are available just prior to bus substitution, traffic was light for all but two trains, and its trend was rapidly down (see table 19). By 1936 the Southern Pacific continued to contract for eleven substitute services providing seventy-seven daily schedules, which carried an average of five passengers each.[73]

In the third type of agreement Pacific Greyhound honored Southern Pacific tickets on its regularly scheduled buses along specified routes, although the Southern Pacific would not honor Pacific Greyhound tickets. Southern Pacific initially entered into such agreements along branch lines where it continued to operate only one or two passenger trains per day but where Pacific Greyhound offered several daily bus trips. This arrangement gave train passengers the option of more frequent bus travel for their return trip. Jones advocated a widespread application of optional routing along Southern Pacific mainlines, but the railroad resisted the program, most likely because it feared loss of traffic on important routes. By 1935 the only important route on which it agreed to establish this arrangement was that between San Francisco and Stockton.[74]

The Santa Fe Railway forced the two carriers into extending this arrangement in late 1935. In October of that year one of its subsidiaries filed applications with the California Railroad Commission to set up and operate a statewide bus system to compete with Pacific Greyhound Lines. The Santa Fe argued that Pacific Greyhound Lines was a statewide bus monopoly controlled by another monopoly, the Southern Pacific Company. According to the Santa Fe, these monopolies victimized the public with excessively high fares and the failure to provide coordinated bus and train service. The Santa Fe proposed to remedy such alleged shortcomings with lower fares and coordinated bus and train service.[75]

The Santa Fe's aggression, which took Travis and the Southern Pacific management by surprise, persuaded the Southern Pacific to allow its passengers to use Pacific Greyhound buses when traveling between northern and southern California via the San Joaquin Valley.[76] However, the program failed to attract traffic. Only about fifty railroad passengers used buses each month on the Stockton route. Those who used the Fresno to Los Angeles route amounted to about three-tenths of a percent of the eligible rail passengers.[77]

Only in one instance did a sizable number of rail passengers use bus services. In 1929 the Southern Pacific bought full control of the Northwestern Pacific, which operated electric suburban trains in Marin County and steam trains as far north as Eureka.[78] In June 1935 the Northwestern Pacific discontinued all of its remaining nonelectric passenger trains except for two and entered into an agreement with Pacific Greyhound Lines. The bus company increased the amount of its bus service in the Northwestern Pacific territory, and it and the railroad established uniform fares and honored each others' tickets between all mutual points south of Ukiah.[79] They divided the profits or losses among themselves.[80] Under these arrangements about fifty passengers per day bought Northwestern Pacific tickets for travel in the affected territory and traveled one way by train and one way by bus.[81]

The examination of Pacific Greyhound's relations with Southern Pacific, their results, and the sources of Pacific Greyhound's substantial profits lend little support to the argument that General Motors, through the Greyhound Corporation, used its economic muscle to force railroads out of the passenger business. In the early 1930s Pacific Greyhound fare policies protected important rail markets. Pacific Greyhound eventually started fare competition in these markets; however, the Santa Fe Railway, rather than General Motors, caused this changed attitude. In the instances where Southern Pacific and Pacific Greyhound cooperated to replace trains with buses, few passengers rode trains. In most cases, the replacement bus service itself shortly disappeared for want of patronage. Southern Pacific refused to cooperate with Pacific Greyhound in important markets until the Santa Fe forced it to, and when it did, few rail passengers took advantage of the added bus schedules available to them. Both bus and rail markets grew after 1933, but they seemed to draw on different segments of the public. When

Pacific Greyhound lowered its fares in rail corridors, it increased its traffic, but not at the expense of the railroad. Its profits came from the increased traffic combined with increasing profit margins on each passenger carried. The latter derived from management's accurate analysis of the costs and revenues of each service, its consequent efforts to lower costs while simultaneously raising revenues for each service, its discontinuing those services where this was not possible, and its expanding the scope of those where it was.

The Greyhound Corporation offered this type of relationship to other railroads as well, and by 1936 five other railroads participated in Greyhound operating subsidiaries. With the railroad capital thereby gained, the Greyhound Corporation realized its goal of creating a national bus system by the mid-1930s.[82]

5
Rising Deficits in a Rebounding Market: Rail Passenger Strategy, 1930–1941

Although the company's passenger operating ratio stood at 84 in 1929, Southern Pacific's vice president of passenger traffic, Felix S. McGinnis, pointed to the company's recent passenger accomplishments with pride. The ratio was moving in the right direction, while traffic was stabilizing. The company's policies of providing faster service, more luxurious accommodations, and lower fares, and of eliminating rural local trains, seemed to be bearing fruit. McGinnis was cautiously optimistic that such policies, together with improved coach accommodations that offered passengers many of the amenities of Pullman travel, as well as improved amenities for women travelers, would ensure demand for the foreseeable future.[1]

The Depression soon proved McGinnis's optimism to be misplaced. The economic downturn reduced total intercity travel demand relatively little, but it savaged rail passenger demand. Under duress of the economic calamity, many of the remaining rail travelers broke old habits and switched to automobiles, which they already owned. The Depression showed that during the 1930s rail managers needed to find a better formula for the passenger train, taking into account the cheapness of using the auto and the ever faster driving conditions being developed, particularly in California.

California's rail managers only partly met the challenge. Their actions during the 1930s showed the existence of a significant latent demand for railroad passenger service in certain markets, but their inadequate infrastructure prevented them from fully taking advantage of the potential market. Their cost ignorance also led them astray. While they did tap part of the market, they lost money doing so. The new trains that they developed during the latter half of the decade cost much more to operate than they anticipated.

Management began the 1930s by misreading the cause of passenger demand reduction. As industrial production fell in 1930, few if any people in American society foresaw the enormity of the economic decline that lay ahead. Day after day for three disheartening years retail sales, rail car loadings, industrial production, the rate of employment, and other indicators of economic health dropped ever lower. Between 1929 and 1933 California business activity plummeted by a devastating 56 percent, as measured by indicators used by the business community.[2]

The Depression hit the California passenger train industry particularly hard. Revenues from passengers traveling within the state dropped by 64 percent, while revenues from passengers traveling to and from the state dropped by 68 percent (see table 20). Nationally, rail revenues declined by 60 percent.[3] Railroad managers attributed this stunning drop to the decline in business activity, and they were confident that demand would bounce back when the economy turned around. They ignored abundant evidence suggesting that not just the Depression but also automobile competition played a significant role in the sudden drop in rail passenger demand.

The Lynds' famous study of Muncie, Indiana ("Middletown"), revealed that the Depression least affected auto ownership and driving. Gasoline sales fell hardly at all in Muncie between 1929 and 1933. Other statistics show that for the nation as a whole, passenger miles of intercity driving declined by only 11 percent over the same period. Figures are not available showing intercity driving in California, but auto ownership in the state declined by only 7 percent between 1929 and 1933.[4] These figures suggest that rail revenues dropped so significantly not because the economic downturn forced many passengers to stop traveling, but because it induced them to switch to autos. Warren Belasco's history of the motel in American life supports this contention by showing that as companies cut back expense accounts after 1928, businesspeople increasingly gave up using Pullman cars on overnight trains in favor of driving and sleeping in inexpensive but congenial tourist courts.[5] By 1933 the auto accounted for more than 90 percent of intercity travel in the United States.[6]

While McGinnis believed that the public demanded faster and more luxurious trains, they actually got slower, fewer, and more spartan trains during the initial years of the Depression. Such cutbacks reflected Southern Pacific management's belief that the downturn in passengers merely reflected the downturn in the economy. When the economy revived, managers intended to restore cutback services to accommodate the flood of passengers who would return to the rails. As the Depression continued the company responded to falling passenger lists by shortening its major trains and reducing dining and observation car assignments. When trains shrank to four or five cars, the company sometimes combined them with other short trains, as it did in 1931 when it combined the two overnight limited trains running through the San Joaquin Valley, the *West Coast* and the *Owl*. To make one train do the work previously performed by two, the company added stops and switched cars into and out of the train en route. Both practices added time to schedules. In 1931 the company slowed down the prestigious *Daylight* by forty-five minutes so that it could make some of the stops of a discontinued local train. With this change, even Pacific Greyhound buses beat the *Daylight*'s slow twelve and a half hour schedule.[7]

The Southern Pacific also continued eliminating branch line trains. Its investment in Pacific Greyhound Lines made such discontinuances easier, because the bus company now provided the comprehensive passenger service that the railroad previously felt obligated to provide. Where Pacific Greyhound already operated regular bus service along the route in question, the railroad did not contract for substitute bus service. By 1935 the company eliminated more than 40 percent of the train miles that it operated in 1929; figure 5.1 shows the results in central California.

Although the Santa Fe initially did not cut back its passenger operations to and within California as much as the Southern Pacific did, by 1933 it faced more radical cuts.[8] McGinnis later testified that he was privy to a 1933 Santa Fe passenger traffic manager recommendation that the Santa Fe abandon its entire passenger operations north of Barstow. This move would have eliminated all Santa Fe branch line gas-electric car service in the San Joaquin Valley, which served largely a token function, as well as mainline passenger service to and from San Francisco. By this time the mainline service consisted of two local steam trains a day that connected with through Los Angeles to Chicago trains at Barstow. McGinnis explained that the Santa Fe's vice president of traffic, who presided over freight as well as passenger traffic, considered this recommendation but rejected it. As did most in the railroad industry, the Santa Fe traffic officer believed that complete passenger discontinuance would irreparably damage the company's prestige in the San Joaquin Valley and the Bay Area and hinder its efforts to solicit what freight remained in the dark year of 1933.[9] However, Santa Fe management remained gravely concerned about its passenger service, whose operating ratio reached 139 in 1933, considerably above the 110 ratio of the Southern Pacific for that year.[10]

The one positive move that railroad management made during the early years of the Depression was to reduce fares. When the economy turned down in 1929 the official regulated fare remained at 3.6 cents per passenger mile throughout the United States. In subsequent Depression years people increasingly refused to pay such a high fare, although their reluctance varied

5.1 Southern Pacific passenger train services in central California, ca. 1935. Source: SFC, exhibit 626

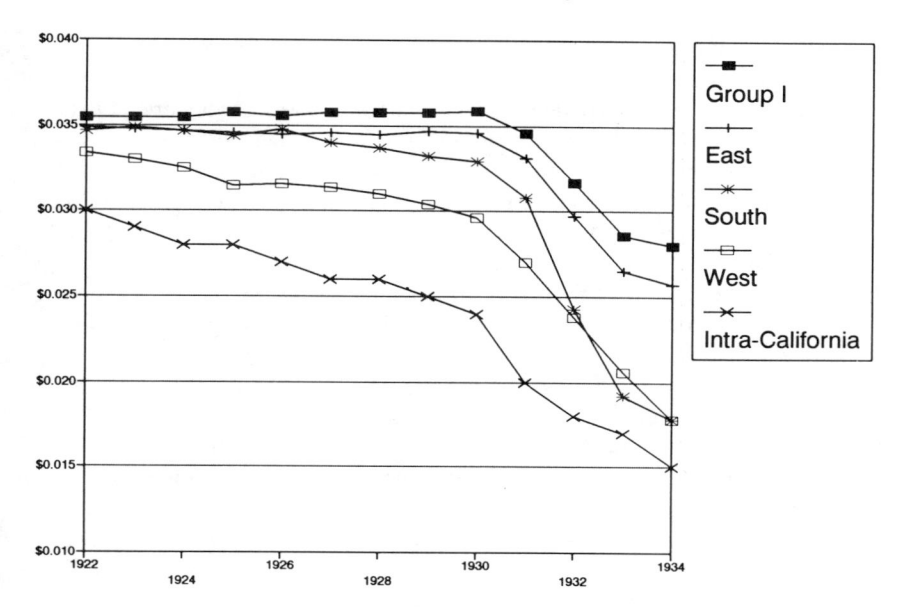

5.2 Passenger fare yields in U.S. regions, 1922–1935. Group 1 includes the Pennsylvania Railroad, the New York Central, and the New Haven. Source: Table 24

with regions. In the Northeast, where both incomes and train speeds exceeded those in other parts of the country, passengers offered less resistance to high fares. Poverty and poor train service resulted in less tolerance for high fares in the South, as did slow trains in the West. To keep passengers on trains, passenger traffic officers had to offer discounts, usually on round trip and excursion tickets. The effect of such discounts on the fare yield per passenger mile in different regions of the country clearly stands out in figure 5.2.

Southern Pacific management slashed round trip and excursion fares during the early years of the Depression. By 1933 the company offered one-dollar day return fares on several services out of San Francisco. Over most of the system the price of a round-trip ticket exceeded that of a one-way ticket by only 10 percent. Few passengers continued to buy the standard one-way ticket.[11]

As the public abandoned using one-way tickets, some western railroads sought to break with national practice and formally lower western rail fares. Working through the Association of Western Traffic Officers, they prepared a fare reduction proposal that the association approved in 1933. While eastern lines opposed western fare reductions, the ICC approved lowering the basic one-way fare in the West from 3.6 cents per passenger mile to 2 cents for travel in coaches and 3 cents for travel in sleeping cars (not including the space charge). The proposal, which took effect 1 December 1933, also eliminated the Pullman surcharge. In order to better compete with buses and coastal steamers for the economy-minded long distance traveler, the Southern Pacific unilaterally went further. All along the Pacific Coast where other railroads did not compete, it applied the regular coach fare to tourist sleeping cars.[12]

Coinciding with an upturn in economic indicators, the 1933 western fare reduction reversed the trend of declining passenger traffic and revenues for the Southern Pacific. Passenger miles rebounded significantly, and although gross revenues in 1934 failed to exceed the average of the previous three years, they at least did not decline below the depressing figure for 1933, and by the end of the year they showed a slight upward trend.[13] The passenger operating ratio also dipped from 110 in 1933 to 107 in 1934.

Southern Pacific management responded to the encouraging reversal in trends with two measures. Beginning in 1933 it cooperated with the Pullman Company to air condition some of its trains. It also revived its efforts begun in the late 1920s to improve coach conditions. By 1936 the company advertised air-conditioned dining cars, sleepers, and coaches on most principal trains operating on the Coast Line and on interstate routes. After the Santa Fe filed its bus applications in late 1935, the Southern Pacific also hurriedly air conditioned its trains in the San Joaquin Valley. It neglected its important Oakland to Sacramento route, which did not receive air-conditioned equipment prior to World War II.[14]

Coach improvements included not only air conditioning but also reclining easy chairs and large men's and women's lounges approximately the size of the men's smoking and dressing lounge in the standard Pullman sleeping car. Capacity of the refurbished coaches ranged from forty-four to fifty seats, compared to seventy to ninety seats in the unrefurbished coaches. Generally, the company assigned refurbished coaches to the same trains that it air conditioned.[15]

The improvement in economic indicators and the general fare reduction in 1933 failed to revive the Santa Fe's passenger operations as much as they did the Southern Pacific's. After declining a staggering 77 percent between 1929 and 1933, the Santa Fe's intrastate passenger revenue increased only slightly in 1934, and the road's transcontinental passenger revenue continued to decline. As the Santa Fe's passenger operating ratio climbed from the alarming figure of 139 in 1933 to an even more dismaying 143 in 1934, management examined the experience of other American railroads in search of a new passenger strategy.[16] Its attention turned to glowing reports emanating from the South on how radical fare reductions could revive passenger service.

During the 1920s coach traffic had dropped precipitously throughout the South. The Southern Railway, the region's largest railroad, discontinued coach trains as revenues dropped below out-of-pocket costs. By the end of the 1920s the Southern's management determined that if the trend persisted, it would discontinue its last coach passenger train in 1934 or 1935.[17]

To avoid such a loss of prestige, the Southern's management began fare reduction experiments in the late 1920s. Because competing railroads in the South opposed fare reductions, the Southern confined its experiments to its lines connecting points of principal population where no other railroad operated. In such markets the Southern's management hoped to increase gross revenues. While a lowered fare would reduce revenue from each existing passenger, it would induce additional passengers to ride. The Southern's management believed that reduced fares would induce so many new passengers to ride that their revenue would more than compensate for lost revenue from old passengers. It also believed that it had so much capacity on its trains that the new passengers would cost the company little to carry. Thus, the Southern Railway anticipated increased gross revenues with little increase in cost, resulting in a reduced passenger deficit.[18]

Such results eluded the company for several years. Each time the company reduced fares, it gained more passengers, but not enough to increase gross revenues. Out of desperation the company reduced fares even further. In 1932 it tried the extraordinarily low fare of 1.5 cents per mile on its route between Winston-Salem and Goldsboro, North Carolina. This effort yielded success. The reduction increased the number of passengers by about 200 percent and gross revenues by 68 percent.[19]

The Goldsboro experiment convinced the Southern's management that a threshold fare existed between 2.0 and 1.5 cents below which coach rail service was attractive and above which it was not. Management reasoned that it should set all of its coach fares at the low level and in 1933 petitioned the ICC for a systemwide fare reduction to 1.5 cents in coaches and 3.0 cents in Pullmans, with no Pullman surcharge. Despite its unilateral action and vehement opposition from all other railroads (as well as bus companies) in the South, the Southern received enthusiastic ICC approval and reduced its fares in December 1933. All other southern railroads and bus companies felt compelled to meet the new low rates.[20]

The low fares succeeded in attracting enough new passengers to increase gross revenues, according to a study performed by the federal coordinator of transportation. Congress established the coordinator's office in 1933 at the behest of railroad security owners, who wanted to achieve cost savings by forcing greater cooperation among railroads.[21] Much of the office's attention focused on ways to reduce the passenger deficit, and it carefully monitored results of the southern fare reductions. It found that the new low fares increased coach passenger miles for all southern railroads by 70 percent and coach revenues by 8 percent in 1934, compared to the average of 1931, 1932, and 1933. During the same test period, the eastern carriers, who kept the high fares of the 1920s, experienced no change in coach passenger miles and an 18 percent drop in coach revenues as more passengers rode on discounted tickets. In the West, where the basic one-way fare fell to 2.0 cents, coach passenger miles increased by 4 percent but coach revenue declined by 26 percent.[22]

The federal coordinator concurred with the Southern Railway that a ceiling for coach fares existed. At fares much above 1.5 cents a mile passengers would not ride coach trains. This ceiling was determined by what the public perceived the cost of driving a car to be. Surveys by the federal coordinator's office as well as those conducted at the University of Iowa revealed that the public perceived the cost of driving an auto at about 1.2 cents per passenger mile. If fares exceeded this value by very much, the public would not use trains.[23]

These results convinced the Santa Fe management to replicate the Southern Railway experiment on its own line between Los Angeles and San Diego. In 1931 the Santa Fe received an average daily revenue of $1,244 from passengers traveling between downtown Los Angeles and San Diego. The average fare yield was 2.3 cents per passenger mile. By the beginning of 1933 the carrier grossed only $491 per day on a fare yield of 2.0 cents. Based on the Southern Railway experience, the Santa Fe radically reduced the fare to 1.0 cent per mile in mid-1934.[24]

The results gratified management. After the substantially discounted fares went into effect, passenger miles increased by approximately 120 percent, while gross revenues increased by 10 percent over the nadir of 1933. In 1935 a major exposition opened in San Diego and led to a much greater increase in passenger miles, which then exceeded levels reached in the 1920s. Gross revenues amounted to several times their 1933 level. Many of the new or regained passengers drove to the Santa Fe station in Los Angeles, compelling the railroad to pave the lovely gardens on the station grounds in order to provide parking spaces. After the exposition closed, gross revenues settled to a level about 40 percent greater than in 1933 and passenger miles to a level about 2.8 times greater.[25]

In the eyes of the Santa Fe management, the San Diego line experience brilliantly contrasted to the railroad's otherwise worsening passenger performance. Even as the economy continued to improve, the Santa Fe passenger operating ratio climbed still higher, reaching 145 in 1935. A stunned management resolved to do something about the deplorable state of its passenger operations and concluded on the basis of its San Diego line experiment that systemwide low fares would figure prominently in a new passenger strategy.

Management also embraced faster trains as another important part of a new passenger strategy. Many rail officials viewed higher speed as a means for protecting earnings. Spokespeople for the New York Central, the Pennsylvania, and the Chicago, North Shore & Milwaukee all claimed that the higher speeds of their services compared to those of most railroads protected their earnings from auto competition.[26] In the mid-1930s Santa Fe managers also stated this view. The company believed that travel between large cities constituted the only market for rail passenger service, and very fast trains were required to tap this market.[27]

To speed up its passenger service, the Santa Fe proposed using new high-speed diesel streamliners as well as buses. Both the Union Pacific and the Chicago, Burlington & Quincy inaugurated short, lightweight, high-speed diesel coach trains in 1934. The Union Pacific's aluminum M-10000 and the Burlington's stainless steel *Pioneer Zephyr* exhibited low weight per seat, low operating and maintenance costs, and high public appeal.[28] According to a special study conducted by the engineering firm of Coverdale & Colpitts, they earned extraordinary profits.[29] Highly publicized, the fast and flashy little trains captured the public imagination during the dreary days of the mid-Depression. They sold the Santa Fe management on the concept of experimenting with diesel power and fast, streamlined trains.[30]

The company intended to use buses in two ways. They could help in speeding up limited trains between major cities by serving unimportant intermediate stops previously served by the limiteds. Buses also could extend service to small towns not on the railroad line. Pacific Greyhound's 30 percent return on investment convinced Santa Fe's management that a local traffic potential still existed, but only buses could tap it profitably.[31]

In mid-1935 Santa Fe's management began to act on a new passenger strategy based on these ideas. It quickly purchased two large regional bus systems in the Midwest and a couple of smaller systems that had remained independent of the Greyhound system and reorganized them under the trade name of the Santa Fe Trail System. The railroad then extended Santa Fe Trail routes east and west along the main Santa Fe rail routes between Chicago, Los Angeles, San Francisco, and San Diego.[32]

The Santa Fe acted quickly in making these purchases and extensions in order to escape provisions of a congressional bill that was about to become law. In the Motor Carrier Act of 1935 Congress extended jurisdiction of the ICC over the intercity bus industry, which previously was unregulated at the national level. If the ICC restricted entry into the bus industry, as the California Railroad Commission generally had done since 1917 within California, it would deny the Santa Fe's attempts to start bus service. To avoid this possibility, the Santa Fe purchased and extended bus lines before the act became effective. In order to move this rapidly, the railroad had to refrain from carrying intra-California passengers on its buses. The carriage of intrastate passengers required California Railroad Commission approval, which Santa Fe management feared would come slowly, if at all. Because of this restriction a passenger at the end of 1935 could board a Santa Fe Trails bus in San Diego and ride to Chicago but not to any point in California.[33]

Upon establishing the Santa Fe Trail System, Santa Fe management turned its attention to implementing a bold plan for revitalizing the railroad's presence within California. It first organized a California bus subsidiary, the Santa Fe Transportation Company. In October 1935 the subsidiary filed applications with the California Railroad Commission for certificates to operate buses competing with Pacific Greyhound Lines between San Francisco, Los Angeles, and San Diego via the San Joaquin Valley. The applications also requested permission to charge a uniform fare of 1.5 cents per mile based on the highway distance between two points. The low rate, which considerably undercut then prevailing Pacific Greyhound and Southern Pacific rates, would apply to Santa Fe buses and trains alike, and passengers could freely transfer between the two.[34]

Shortly after asking the state commission to allow statewide bus competition, the Santa Fe revealed that it planned to do still more. If the railroad commission approved the bus and fare reduction applications, the Santa Fe promised to inaugurate two daily high-speed diesel streamliners between Bakersfield and Oakland, and another two between Los Angeles and San Diego. Santa Fe Trails buses would feed passengers to the streamliners. In addition, buses and trains would work together to provide a fast through service between Los Angeles and San Francisco. A through passenger would travel on a modern, air-conditioned bus over the new high-speed highway from Los Angeles to Bakersfield, continue on a diesel streamlined train to Oakland, and complete the journey by bus over the new Bay Bridge into San Francisco. In all the passenger would spend only nine and a half hours completing this trip, three hours faster than if he or she used the fastest Southern Pacific train and about as fast as the commonly perceived driving time.[35]

These proposals stunned both the Southern Pacific and Pacific Greyhound Lines managements. Neither had any hint of what the Santa Fe intended until it filed its applications. Since the early part of the century until the renegade Southern Railway broke with tradition, railroads rarely acted unilaterally in matters affecting other railroads. They acted cooperatively through traffic and executive associations. For this reason the Southern Pacific and Pacific Greyhound Lines kept the Santa Fe informed of their plans and on two occasions invited the Santa Fe to join in control of the bus operation. The Santa Fe still was welcome to buy in.[36] In the eyes of the Southern Pacific and Pacific Greyhound as well as prevailing business etiquette, joint ownership rather than a competing bus operation was the proper way for the Santa Fe to reap the profits of buses. The contrary actions of Santa Fe's management seemed to the Southern Pacific and Pacific Greyhound Lines managements to be a betrayal, and they reacted accordingly.

Not surprisingly, both carriers opposed the applications and attempted to marshal California business sentiment against the Chicago-based Santa Fe. In the World War I era Southern Pacific president William Sproule had successfully used a similar tactic against the Union Pacific over control of the Central Pacific. Recalling the earlier campaign, Southern Pacific president A. D. McDonald, McGinnis, and other officers visited chambers of commerce and business groups in every community affected by the proposals. They tirelessly argued that the Santa Fe plan would do no more than spread existing traffic more thinly over a duplicative and costlier transportation system. Such waste would further weaken the already financially wobbly Southern Pacific and, because the company still was one of California's most important business institutions, would irreparably harm the state. California would not even benefit from low rates, they argued. Heavy financial losses would force the Santa Fe to raise rates and also withdraw its streamliners. Everybody would lose.[37]

Travis and other Pacific Greyhound officers also visited business groups, arguing that the Santa Fe intended to drive Pacific Greyhound Lines out of business and then cut back its bus service in favor of trains, much as the Pacific Electric Railway did with Motor Transit. The Santa Fe thus would deprive the public of a valuable form of transportation. Travis added that the Santa Fe management could not possibly make money operating buses at fares of 1.5 cents per mile because, being railroad men, they could not figure out how to operate at a low enough cost.[38]

To press its case the Santa Fe in turn raised the specter of the Southern Pacific octopus. Its officers also lobbied business groups throughout the state and angrily charged that the monopolistic combination of the Southern Pacific and Pacific Greyhound Lines stifled transportation innovation in California while extorting excessive fares from the public. It exposed

Pacific Greyhound's practice of charging rates based on circuitous railroad distance. Santa Fe officers cited examples of such rates not only between Los Angeles and Bakersfield, but between Los Angeles and San Francisco and all San Joaquin Valley points. In all of these cases bus fares were based on the railroad distance rather than the much shorter highway distance. Competition provided the only protection of the public from such abuses, the Santa Fe argued. Moreover, improved service at lower fares would stimulate much greater travel to the benefit of everybody, including the Southern Pacific and Pacific Greyhound Lines.[39]

Such arguments raged before the railroad commission for two and a half years. In the meantime, the Southern Pacific and Pacific Greyhound Lines hurriedly improved their services. To complement its numerous fourteen-hour schedules between Los Angeles and San Francisco via the San Joaquin Valley, Pacific Greyhound added several daily express buses running on a twelve and a half hour schedule. It also lowered its fares in mid-1936 and based the new fares on the highway distance. In February 1936 the Southern Pacific split and speeded up previously consolidated through trains in the San Joaquin Valley and added new service between San Francisco and Fresno. It also restored a daily gas-electric train running east-west between Armona and Porterville. In addition it accelerated the schedule of the Coast Line's *Daylight* between San Francisco and Los Angeles by one and a half hours and added a new local train to that route. It also air conditioned most of its through trains in the San Joaquin Valley and along the coast. Southern Pacific's management claimed that it restored service because traffic warranted it and not because of the Santa Fe initiative.[40]

In addition to these service changes, the Southern Pacific invested $2.4 million in a pair of new streamlined trains to operate between San Francisco and Los Angeles. According to Southern Pacific historian Don Hofsommer, the company's marketing consultant recommended in 1933 that the company invest in high-speed, lightweight motor trains to meet auto competition. The consultant placed highest priority on the Oakland to Sacramento route, where the Southern Pacific carried the greatest number of passengers on its entire system, and on the San Francisco to Los Angeles route.[41] Richard Wright's history of the *Daylight* shows that the Southern Pacific's Office of the General Superintendent prepared drawings in 1933 for a low-cost, lightweight, high-speed motor train consistent with the consultant's recommendations.[42]

Despite the recommendations and engineering work, Southern Pacific management deferred action until spurred by the Santa Fe initiative more than two years later, and then it responded only to meet the Santa Fe competitive threat. A month and a half after the Santa Fe filed its applications,

Southern Pacific president A. D. McDonald decided to build a new train for service between San Francisco and Los Angeles. He ignored the Sacramento route. He also rejected the idea of an economy high-performance train because he did not think the design looked sufficiently like a train ought to look. He ordered instead that his mechanical department design a more luxurious and more conventional-looking streamlined train of individual cars of lightweight construction, pulled by a massive but streamlined steam locomotive. He wanted the new train to offer about five hundred spacious seats, with large and richly appointed men's and women's lounges in every car, and first-rate dining and lounge services. Rather than costing $1,400 per seat to build, as would the original economy design, the new Southern Pacific design had to outshine the Santa Fe's proposed trains, which were estimated to cost about $2,300 per seat. Southern Pacific's new luxury *Daylight* ended up costing about $2,800 per seat.[43]

From the time that the new trains entered service in March 1937 on a fast nine and three-quarter hour schedule, Southern Pacific management realized that it had tapped a latent market for rail travel far larger than it anticipated. Revenues per train mile jumped from $2.69 for the old *Daylight* in 1936 to $4.88 for the new, faster *Daylight* in 1938. Coverdale & Colpitts calculated that the new streamliners earned among the highest profits of any streamlined train in the United States prior to World War II.[44]

Despite the *Daylight*'s earnings and a couple of other bright spots, Southern Pacific management viewed its passenger operations with alarm in 1938. Passenger and freight traffic rose rapidly, almost reaching 1929 levels by 1937, but gross revenues rose much less rapidly because of heavily discounted fares and freight rates. Costs grew in proportion to traffic rather than revenues. Consequently, the passenger deficit worsened as the economy improved. From a low of 107 in 1934, the passenger operating ratio climbed to 112 in 1936 and 118 in 1937. After a sharp recession reduced the company's profits by 95 percent in late 1937 compared to 1936, and the Santa Fe won its fight before the Railroad Commission in April 1938, the Southern Pacific management reevaluated its passenger strategy.[45]

Up to this time the company continued to operate some unprofitable passenger services for the benefit of businesspeople. Its electric and steam suburban operations in the Bay Area fell into this category, as did its subsidiary Pacific Electric Railway in Los Angeles. The company also continued to operate several local trains in the San Joaquin Valley for the purpose of hauling businesspeople in overnight Pullman cars from various valley towns to Los Angeles and San Francisco. Several passengers used these cars each night, but the trains hauling them grossed only between $0.20 and $0.50 per mile.[46]

During the *Santa Fe Case* Southern Pacific president McDonald argued that one of the benefits that the California public received from the railroad's protected status was the provision of such unprofitable but socially needed services. He strongly implied that if the railroad commission approved the Santa Fe's applications, the Southern Pacific would discontinue the services.[47] These arguments failed to persuade business groups. Despite the Southern Pacific's and Pacific Greyhound's efforts to enlist the support of the California business community, every business group they contacted lined up behind the Santa Fe. Even the San Francisco Chamber of Commerce, in which McGinnis prominently participated, rejected the Southern Pacific's pleas and backed the Santa Fe. In supporting the Santa Fe, the spokespeople of almost all groups found no fault with Southern Pacific's service and regretted any financial harm that might befall Southern Pacific as a consequence of competition. However, they believed the short term improvements brought by competition would outweigh any longer term dire consequences predicted by Southern Pacific.[48]

As the Greyhound executive Cloyd Kimball later recounted, the position taken by the state's business groups leading to the railroad commission's April 1938 decision favoring the Santa Fe embittered Pacific Greyhound president Buck Travis. As a consequence, Travis effectively turned the reins of his business over to his longtime colleague, Fred Ackerman.[49] Given Southern Pacific's careful cultivation of California business interests since 1911, it is likely that company's managers felt similarly.

In any event, the company began discontinuing money-losing services, beginning with nonmainline passenger trains. By the end of the next year it eliminated all local Pullman services and remaining local trains in the San Joaquin Valley. It also axed its slow Oakland to Stockton trains, which the new, faster Santa Fe service made redundant. Local trains to Santa Barbara and Santa Cruz also disappeared.[50]

The remaining electric services also began to go, but the decision to sell or abandon them was not easy. Through the 1920s Southern Pacific sought to end its East Bay electric deficits by merging its electric lines with those of the rival Key System into a jointly owned subsidiary. According to McDonald, Southern Pacific's electric railway employees blocked this proposal, which meant less liberal work rules for them. Management did not think the price of a systemwide strike was worth paying to resolve this issue, so the company let the status quo continue until 1933. Then McDonald directed the company's general vice president, Frank L. Burckhalter, to study the electric problem. After finding labor still intransigent, Burckhalter recommended that the company completely abandon the East Bay electric operation. According to Danny McGanny, Southern Pacific vice president of research during the 1960s, McGinnis objected to the recommendation, and McDonald put off making a decision.[51]

McDonald apparently decided after the *Santa Fe Case* decision. In January 1939 Southern Pacific's Bay Area electric trains began operating as a wholly owned subsidiary company called the Interurban Electric Railway (IER). In March 1940 IER applied to discontinue all electric service. McDonald's observations on this discontinuance reveal the parent company's new policy of ending cross subsidiaries:

> The Interurban Electric losses have exhausted its financial resources; and the Southern Pacific Co. is unwilling to continue making advances to the Interurban to enable it to continue operations. . . . Withdrawal of support for the Interurban Electric Railway is another step in the policy the Southern Pacific Company has adopted to strengthen its financial position and thus improve its ability to meet the needs of its major transportation services. Evidence of this policy will be found in the recent disposition by Southern Pacific of its interest in street railway systems in San Jose, Stockton and Fresno, in the contemplated abandonment of interurban service by the Northwestern Pacific, in substitution of motor coaches and abandonment by the Pacific Electric of substantial parts of its rail lines, in withdrawal of financial support from the Southern Pacific Railroad Company of Mexico, and now in the abandonment of the Interurban Electric. . . . Because these unprofitable phases of service are no longer generally desired by the public, as indicated by lack of patronage, and because they constitute a drag on our efforts to provide modern service of the type that the public does want, we are asking and expect to have the support and cooperation of the public, in its own interest and for the greatest good of the greatest number, in working out these transitions in transportation services.[52]

McDonald's statement contrasts markedly from his position three years earlier when he testified, "[The Southern Pacific] has provided at great capital outlay, and is operating at a loss, interurban service which is indispensable and of great value in promoting general welfare."[53] The utility of the interurban service changed little between 1937 and 1940; what changed was Southern Pacific's willingness to operate services at a loss for the general welfare.

The company readily received railroad commission approval and, except for the more heavily traveled lines of the Pacific Electric, discontinued its last electric train in mid-1941. Only two significant Southern Pacific passenger operations remained outside of mainline passenger services. The company continued to operate money-losing commuter service to the wealthy suburbs south of San Francisco, where most Southern Pacific executives lived, and it continued heavily patronized trains between Oakland and Sacramento.[54]

While the Southern Pacific discontinued money-losing passenger services, it continued to improve its mainline trains. With the inauguration of the once-weekly *City of San Francisco* in 1936 and the new *Daylight* in 1937, the glamorous streamliner stole the spotlight from the company's intercity passenger improvements. The company initially experimented with streamliners reluctantly. As already recounted, the steamlined *Daylight* resulted from the Santa Fe California initiative. Indirectly, the Santa Fe also provided the creative impulse that led to the *City of San Francisco*. Maury Klein shows that in 1936 the Union Pacific inaugurated the *City of Los Angeles* to meet the competition of the thirty-nine and three-quarter hour Santa Fe *Super Chief* between Chicago and Los Angeles. Having favored Los Angeles with a fast streamliner, the Union Pacific then was compelled to also provide San Francisco with an equally fast train.[55]

Results of the streamliners quickly proved encouraging. Often attracting sellout crowds, the diesel-powered *City of San Francisco* averaged about 57 miles an hour for the 2,260-mile trip and grossed more than $4.00 per train mile. While the *Daylight* averaged only 48 miles an hour for its 470-mile trip, it beat the fastest previous train by one and a half hours and grossed more than $5.00 per train mile. The experience of the *City of San Francisco* and the *Daylight* convinced management to invest in more such trains, although it did so sparingly, usually when prompted by a competitive threat. In late 1937 it placed two streamliners in service between Houston and Dallas to meet streamlined competition from the Burlington–Rock Island. It also purchased additional streamlined cars and locomotives for transcontinental services. By the end of the year it had spent almost $10 million in equipment improvements. In 1940 it added a second pair of *Daylights* to the Coast Line, and in 1941 it reequipped its premier San Francisco to Los Angeles overnight train, the *Lark,* with streamlined equipment. The Southern Pacific also cooperated with the Union Pacific and the Chicago & Northwestern in building additional larger streamliners for the *City of San Francisco* service to increase its frequency to three times a week.[56]

To meet the Santa Fe challenge in the San Joaquin Valley, the Southern Pacific considered several options. It evaluated its new Dallas to Houston streamlined service as a failure and considered transferring the streamlined trains from Texas to the San Joaquin Valley. McDonald ultimately rejected this option because of the loss of prestige the Southern Pacific would suffer in Texas. He also considered but rejected purchasing one or more Rock Island streamliners, which his staff thought were not doing well. He finally decided to build two new trains patterned after the *Daylight*. Named the *San Joaquin Daylight,* the new trains began daily service between Los Angeles and Oakland in July 1941 on a twelve-hour schedule.[57]

The company improved other mainline trains as well. For starters, it speeded them up. By the end of the 1930s most of its mainline trains ran modestly faster than a decade earlier, reflecting the speed demands of a more auto-oriented public (see table 21).

The company also made a large effort to regain the high-volume economy trade, which it lost in the 1920s. To attract such passengers, the company began in 1937 to rebuild old heavy steel coaches to approximate the interior accommodations of the new streamlined coaches. It combined the rebuilt coaches and tourist sleepers with informal dining and lounge cars and ultra-low fares to offer economical but comfortable transcontinental train travel for those not liking the stuffy formality and prices of the first-class trains. This concept in train travel had been promoted in the *Passenger Traffic Report*, released in January 1935. The Union Pacific then pioneered the economy train with the May 1936 introduction of the *Challenger* between Los Angeles and Chicago. The Southern Pacific became involved in 1937, after the early popularity of the *Challenger* convinced it and the Union Pacific to provide similar service between Chicago and San Francisco. Thereafter the Southern Pacific rapidly introduced economy trains to all of its mainlines and advertised a train on every mainline for every purse and taste.[58]

The Santa Fe's California improvements began to appear in 1938. In March of that year the company inaugurated twice-daily high-speed diesel train service between Los Angeles and San Diego, and on 1 July 1938 it began coordinated bus and rail service between Los Angeles and San Francisco with the new 1.5 cent fare. The through fare between Los Angeles and San Francisco fell from $9.00 to $6.00, which the Southern Pacific was forced to meet on its *Daylight*. Under the name of Santa Fe Trailways, the Santa Fe also started a comprehensive network of bus services competing with Pacific Greyhound Lines between San Francisco and San Diego. By this time the Santa Fe joined with several other railroad-owned and independent bus systems to form a national marketing organization called the National Trailways System. Members of the system painted their buses the same colors, coordinated their schedules, provided through services and fares, used common terminals, and published joint timetables. Collectively, National Trailways members offered the public a bus system comparable to that of the Greyhound Corporation.[59]

Contrary to the Southern Pacific's dire predictions, the greatly improved service and lowered fares generated a large amount of new traffic and revenues. The *Golden Gates* and *San Diegans* carried about as much traffic as Santa Fe witnesses predicted during the *Santa Fe Case*. Most of this traffic was new to the Santa Fe and did not merely transfer from older

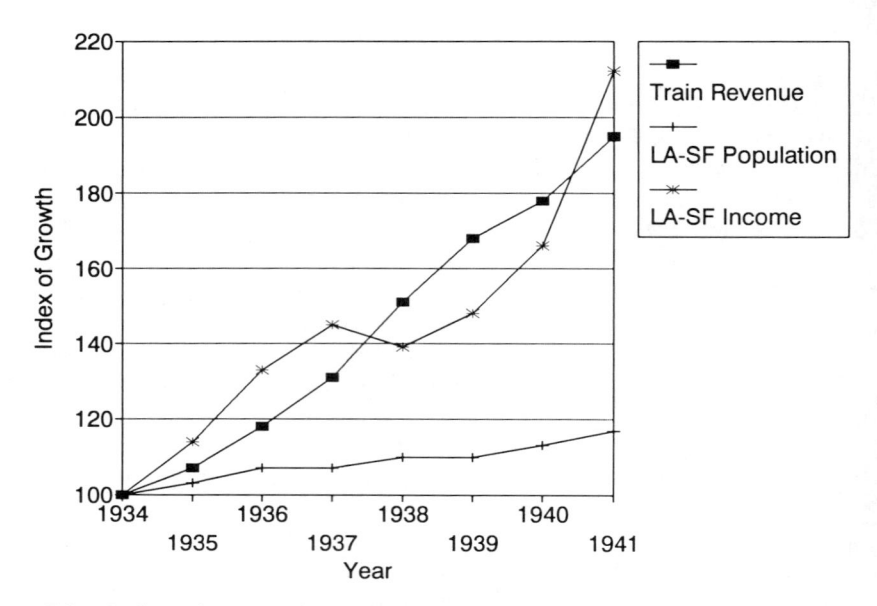

5.3 Indices of growth of Los Angeles to San Francisco passenger train revenues, area population, and area income, 1934–1941. Source: Table 25

trains. The railroad's revenues from intra-California trains increased from $500,000 in 1937 to $1.4 million in 1939 and reached $1.8 million in 1941. Coverdale & Colpitts pronounced both services highly profitable. At the same time, the earnings of Southern Pacific trains stayed the same or, as in the case of the *Daylight*, substantially increased because of the reduced fare. As figure 5.3 shows, the California rail improvements that the Santa Fe initiated, and those that it induced the Southern Pacific to make, caused a modest revival of rail importance in the several markets between Los Angeles and San Francisco. Despite rising air competition and improved highways, rail revenues per capita nearly doubled between 1934 and 1941.[60] These and the San Diego train improvements stopped the historic decline in intra-California rail passenger demand prior to World War II (figure 5.4).

The Santa Fe and the Southern Pacific achieved these impressive traffic increases without major improvements to their tracks and facilities. About the only significant improvement that the Southern Pacific made allowed the *Daylight* to meet its intended nine and three-quarter hour schedule. In 1937 the company laid eighty new track miles of heavier rail on the Coast Line, realigned curves over Cuesta Grade and near Santa Margarita, and constructed nine miles of additional sidings. It also constructed new maintenance facilities in Los Angeles and San Francisco to service the new

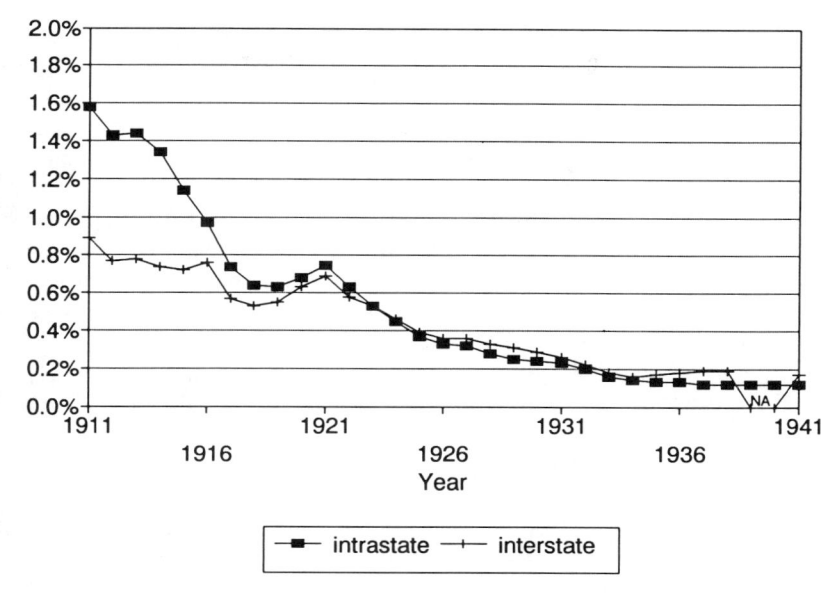

5.4 California passenger revenues as a percentage of California income, 1911–1941. Source: Table 20

trains.[61] In order to enhance high-speed train service, the Santa Fe also worked cooperatively with the California Division of Highways's realignment of U.S. 101 to straighten some curves on its San Diego line.[62] While the improvements to the Southern Pacific and Santa Fe lines were desirable, they paled in comparison to the new high-speed, shorter distance highways that the California Highway Commission feverishly constructed over mountain passes on California's trunk routes during the 1930s.[63]

The Southern Pacific and Santa Fe also invested heavily in Los Angeles's new Union Station, opened in 1939, although the investment probably worsened rather than improved passenger service performance. After years of struggle in the courts and regulatory commissions, the City of Los Angeles forced the three major intercity railroads serving the city to build a union station. With the most passenger trains operating into Los Angeles, the Southern Pacific contributed 44 percent of the $11 million construction cost. While architecturally striking, the new terminal did not significantly improve the quality of the state's passenger service. I have not found operating cost figures of the new terminal, but Carl Condit's penetrating work on terminals in Cincinnati suggests that the new terminal cost more to operate than the two passenger terminals that it replaced.[64]

The net result of the Southern Pacific's passenger strategy in the late

1930s proved disappointing. The deletion of money-losing passenger services and the improvement of money-making trains failed to end passenger service financial woes. Although the passenger operating ratio dropped from 119 in 1938 to 109 in 1939, it rose again to 117 in 1940. Only as war threatened in 1941 did swelling war-related traffic mask this trend, bringing the operating ratio down to 105.

How the Santa Fe management evaluated its improvements is not known, but records exist showing how Southern Pacific management viewed them. During the first several weeks of *Golden Gate* operation, Southern Pacific employed clandestine agents to ride on Santa Fe's bus/train service and make daily reports to A. D. McDonald. McDonald in turn had his staff analyze the reports and periodically summarized the analyses for board chairman Hale Holden in New York. McDonald concluded that when all costs were considered, including those of the connecting buses, the service failed to cover its operating and equipment costs, but that the Santa Fe had scored an incalculable publicity coup that would lead to a growth of Santa Fe freight revenues in the San Joaquin Valley. This scared McDonald, because the Southern Pacific still dominated rail freight movement in the San Joaquin Valley and the Bay Area, meaning that it potentially could lose much to the Santa Fe.[65] He believed that the Santa Fe viewed the service in this manner and thought increased freight revenue would more than compensate for added passenger deficits.[66] His observation, "The situation points to the need of some positive action on the part of Southern Pacific if we are to counteract the prestige which the Santa Fe has undoubtedly gained, and hold to our own line our rightful proportion of San Joaquin Valley traffic—both freight and passenger," led to Southern Pacific's investment in the *San Joaquin Daylight* in 1941.[67] Clearly Pratt's 1901 assertion that railroads operated passenger trains to advertise freight service still prevailed in 1938.

While the Santa Fe generally succeeded with its California passenger rail improvement program, its overall passenger indicators must have disappointed management. Since 1936 the company operated the *Super Chief,* a weekly diesel-powered high-speed luxury train between Chicago and Los Angeles. In 1938 it outfitted its premier daily train on the run with streamlined cars. It also inaugurated lightweight high-speed economy day trains between Chicago and Kansas City, as well as a novel weekly high-speed streamlined coach train from Chicago to Los Angeles. Coverdale & Colpitts reported that all of these trains attracted heavy passenger loadings and earned high returns on investments. Yet revenues from all Santa Fe interstate trains into and out of Los Angeles grew only by 11 percent between 1936 and 1937 and then remained largely static through 1940. The passenger operating ratio declined from 138 in 1937 to 129 a year later, coinciding with the introduction of diesel trains in California and in the Midwest, and it declined further to 123 in 1940. The economies of streamlined operation or, more probably, diesel operation may have contributed to this improvement, but considering the large profits that Coverdale & Colpitts attributed to the streamliners, the passenger deficit remained remarkably high.[68]

When Santa Fe Trailways started its California service in 1938 Pacific Greyhound revenues dropped up to 40 percent in important markets. According to Pacific Greyhound executive Cloyd Kimball, the Santa Fe captured about half of the bus business in its markets and held onto this share before World War II. Travis threatened to drop the bus fare between Los Angeles and San Francisco to $5.00. Whether or not this happened is not clear. It is clear, however, that while Santa Fe Trailways carried about half the traffic in its markets, which also were Pacific Greyhound's most lucrative markets, Pacific Greyhound's profitability remained at its high 1936 level until World War II.[69] At the same time, Santa Fe Trailways lost money. By the end of World War II, Santa Fe showed little interest in the bus business, which by this time, according to Kimball, it managed without competitive zeal. It made no attempt to hold on to the business it had captured from Pacific Greyhound and quickly sold out. Despite the Santa Fe's marketing success with buses, Travis proved correct: the railroad could not make money in the bus business.[70]

Responding to a devastating collapse in demand at the beginning of the decade, Southern Pacific and Santa Fe managements during the 1930s greatly altered the character of the late 1920s passenger train. The Southern Pacific in particular accelerated its shift away from short distance trains by eliminating most of them in favor of buses. On the other hand, it speeded up and added more luxurious accommodations to its longer distance trains operating between large cities, while charging ever lower fares. Through such actions the Southern Pacific operated far fewer trains, but each train carried more cars, offered more amenities, operated at faster speeds, and carried its passengers over greater distances. Although the number of passengers using the Southern Pacific declined substantially over the decade, the fact that each passenger rode much farther resulted in approximately the same number of passenger miles using the Southern Pacific in 1939 as in 1927.[71]

The Santa Fe's management followed a similar strategy, but it emphasized considerably more than the Southern Pacific high-speed coach trains offering comfortable but not posh accommodations. It also reversed its strategy of the 1920s and first half of the 1930s by turning more of its attention to shorter distance markets, most notably that between Los Angeles and San Diego and those between the San Joaquin Valley towns and California's two major metropolitan areas. Its efforts boosted gross intra-California passenger revenues to the level of 1928, but the company had to work much harder and incur greater expense to get the revenue. Because fares in 1941 were much lower than those in 1928, the number of passenger miles producing the revenue approached the passenger miles of the peak year of 1913.[72]

Curiously, the Southern Pacific's passenger improvements failed to reduce the company's passenger deficit, while the Santa Fe's efforts produced only modest improvements. In 1940, the last year before war-related traffic affected statistics, the Southern Pacific's passenger operating ratio stood as high as at any time during the 1930s and exceeded the deplorably high level of 1933 by a wide margin. That the company lost more money on a passenger volume 60 percent greater than that of the bleak year of 1933 should have alarmed management. While the Santa Fe's efforts reduced its passenger operating ratio by about 15 points, it still stood at the unacceptably high level of 123 on the eve of World War II.

In many respects the California passenger experience of the Southern Pacific and the Santa Fe paralleled that of Pacific Greyhound Lines. All three faced a public demanding ever lower fares. All three faced declining traffic to about 1933 and then rebounding passenger volumes. All three improved service to capture the increasing traffic potential after 1933. Their experiences differed only in profitability. Whereas Pacific Greyhound Lines made a 30 percent return on investment under these conditions, both railroads lost substantial sums on their increasing passenger business. Why this was so begs explanation.

6
What Went Wrong

A paradox confronted Southern Pacific and Santa Fe managers at the end of the 1930s. Even as they implemented passenger improvement measures, which when examined individually seemed highly profitable, each company's passenger deficit stubbornly persisted. Either their efforts achieved much less than their apparent success, or the ICC definition of the passenger deficit bore little resemblance to reality.

During the 1950s and 60s many railroad critics argued the latter view. According to them, the ICC formula yielded an overly pessimistic picture of passenger train finances because it included allocated fixed expenses that critics thought would continue if the passenger trains were eliminated.[1] The economic historians George Hilton and John Due reached similar conclusions from their study of electric interurban railways. In studying the financial effect that passenger service abandonment had on electric interurban railway companies that continued to provide freight service, Hilton and Due found that the costs actually saved approximated the predicted cost savings based on out-of-pocket cost calculations.[2]

After studying the evolution of costing on the Southern Pacific in relation to recent cost analysis work, I come to different conclusions. I argue here that cost estimates based on the ICC formula approximated reality much more closely than did railroad out-of-pocket costing methods for mainline passenger services on heavily used railroads. Hilton's and Due's conclusions pertained to lightly used railways. Most of the cases in their sample had minimal capacity, and what freight and passenger service remained at the time of passenger abandonment used only a small fraction of the capacity. In such cases most allocated joint costs are fixed. In addition, Hilton and Due point out that in most cases management failed to properly maintain passenger service, which understated passenger costs.

These conditions prevailed to a far lesser extent for mainline passenger service. Mainlines of major railroads were built for much greater capacity than interurban lines, and passenger and freight trains used most of the capacity. Changes in the volume of either passenger or freight service changed the magnitude of joint expenses commonly thought of as being fixed. In this chapter I contend that the passenger deficit was real and persisted because management failed to consider the impact of individual trains on what were thought of as fixed costs. Consequently, individual trains earned smaller profits than management thought. In many cases, they earned deficits. Excessive tare weight per passenger primarily accounted for this problem. Traditional railroad accounting failed to show the cost consequences of the tare weight factor, which in reality became an ever greater liability as trains became faster and as fares fell. Because of such cost ignorance, managements wasted millions of dollars on investments in inappropriate streamlined train designs. They also upgraded hundreds of old battleshiplike cars with relatively luxurious and low density accommodations. The cars should have been junked. These factors explain much about the inability of U.S. railroad managers to operate their passenger service profitably in the days before airline competition.

Another factor contributed to the relatively poor financial performance of California passenger service. The primitive development of railroad infrastructure, particularly over the mountain passes that separated the various populated regions of the state, wasted passengers' time, which depressed potential revenue. It also increased operating expenses.

Of the two explanations for the failure of California passenger service, the cost explanation is the more applicable to the general passenger train problem of the United States in the 1930s, and I will address it at some length. In his study of U.S. passenger train costing on behalf of the Harvard business school in the mid-1950s, Dwight Ladd identified Southern Pacific's costing methods as the most advanced in an industry otherwise characterized by deplorably bad cost information.[3] Southern Pacific passenger management had only recently adopted the methods, but the company's Bureau of Transportation Research had developed them more than thirty years earlier. The evolution of these costing methods sheds light on inadequacies of passenger decision making before World War II, not only for the Southern Pacific but for the U.S. railroad industry as a whole.

When Congress returned railroads to private control in March 1920, Southern Pacific established a small office, the Bureau of Transportation Research, to prepare exhibits for court cases and regulatory hearings. Much of the bureau's work centered on Section 4 cases. Section 4 was the chapter of the Interstate Commerce Act that prohibited long haul/short haul rate discrimination. Railroads could petition the commission for specific waivers to Section 4, but they had to demonstrate that they would not lose money by carrying new traffic attracted by lowered rates.

Section 4 cases figured importantly in railroad freight rate-making strategy. The industry typically requested that the ICC grant it blanket freight rate increases in order to improve its financial standing. High railroad freight rates then encouraged shippers to seek other forms of transportation. Only when a shipper or region succeeded in finding an alternative would a railroad then propose to selectively lower rates for that shipper or region. Doing so typically ran afoul of the long haul/short haul discrimination provision of the ICC, prompting the railroad to apply for a waiver. The practice of individual railroad companies seeking Section 4 waivers to regain traffic that competitors had taken away at the same time that they were requesting general rate increases created resentment in the business community against railroads. Reflecting such resentment, Congress placed increasing burdens on railroads to demonstrate that lowered rates were in fact compensatory. The Transportation Act of 1920 strengthened this requirement, prompting the railroads to place greater effort in cost finding.

Southern Pacific's cost finding work progressed when the company was confronted with a unique opportunity for gaining traffic if a Section 4 waiver could be obtained.[4] This case involved water-competitive freight traffic between California and Oregon. During the mid-1920s coastal steamers hauled about 60 percent of the freight moving between California and Oregon, in part because of the lengthy travel times and high cost of moving traffic over Southern Pacific's sinuous and grade-ridden route between those points.[5] Prior to the 1926 opening of a new, more competitive line, the railroad petitioned for a Section 4 waiver for lowered freight rates between San Francisco and Portland in order to capture more of the high-volume market from steamships. Its efforts ran afoul of its inability to demonstrate that costs were less than its proposed water-competitive rates.[6]

Two interest groups objected to the proposed rate reductions: railroad shippers located at interior points and steamship operators. Both groups feared that the proposed rates were so low that the railroad would spend much more to carry the large volume of new traffic than it would get in revenue. Steamship operators viewed this as predatory pricing designed to drive them out of business. Shippers at interior points feared that they would be the ones who would have to pay for the railroad deficits. The fact that the western railroads at the time were petitioning the ICC for higher general freight rates convinced shippers at interior points that selected rate discounts to win competitive traffic did not pay. The Southern Pacific failed to win its case because it could not assuage such legitimate fears of shippers or the ICC.[7]

Six years later the Southern Pacific again sought Section 4 relief in the California to Oregon market and won its case on the strength of progress that one of its executive staffers made in cost analysis.⁸ Professor Clarence Day graduated in civil engineering from the University of California in 1905. For the following fifteen years he worked in Southern Pacific's chief engineer's office on the location of railroads and the economics of the operation of alternative routes. In 1920 he took a three-year leave of absence to become a professor of railway engineering at the Pei Yang University, Tiensien, China, where he taught railway engineering and the economics of railway engineering. Upon returning to Southern Pacific in 1923, he resumed his previous duties until promoted to office engineer in the general manager's office in 1925. There he conducted his first operating cost analyses. He soon transferred to the company's Bureau of Transportation Research, where he refined and continued his work.⁹

Day advanced the costing work of the ICC's M. O. Lorenz, who a decade earlier cast doubt on the traditional railroad economics paradigm holding that most costs are fixed. Day sought to determine with more precision than Lorenz had done how much each cost account went up or down when the railroad moved more or less freight. Using a statistical technique called regression analysis, combined with interviews with managers responsible for different areas of Southern Pacific costs on each division, he studied the relationship between traffic volume and the magnitude of each cost account on each division. Day's use of regression analysis probably marked its first use in the railroad industry.¹⁰ Such methods led Day in 1937 to observe that as a rough rule of thumb, the variable expenses from operating an average length train were about 60 percent of the ICC fully allocated cost per train mile. To determine how much the operation of a new train added to the railroad's annual operating costs, he used the 60 percent figure and added to it allowances for terminal expenses, depreciation, interest, and taxes.¹¹

Day also concluded that long, heavy trains cost much more to operate than short, light trains. For a train of average length, one could very roughly estimate the added operating expense of adding an extra car as 60 percent of the ICC fully allocated cost per car mile.¹²

Day's work almost resulted in the development of a general costing procedure that could have immensely helped management, but the railroad siege mentality prevented this work from coming to fruition. In 1935 the California legislature placed for-hire trucks under the jurisdiction of the California Railroad Commission.¹³ The legislation directed that truckers base their rates on the marginal or out-of-pocket costs of truck operations. Truckers agreed to this provision but demanded that a similar standard be applied to rail rates.

The commission acceded to their demands and launched a study of railroad marginal costs. To direct the study, it hired Dr. Ford K. Edwards, formerly a transportation economist at the University of Southern California.[14] The Edwards study zeroed in on refining the cost variability research that Day previously developed.[15] In doing so, the study tied together what Edwards termed the best railroad cost variability work that then existed. In addition to Day's work, this included that of the ICC's M. O. Lorenz and Arthur White. White previously worked as the federal coordinator's chief statistician and prior to 1933 was a colleague in the Southern Pacific executive office with Day. Edwards called White's earlier cost analysis work with the federal coordinator's office pathbreaking.[16] Lorenz, White, and Day worked together on the Edwards study, with the full support of the Southern Pacific. The railroad's Sacramento shops were made available for engineering experiments on cost variability.[17]

Unfortunately, the study did not get beyond the stage of developing a general formula for finding the cost of operating different trains, a necessary first step in product costing. According to the Greyhound executive Cloyd Kimball, Southern Pacific killed the study. Kimball was in a position to know. He had been one of Edward's students at the University of Southern California and after graduation went to work for California's trucking industry. When Edwards went to the railroad commission, Kimball followed and participated in the study. According to Kimball, Southern Pacific came to fear the potential political repercussions of the study. At the time most railroad rates still bore no relation to the cost of providing the service. Southern Pacific feared that those shippers who were paying rates far above the cost of their service would exert political pressure to have their rates legislated downward once they discovered the truth. On the other hand, those shippers who were paying rates far below the cost of their service would exert political pressure to have their rates frozen in place. The cold light of truth would force the railroad into bankruptcy, according to this reasoning.[18] Ladd found that as late as 1956 many American railroads resisted the development of accurate passenger train costs for fear that such information could be misused if it got into the wrong hands.[19]

Had management applied Day's work to passenger service in the 1920s and 1930s, it would have concluded that trains cost more to operate than it thought. In 1937, for example, the ICC fully allocated cost per passenger train mile on the Southern Pacific was $2.35. This number is the cost of Southern Pacific's passenger operations in 1937 calculated by the ICC formula, divided by the annual passenger train miles in 1937. Day's reasoning implied that if Southern Pacific ran a passenger train one additional mile, the company's annual operating costs would increase by 60 percent of $2.35, or $1.41. Interest and taxes would add another 25 cents to this figure, bringing it to $1.66. Terminals expenses would add still more. Day's reasoning also implied that if the company added one car to the train, which averaged 9.1 cars in 1937, the company's annual expenses would increase by 15 cents.

Later cost analyses show that even Day's estimates understated the impact of passenger train operations on the company's operating costs. In the mid-1950s John R. Meyer and a group of Harvard economists studied the passenger burden on behalf of the Aeronautical Research Foundation for the Association of American Railroads.[20] Using regression analysis, they analyzed the variability of major railroad cost accounts with explanatory variables describing both freight and passenger traffic. Their work differed from Day's 1928 work, which the ICC still used in the 1950s, by making the tests for variability before rather than after separating each account into freight and passenger related costs according to ICC formulas. By doing so, they avoided the controversy surrounding the formulas.

According to ICC hearing examiner Howard Hosmer, the Meyer et al. study offered an independent check on the ICC passenger costing formula, and it showed that the ICC formula understated the passenger burden.[21] Later works by scholars such as Theodore Keeler, Ann Friedlaender, and Richard Spady used refined methods but came to generally the same conclusions as did Meyer and his group. Friedlaender and Spady, for example, received intuitively plausible results, including indications that freight loss and damage costs rose when passenger service was discontinued, presumably because railroads cut back too much on maintenance or became too sloppy in their operations. In spite of such external economies of passenger operations, the results show that for roads such as the Santa Fe in 1968, running a passenger train one extra mile added more to the company's annual operating costs than indicated by the ICC fully allocated cost per train mile. These researchers' works also generally corroborated Lorenz's findings of roughly seventy years earlier.[22]

This body of work suggests that once traffic has built up to rather minimal mainline densities, a total of about six or seven mainline freights a day, still more traffic requires longer and more trains, producing greater motive power and car maintenance costs and more wear and tear on existing facilities. At the same time, it requires more yard and terminal facilities, more passing sidings, and more shops. All of these additional facilities and equipment must be operated and maintained. Costs from such sources rise about as fast as traffic, such that whether six or twenty trains a day are operated, unit costs are about the same.

Moreover, the process is reversible. At any given time large railroads have facilities in need of replacement. At times of traffic reduction, replacement can be foregone. Yards, sidings, second tracks, roundhouses, and shops also can be operated and maintained at reduced capacity. Some such facilities and rolling stock can be mothballed altogether, thereby almost completely eliminating their ongoing expenses, or they can be abandoned. Even some debt interest can be reduced. A sizable part of debt is for rolling stock, which can be sold or returned to the lender. The ability of a railroad to reduce operating expenses and adjust a supposedly fixed plant in the face of traffic reduction is far greater than is commonly thought, as the Great Depression showed.

The work from Lorenz through Meyer and his colleagues suggests that passenger trains operating on freight mainlines fit into this characterization with an important difference: passenger trains added to costs more than freight trains of equivalent weight. Thus, fluctuations in the volume of passenger service in the context of an already moderate traffic volume had significant impacts on the corporate bottom line. According to this work, passenger operations cost the Southern Pacific in 1937 at least $2.35 per train mile to operate a train nine cars long, and $0.26 for every additional car.[23]

Unfortunately, railroad methods for estimating the direct or out-of-pocket costs of passenger trains captured only a small part of the linkages between added services and added activities on the railroad caused by those services. This condition prevailed even on the Southern Pacific, where Day developed his more advanced cost finding techniques. As described in chapter 3, Southern Pacific accounting forms of the early 1920s, for example, showed the out-of-pocket cost of running passenger trains at between only $0.30 and $0.50 per train mile, while the average cost based on the ICC method was about $2.50 per train mile.

By the 1920s and through the mid-1930s, Southern Pacific and Santa Fe managements revised their estimates of out-of-pocket costs upward to about $1.00 a train mile for steam trains. Both managements estimated costs similarly. In addition to crew wages and fuel expenses, they included allowances for maintenance of way, and for locomotive and car maintenance expenses. Neither allowed for depreciation or interest on rolling stock, though one study did include a special category for ice-activated air conditioning that contained operating costs, depreciation, and interest. The Santa Fe prepared its estimates from division accounts, using solely related passenger expenses from most accounts divided by the number of passenger train miles in the division to obtain an average cost per mile. For locomotive repairs, it used allocated passenger costs. For maintenance of way and structures, it used one-third of fully allocated passenger expenses, following the then accepted assumption that one-third of maintenance of way and structure expenses varied with the amount of traffic over the line. These calculations produced an out-of-pocket cost per train mile. The Southern Pacific used similar methods with just a couple of exceptions. It allowed for lower cost of motor car fuel and maintenance, while the Santa Fe did not. The Southern Pacific discontinuance applications also noted that the passenger trains imposed delay costs upon freight traffic, but it made no attempt to quantify those costs.[24] By the mid-1930s the conception that both Southern Pacific and Santa Fe management had of the marginal cost of running a passenger train one mile—about $1.00—was more than double the figure of the early 1920s, but it was still less than half the ICC fully allocated passenger cost per train mile. The latter more accurately reflected the true out-of-pocket expenses of operating mainline passenger trains on railroads with both heavy freight and passenger traffic.

An exchange during the *Santa Fe Case* between Southern Pacific vice president of passenger traffic Felix S. McGinnis and Santa Fe counsel Allan Matthew illustrates the state of Southern Pacific passenger train costing in 1937. Matthew asked McGinnis, "You do not keep figures of net revenues from handling passenger trains, do you?" McGinnis replied, "We do not figure them, except in one instance, that happens to be the streamliner, the *City of San Francisco,* and we can figure a net revenue for that train."[25] Pacific Greyhound counsel Earl Bagby pursued this line of questioning when he asked McGinnis, "Well, as to the steam trains under the accounting procedure established by the I.C.C. and with their allocations, do you not have a bookkeeping account that indicates net revenue from passenger train operations?" McGinnis understood Bagby to mean the net for individual trains. He replied, "It probably could be obtained, but we do not have it."[26]

This type of questioning continued until Southern Pacific counsel objected that McGinnis was not a cost witness. Clarence Day was placed on the stand for that purpose. In cross examining Day, Matthew discovered that Day conducted special cost studies for specific freight rate cases but to that time had not performed any cost analysis of Southern Pacific passenger service.[27]

Interest in new streamliners spurred the development of more complete passenger train costing in the mid-1930s. In the *Santa Fe Case* the Southern Pacific requested that the Santa Fe provide an economic analysis of the proposed streamlined train. Santa Fe's valuation engineer, Joseph Weidel, argued that the company would earn a healthy return on its streamliner investment, even under moderate usage. The method Weidel used for estimating operating expenses represented an advancement over earlier methods and reflected a new idea that longer and heavier trains cost more to operate. Engineering consultants had prepared operating cost analyses for three-unit *Zephyrs* then being used by the Chicago, Burlington & Quincy. While the train Weidel proposed for the Santa Fe was not like the *Zephyr*, he based his estimates on the *Zephyr*'s costs with appropriate modifications. Weidel's proposed train would be composed of a diesel locomotive and six detachable cars generally similar to those in the new *Abraham Lincoln* running between Chicago and St. Louis, except made out of stainless steel. The Budd Company had already built a prototype car. His proposed train was calculated to be 3.46 times heavier than the three-unit *Zephyr*. Weidel reasoned that crew costs for his train would be the same as those for the *Zephyr*, except that he added expenses for a locomotive fireman, which he thought the unions would demand, and an extra brakeman required by California's full crew law. He estimated that remaining operating and maintenance expenses would be 3.46 times greater than those for the *Zephyr*, because he reasoned such costs varied by weight. To the result, he added depreciation, interest, and taxes, arriving at a $0.97 figure.[28]

Southern Pacific's skepticism of these projections revealed that it still made no analysis of its own passenger rolling stock investments. In early 1937 Day took the stand to dispute Weidel's economic analysis for Santa Fe's proposed streamliner by arguing that it was too low. Under cross examination, he revealed that neither he nor anyone else in Southern Pacific's management performed cost analysis for Southern Pacific's *Daylights*.[29] Moreover, the Southern Pacific made no estimate of the load factor of the proposed train, nor of the extent to which traffic would be diverted from other trains.[30]

However, Southern Pacific was taking the first steps in cost analysis that would later enable the company to perform estimates on the return on investment of proposed rolling stock. The accounting department began issuing monthly statements for at least those trains for which the company had made large investments in rolling stock. As McGinnis stated, the company in 1937 was compiling net revenue statistics for the *City of San Francisco*, which was a lightweight diesel streamliner that the Southern Pacific operated jointly with the Union Pacific and Chicago & Northwestern since 1936. As the company invested in additional streamliners, it began to monitor their financial performance as well, recording both expenses and revenues. For example, the accounting department showed that the thirteen-car *Daylight* cost $2.77 per train mile to operate for the first seven months of 1938, while it grossed $5.37 per train mile.[31] The cost figure is not too much below the 1937 fully allocated cost of $3.35 per train mile for a thirteen-car train.

In the light of what is now known about the behavior of railroad costs,

Southern Pacific's evolution of passenger cost analysis shows that until the time of the *Daylight* management significantly underestimated the cost implications of its passenger decisions. As a consequence, management failed to improve rail passenger productivity as much as it might have. Its management of load factors (the proportion of saleable space sold) provides a striking example of such failure.

Although the Pullman Company kept records on how many passengers occupied its sleeping cars, railroads did not monitor the load factor of their coaches in the mid-1930s.[32] Day revealed this fact when he testified that the federal coordinator's special study of occupancy of coaches on specific trains constituted the first instance of the gathering of this information in the railroad industry. He believed the information was accurate and valuable, and in 1936 he collected additional information that was comparable to the 1933 data. This information showed that the coach load factors of most leading trains failed to reach 30 percent in 1933. The *Daylight,* Southern Pacific's most heavily traveled coach train, had a load factor of only 34 percent. Despite substantial growth of passengers using the train, the *Daylight*'s load factor still averaged about 34 percent in 1936 because managers added cars to the train to accommodate the added passengers.[33]

The Southern Pacific's negligence in this area typified that of most railroads. Day testified that he had attempted to obtain load factor information from both the Santa Fe and the Chicago, Burlington & Quincy, but had received written replies from both roads that they compiled no such statistics.[34] Railroads in the East neglected this aspect of passenger management, too. Raymond D. Swenk, general superintendent in the operating department of the Pennsylvania Railroad, the nation's largest passenger carrier, managed the capacity of his system's passenger trains. He described how statistics of passenger miles and coach car miles published by the Interstate Commerce Commission were useless for computing coach load factors. However, he saw no need to collect load factor information himself. He had not even bothered to look at the federal coordinator's occupancy figures for his trains because he erroneously thought they were the same as those published by the Interstate Commerce Commission.[35] Witnesses for the New York Central, the nation's other major passenger carrier, testified similarly in the same hearing.

The railroads' casual attitude toward managing load factors contrasts vividly with the urgency with which Pacific Greyhound Lines managed this statistic. To Pacific Greyhound Lines, as to airlines today, profits or losses depended on how high managers kept the load factor. In 1936 Pacific Greyhound Lines maintained an average load factor of 60 percent on all of its buses competing with the *Daylight,* while it maintained a systemwide load factor of more than 50 percent. Had the Southern Pacific done as well, it likely would not have had a passenger deficit.

Designs of the new streamliners also reflected railroad managements' nonchalance about load factors. When Pacific Greyhound Lines invested in a new bus design, it bought not only a more comfortable and attractive vehicle, but also a more efficient vehicle that carried more passengers per unit of weight. For all of this it paid hardly more than for the old buses that it replaced. When the railroads invested in streamliners, they generally bought trains less efficient in terms of tare weight per seat than the old trains they replaced. This, too, contributed to the passenger deficit. A typical nine-car pre-streamlined coach train of the mid-1930s, including a baggage and a dining car, weighed about 2.1 tons per seat. Generally weighing less than one ton per seat, the first generation streamliners greatly improved on this while offering spacious reclining seats, attractive meal and lounge service, and air conditioning. They represented a great step forward, returning passenger trains to the tare weight efficiency of the wooden trains of the 1910 era while offering incomparably more comfortable accommodations and greater speed in the process.[36] However, the second generation streamliners ordered by the Santa Fe and the Southern Pacific improved on amenities by eliminating the breakthroughs in efficiency of the first generation streamliners. The Santa Fe's *Golden Gates* weighed about 2.5 tons per seat, while the *Daylight* weighed about 2.3 tons. They also cost three times more to buy than the old trains they replaced.[37]

Such high tare weights, purchased at high cost, adversely affected passenger profitability. As the cost analyses since the 1950s show, not so much the length but the weight of a passenger train contributed to its operating costs. A train weighing twice what another train weighed per seat cost almost twice as much to move a passenger one mile, if they both had the same load factor. Railroad negligence in using the investment in streamliners to reduce tare weight therefore contributed to unnecessarily high operating costs.

That the *Daylight* earned substantial profits fails to detract from the argument. If management had invested in more efficient equipment, the *Daylight* could have netted more, and management could have converted other services that were unprofitable into profitable ones. Figure 6.1 shows how. The figure shows the April 1938 gross revenues for major trains on the Southern Pacific system. Costs are not shown, but we can roughly estimate them. From what we now know about the way costs behaved, the ICC fully allocated cost per train mile was a reasonable proxy for how much the Southern Pacific spent to run an average train one mile. In 1938 this figure was about $2.30 for a nine-car train. We reasonably can assume that most

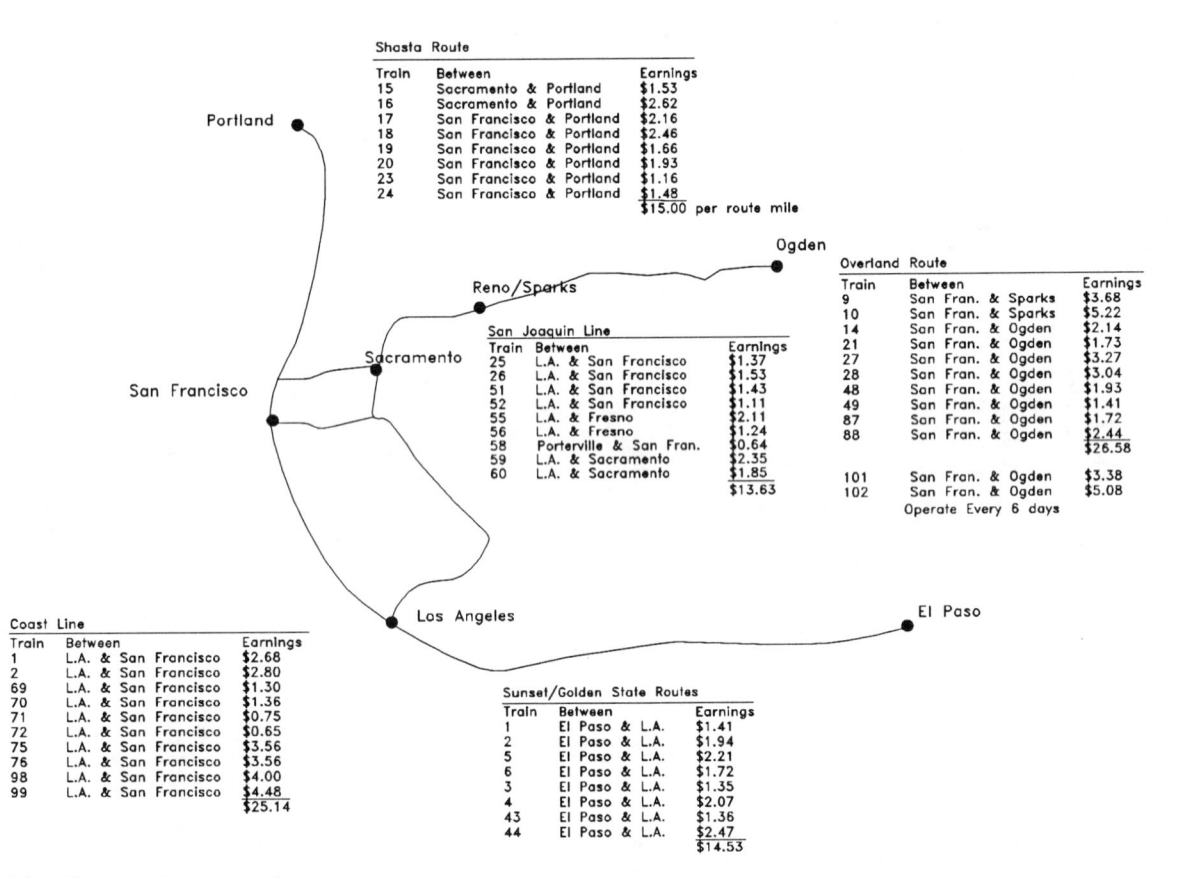

Shasta Route

Train	Between	Earnings
15	Sacramento & Portland	$1.53
16	Sacramento & Portland	$2.62
17	San Francisco & Portland	$2.16
18	San Francisco & Portland	$2.46
19	San Francisco & Portland	$1.66
20	San Francisco & Portland	$1.93
23	San Francisco & Portland	$1.16
24	San Francisco & Portland	$1.48
		$15.00 per route mile

San Joaquin Line

Train	Between	Earnings
25	L.A. & San Francisco	$1.37
26	L.A. & San Francisco	$1.53
51	L.A. & San Francisco	$1.43
52	L.A. & San Francisco	$1.11
55	L.A. & Fresno	$2.11
56	L.A. & Fresno	$1.24
58	Porterville & San Fran.	$0.64
59	L.A. & Sacramento	$2.35
60	L.A. & Sacramento	$1.85
		$13.63

Overland Route

Train	Between	Earnings
9	San Fran. & Sparks	$3.68
10	San Fran. & Sparks	$5.22
14	San Fran. & Ogden	$2.14
21	San Fran. & Ogden	$1.73
27	San Fran. & Ogden	$3.27
28	San Fran. & Ogden	$3.04
48	San Fran. & Ogden	$1.93
49	San Fran. & Ogden	$1.41
87	San Fran. & Ogden	$1.72
88	San Fran. & Ogden	$2.44
		$26.58
101	San Fran. & Ogden	$3.38
102	San Fran. & Ogden	$5.08
	Operate Every 6 days	

Sunset/Golden State Routes

Train	Between	Earnings
1	El Paso & L.A.	$1.41
2	El Paso & L.A.	$1.94
5	El Paso & L.A.	$2.21
6	El Paso & L.A.	$1.72
3	El Paso & L.A.	$1.35
4	El Paso & L.A.	$2.07
43	El Paso & L.A.	$1.36
44	El Paso & L.A.	$2.47
		$14.53

Coast Line

Train	Between	Earnings
1	L.A. & San Francisco	$2.68
2	L.A. & San Francisco	$2.80
69	L.A. & San Francisco	$1.30
70	L.A. & San Francisco	$1.36
71	L.A. & San Francisco	$0.75
72	L.A. & San Francisco	$0.65
75	L.A. & San Francisco	$3.56
76	L.A. & San Francisco	$3.56
98	L.A. & San Francisco	$4.00
99	L.A. & San Francisco	$4.48
		$25.14

6.1 Gross earnings for major trains on the Southern Pacific, Pacific Lines, 1938. Source: TWR: Train earning comparisons, 1 May 1938 mainline trains were of average length or longer and therefore cost $2.30 or more per mile to operate. Comparing this number to the revenues in figure 6.1, we see that most Southern Pacific mainline trains lost money. This need not have been. Had management carried the same number of passengers and items of mail, express, and baggage in shorter trains weighing substantially less, it could have reduced the operating costs of many trains to below revenues.

In a sense, then, railroad management wasted some of the investment it placed in streamliners by ordering equipment that failed to reach its productivity potential. Southern Pacific management compounded this lost opportunity by placing some of its expensive new trains in markets of insufficient size to make them pay, or by emphasizing the wrong attributes to stimulate new traffic. The Texas streamliners illustrate the first point. They grossed only about $1.50 per train mile, and while this figure probably exceeded considerably the revenues of the trains they replaced, in the opinion of Southern Pacific's management it failed to cover costs. Before World War II Dallas and Houston each contained about 300,000 people, populations not large enough to support competitive rail service.[38]

The *Lark*, the crack overnight train between Los Angeles and San Francisco, illustrates the second point. While its gross revenue was much higher than that of the Texas service, the revenue failed to improve after the company invested heavily to equip the train with ultra-luxurious streamlined cars in 1941. Several factors contributed to the lack of earnings response to the investment. First, the investment bought luxury but not shorter travel time. This emphasis was mistaken. The public responded enthusiastically to earlier streamliners in large part because the new trains saved considerable amounts of time for each passenger. In contrast the *Lark* continued on its leisurely twelve-hour schedule. Second, competition from Southern Pacific's faster daytime trains as well as airlines ate into the *Lark*'s demand. In 1933 the approximately 10,000 passengers riding in five-seat planes between Los Angeles and San Francisco constituted about 5 percent of the public mode market, but by 1937 airlines provided much greater capacity and comfort. Eight daily United Airlines flights flew nonstop between the two cities in two hours, while another three stopped at Bakersfield and Fresno en route. Capacities ranged from ten passengers for older model planes to twenty-one passengers for the new DC-3s. Many schedules ran in sections, particularly on weekends, indicating heavy passenger loads.[39] Because air competition intensified during the next four years and drew most heavily from the Pullman market, it is not surprising that inauguration of ultra-luxury equipment on the *Lark* between March and July 1941 failed to increase its revenues significantly.[40] Southern Pacific's transcontinental

Pullman revenues also suddenly turned down in 1940, again most likely because of increasing air competition.[41] Investments in luxury equipment to compete with air service could earn no return.

While the Southern Pacific invested heavily in streamliners for some unpromising markets, it ignored its heavy Oakland to Sacramento market, where higher speed streamliners could have earned profits. Through the rejuvenation of its Los Angeles to San Diego service, the Santa Fe showed what could be done with this type of market. After carrying about 75,000 passengers per year in 1933, the Santa Fe through low fares and much higher speeds increased this number to about 500,000 passengers per year in 1941. The streamliners grossed $2.30 per train mile, and because they used diesel rather than steam power probably cost less than $2.30 to operate.[42] They could have netted considerably more had they been designed with lower tare weights. In contrast, traffic in Southern Pacific's neglected Oakland to Sacramento market declined from around 300,000 passengers per year in 1933 to about 200,000 in 1939.[43]

How Southern Pacific's passenger strategies affected the passenger operating ratio is analyzed in table 22. Dividing passenger expenses by passenger revenues in a given year yields the operating ratio. Table 22 shows the trend in expenses and revenues from 1927 through 1941 for the years for which data could be found. It does this by examining two statistics. One shows the resources that the Southern Pacific spent to move a passenger car one mile. These are costs per car mile, adjusted for changes in the price of fuel, materials, and labor. The other statistic shows revenues that the car mile grossed, again adjusted for changing price levels. Division of the adjusted cost per car mile by the adjusted revenue per car mile shows the resources that the railroad spent to earn a dollar in revenue. This is the same as the passenger operating ratio and corresponds to the Southern Pacific passenger operating ratios shown in table 23.

Table 22 reveals that from 1927 through 1941 the Southern Pacific improved its efficiency in moving a passenger car one mile—by almost as much as did Pacific Greyhound Lines through 1935 (see chapter 4). There are two likely causes for the improved efficiency. The moderate drop in the cost per car mile between 1933 and 1935 no doubt resulted from better use of resources as expanding passenger traffic took advantage of a greatly underutilized physical plant. The improvement between 1938 and 1939 probably reflects the severe economy measures that the company began enacting in 1938 as well as the expanded operation of streamliners and more efficient steam locomotives. Streamliner cars weighed fifty to fifty-five tons, compared to seventy to eighty tons for standard coaches.

The reason that Southern Pacific's passenger operating ratio remained above 100, while Pacific Greyhound earned substantial profits, derives from the revenue per car mile part of the ratio. As passenger fares fell Pacific Greyhound kept up the revenue per bus mile by loading more passengers into each bus. In contrast, while the Southern Pacific improved the productivity of moving a passenger car one mile, it failed to keep up the gross revenue that each car mile brought in, as shown in table 22. In the mid-1930s, as passengers returned to trains, Southern Pacific management added cars to trains, rather than enticing passengers to fill up the seventy to ninety seats typical of standard cars of the period. In the latter part of the decade it invested in streamliners with only forty-five to fifty-five seats in each car, and it rebuilt the interiors of standard cars to the same capacity. These investment policies increased rather than decreased the tare weight per seat and made the trains uneconomical, even when passengers (who paid very low fares) filled most of the seats. In short, the railroad failed in comparison to Pacific Greyhound Lines because of its inability or unwillingness to manage load factors and tare weights.

The failure of both the Southern Pacific and the Santa Fe to significantly improve their intra-California mainlines also contributed to unsuccessful passenger results. Routes over mountain passes connecting both Los Angeles and San Francisco to the San Joaquin Valley possessed two significant shortcomings, which neither railroad addressed. First, with miles of unrelenting tight curves, the old lines forced passenger trains to run at speeds as slow as 20 miles an hour. And the trains ran at the slow speeds miles out of their way: about fifty wasted miles in the case of the route out of Los Angeles, and about fifteen wasted miles in the route out of San Francisco. Passenger trains using these routes required hours more to reach destinations than what the auto-conscious public had become accustomed to. This penalty depressed gross earnings. The old, circuitous lines also cost more to operate than shorter, straighter lines would have cost.

The possibilities of what could have been achieved with improved alignments are illustrated by the results of the only significant realignment that actually occurred. The building of Shasta Dam in the late 1930s necessitated the relocation of Southern Pacific's mainline to Oregon for about thirty-seven miles north of Redding. The old line still followed the original 1884 sinuous alignment along the bottom of the Sacramento River Canyon. To bypass this line, the California state engineer in 1925 located a new thirty-two-mile railroad to the east of the canyon. Under a state contract the Southern Pacific refined the new alignment in 1935, and the U.S. Bureau of Reclamation began constructing the line in the late 1930s. Completed in 1942 at a cost of $17.5 million, the new line eliminated 5,100 degrees of curvature (a reduction of 72 percent) in its thirty-two miles and shortened the route by five miles. It allowed speeds for passenger trains up to 60 miles an hour, in contrast to 20 mile an hour restrictions on many of the curves of the old line. Although the new line was relatively short, its fewer and gentler curves and reduced route permitted passenger trains to save a substantial thirty-three minutes between Redding and Delta.[44]

The Shasta Dam line relocation represented a new type of mountain railroad that contrasted as vividly with the old type of railroad as the new mountain highways of the 1930s contrasted with the 1910-era highway alignments they replaced. Unfortunately, the California Highway Commission generally had no jurisdiction over railroads, and neither the Southern Pacific nor the Santa Fe replaced any of their antiquated railroad alignments.

Improvements to the mountain routes on the main rail corridors in California, similar in nature to the Shasta Dam line relocation, would have made a difference. Such improvements constructed along the 1922 Santa Fe survey between Los Angeles and Bakersfield and from the San Joaquin Valley over Altamont Pass into the Bay Area not only would have speeded up trains, they would have shortened the route between the Bay Area and Los Angeles by fifty to sixty miles as well. The combination of a shorter route and faster speeds would have cut several hours from the schedules of California's passenger trains linking the Bay Area and Los Angeles.

Given the enthusiastic passenger response to the modestly shortened running times of the streamliners, as shown in figure 5.3 of the previous chapter, investments in modern mountain crossings would have increased passenger traffic dramatically within California. If the trains using the new alignments would have been economical high-speed streamliners, such as those of the first generation, the heavy passenger volumes also would have been profitable.[45]

The fundamental problem bedeviling Southern Pacific and Santa Fe passenger service at the end of the 1930s was the failure of their major heavily used trains to earn substantial profits. Managements increased the gross revenue per train mile that each train generated by making the trains longer, which also made them more costly to operate. Typically, the gross revenue that each car mile earned fell short of the cost of moving the car mile, because management placed too few passengers into each car. Tare weights were much too high.

At the same time, both railroads failed to invest in potentially profitable improvements on their routes linking California's major cities. As a consequence, passenger revenues did not reach the magnitudes that they could have, while passenger operating expenses remained higher than they had to. Compounding this problem, the Southern Pacific placed some of its costly streamliners on routes with little traffic potential while it neglected one of its most heavily traveled routes. Desire for prestige rather than profits motivated the company's investment decisions, and the traveling public sometimes suffered as a consequence.

Such decisions and consequences were rooted in the historic relations between railroads and the society that they served in California. Chapter 7 reexamines this relationship and summarizes its impact on California's rail and bus managements.

7
Conclusion

After peaking about 1910 the passenger train's influence in California waned for the next three decades as railroad managements struggled unsuccessfully to meet auto and highway competition. Historians disagree on how competently railroad management responded to the auto threat. Some maintain that rail managers tried but failed to maintain profitable passenger service in the face of overwhelming odds. Nothing managers did to improve passenger service could compensate for the auto's flexibility or low operating cost. Others say that regulation hindered management's ability to respond to a changing market. Still others argue that rail managers could have maintained some amount of profitable passenger service had they so desired. Instead they dumped passenger service when they realized through collusion with General Motors that they could make more money carrying freight resulting from increased auto production.

This examination of how passenger train managers reacted to the changing market after 1910 suggests the rejection of two of the explanations and the acceptance of the third in a modified form. The evidence in California shows that a significant, potentially profitable niche remained for passenger trains after the auto market first became saturated at the end of the 1920s. Rail managers failed to fully exploit it because of their business culture and cost understanding and not because of collusion with General Motors or interference from regulatory authorities in matters such as fares or train discontinuances. Rather than viewing passenger service as a significant source of profit, railroad managers saw it as a means of gaining competitive advantage over other railroads in the pursuit of freight traffic. This view led them to ignore important public preferences through the 1920s. In the early 1930s managements showed greater market sensitivity, but profitability eluded them because of their ignorance of the cost consequences of their passenger decisions. Unnecessarily high costs ultimately led to the passenger train's demise. Management could have created a much lower cost service that met the demands of the public.

Conclusion 153

In this explanation, I find that regulation hindered management little if at all in making short term decisions affecting passenger service. However, government policy more indirectly interfered with management's ability to adapt the passenger train to the auto age. After about 1915 California's rail managements invested relatively little in the main rail routes connecting the state's population centers. As early as 1916 some highway routes proved superior to rail lines in terms of directness and speed. By the late 1930s direct and high-speed superhighways built across all of the mountain passes separating California's major cities rendered the state's trunk rail lines virtually obsolete. Not even streamliners could overcome this handicap fully. This condition arose from government policy that favored other forms of transportation over railroads, and that before World War I actually penalized railroads.

Some observers, such as Albro Martin, excoriate government over this condition. However, I find that railroad managements must take much of the blame. In California, at least, managers failed to recognize the legitimate claims on the control of transportation policy of shippers and developers. Government policy toward the railroads, water transportation, and highways arose as a negative reaction by the state's business groups to railroad management culture that demanded total control. After about 1910 other business groups held more political power than railroads. Railroad management failed to come to terms with this condition, and consequently the railroad industry was afflicted with what management called unfair government policy.

We also can infer that the beliefs of railroad managements about how costs and demand behaved contributed to the primitive quality of the major rail routes in California. The belief of railroad managements that most of their costs were fixed would have led them to underestimate the potential operating cost savings of shorter and less crooked alignments. While managements came to believe that faster services helped retain traffic, their surprise at the response of the public to fast streamliners showed that they greatly underestimated the elasticity of their market with respect to speed. They thus underestimated the gross revenue consequences of infrastructure investments. Had managements better understood their costs and their markets, they may have invested more in their most important rail lines and they likely would have been rewarded with profits.

Management's ineffective response to the auto in California took root during the first two decades of the twentieth century as it confronted two threats to the railroad industry. One threat came from the state's business community. The other, partly related threat came from a stagnating and then falling market.

In the first decade of the century California's rail managers responded to explosive population and economic growth with tremendous investments to modernize and expand the state's railroad systems. Despite such accomplishments, California's business community by 1910 detested the railroad corporations operating in the state, particularly the Southern Pacific. The reason was simple. California's business community wanted to control the transportation system upon which it depended. It wanted more transportation service at lower rates than private rail corporations could profitably provide.

Since the 1860s the Southern Pacific maintained sufficient political power to counter the business community's desires, but about 1910 its political resistance crumbled. Business-backed anti-railroad candidates took control of the state government in that year, while nationally Congress passed legislation strengthening the Interstate Commerce Commission, effectively turning it over to the control of associations of rail users. Business groups nationally and in California used their newfound power to hold rates down during inflationary times, while those in California also championed the expansion of state-subsidized highways paralleling the main railroad routes in the state. At the same time automobile ownership soared in California.

These actions contributed to the second threat facing the managers of California's rail passenger service after 1910: falling demand for that service. The rapid decline in consumer expenditures on passenger trains between 1910 and World War I suggests that the auto dramatically cut into passenger train demand in the era of primitive motorization and the earliest paved roads. At first local trains, which before 1910 experienced the largest usage, bore the brunt of the decline. By World War I local and long distance trains alike experienced falling per capita usage, and the decline persisted almost continuously through the prosperous 1920s and into the Depression.

The railroad industry's management structure and culture influenced the way California's rail managers responded to the twin threats of business community hostility and declining demand. The structure arose in the mid-nineteenth century as the world's first example of a large, multidivisional business organization. Alfred D. Chandler, Jr., views such organizations as the rational response to coordination challenges posed by a complex technology spanning territories of hundreds of miles in length and breadth. Through an elaborate cost accounting system working through a hierarchical but multidivisional management structure, a relatively small team of professional managers could maintain control over the vast enterprises.

As Thomas C. Cochran found, these organizations contained weaknesses. Separation of revenue and cost analysis, reflecting the main structural cleavage between operations and accounting, hid from management

Conclusion

the profitability consequences of its actions. The evidence presented in this book shows that this cleavage contributed to a false paradigm of railroad economics that most operating costs were fixed.

Managers could have surmounted this weakness had not ideology intervened. Railroad managers mistrusted their primary customers—freight shippers and town development interests—believing them to be short-sighted and incapable of understanding the complexities of railroad technology. Only railroad managers understood the ramifications of fare and service policies and therefore bore the burden of deciding what was best for shippers and passengers. Financial ruin would result if managers allowed users to influence railroad affairs through the ICC or government operation. The administration of the ICC under the control of shippers between 1910 and 1917 confirmed railroad managers' fears, convincing them not to cooperate in the development of information on the workings of railroads that might get into the hands of users. When the railroads came under federal control in late 1917, railroad managers reasserted sufficient political power within Woodrow Wilson's administration to prevent shippers from having any say in the government's administration of the railroad industry. After the war railroad managers resisted developing information that would reveal the cost of moving different commodities, because shippers potentially could use such information against them.

Consequently, railroad managers ignored the important work of ICC economists pointing to the falseness of the railroad cost paradigm. By 1914 ICC economists confirmed the costing work of several railroad engineers thirty years earlier showing that most railroad operating costs rose when traffic rose and fell when traffic fell. This meant that high-volume services on which railroads charged low rates probably lost money and were subsidized by lower volume shippers, contrary to what railroad managers argued. The ICC, and in particular Louis D. Brandeis, viewed cross subsidization as the source of railroad inefficiency and financial difficulties and pressured the railroad industry to adopt more advanced cost finding methods to end such abuses. Fearing that more advanced cost finding would further erode their already seriously weakened political power, railroad managers adamantly rebuffed the ICC in these efforts. The ICC succeeded only in forcing railroads to separate costs between freight and passenger service.

The railroad industry's attitudes towards its shippers led California managers to develop responses to falling passenger demand that ignored important market signals until about 1930. Rather than allowing shippers a say in the conduct of the railroad industry, managers sought an accommodation with them. The Southern Pacific, which had been the principle political force in California, responded to the business attacks by cutting back its political activities and assuming a more subservient stance. It sought a social contract with the state's business leaders whereby it provided a comprehensive package of needed transportation services. These included many unprofitable freight and passenger services, but in exchange the railroad received some business interest protection from the threat of new railroad competition from out of state.

Under this accommodation, railroad managers came to view passenger service more as a public relations effort than as a source of profit. Since at least 1900 railroad managers held the view that certain deluxe trains operated as loss leaders for freight service. By 1920 they judged passenger service in general by its direct or indirect utility to the business community. The Santa Fe ruthlessly eliminated rural local trains as usage evaporated, until it operated no more than a token gas-electric service on most lines out of deference to shippers. Its management concentrated on business traffic between Los Angeles and Chicago.

Because of its status as the dominant railroad in California, the Southern Pacific behaved somewhat differently. Businesspeople, who were among the first to own autos, likely quit using rural local trains as the paved state highway system took shape by the beginning of World War I. One can infer that the Southern Pacific management's cessation of investments in new cars, locomotives, and facilities for rural services about that time reflected the loss of usage and prestige of rural services. However, management continued operating such trains for another decade under no duress from the railroad commission, most likely because of the fear that if it did not maintain a comprehensive passenger service, other railroads might be allowed to build routes into California. The Southern Pacific also continued to invest in heavily traveled commuter trains that the business community valued but which lost money. As did the Santa Fe, it continued investing in mainline limited trains.

Railroad management's view of passenger service primarily as a service for business travelers explains the industry's fare practices during the 1920s. The industry enacted the high 3.6 cent fare and the Pullman surcharge in August 1920 under pressure from the ICC as a means of restoring profitability to U.S. passenger operations as a whole. Over the next several years the high coach fare destroyed the nonbusiness-oriented railroad coach trade. This included passengers using all short and long distance coach services, except those short distance coach trains linking large cities such as San Francisco and Sacramento or Los Angeles and San Diego. The latter most likely remained popular with businesspeople in the early 1920s because of congested driving and parking conditions in large cities, and high fares did not matter to them. In contrast, most other coach services, whether short or long distance, catered to budget-minded tourists, migrants, and travelers visiting friends and relatives. These passengers left the rails in droves in the early to mid-1920s as a consequence of the high fares. Many nonbusiness travelers also used Pullman cars at the beginning of the 1920s. They, too, left the rails. Their departure not only dried up traffic on many short distance coach trains, but it resulted in the stagnation of demand even for transcontinental trains operating into the rapidly growing Los Angeles and San Francisco areas.

For almost a decade railroad management did nothing to counter this trend except discontinue coach trains when usage dwindled to the vanishing point. Except for the trains linking Los Angeles and San Diego, the Santa Fe discontinued its relatively few local coach trains that remained after World War I. The Southern Pacific maintained its illusions of providing a comprehensive public transportation service, but it replaced its rural trains with buses beginning in 1927, when traffic dwindled to the vanishing point. Management believed that the modern image of buses reflected favorably on the company in the towns of California, and buses cost far less than trains to operate.

At the end of the 1920s various railroad managements began to break out of this mold and listen more carefully to market signals, and as they did, they became fare conscious and concerned with nonbusiness travelers. To boost sagging traffic on its prestigous San Francisco to Los Angeles all-coach *Daylight*, Southern Pacific management significantly lowered the *Daylight*'s fares in 1927 and was rewarded with an increase in gross revenues. It also began discounting long distance coach and tourist car tickets and recognized the need to improve the comfort of long distance coach travel. Santa Fe's management also discounted long distance coach and tourist car tickets at this time.

These moves at the end of the 1920s anticipated a more market-oriented passenger strategy by the middle 1930s. After 1934 the Santa Fe management oriented its passenger decisions toward increasing passenger volume and profits. Through high speeds, low fares, and greater amenities it attempted to wring more passenger traffic out of its long-favored Los Angeles to Chicago market, but it also aggressively turned its attention again to shorter distance passenger markets in California and the Midwest. The Santa Fe initiative prodded the Southern Pacific into similar market-driven improvements, but the Southern Pacific ignored potentially important markets that lacked effective rail competition, most notably between San Francisco and Sacramento.

Where implemented between cities with large populations, such measures attracted large numbers of passengers back to the rails, but they failed financially. Because rail managers misunderstood how costs behaved, their improvements increased costs as fast or faster than revenues. Managers hoped to make money from the lower fares by concentrating more passengers onto fewer trains, and superficial results showed that they succeeded. Despite fares of less than 1.5 cents a mile in the late 1930s compared to fares of more than 3.2 cents per mile in the late 1920s, the more popular streamliners of the late 1930s grossed as much or more per train mile as the best trains of a decade earlier, which was about $4.50 per train mile.[1] This was possible because the popular coach streamliners at the end of the 1930s averaged about 300 to 500 passengers spread over thirteen to eighteen cars, while the typical limited train of the late 1920s carried only 100 to 150 passengers in seven to nine cars.

Despite the appearance of success of individual passenger strategies, the financial position of California's passenger service significantly worsened in the later period. In the late 1920s passenger service earned enough to cover operating costs, if not enough to provide an adequate return on investment. A decade later passenger service failed to come close to earning its operating costs. The culprit in the later period was not branch line or commuter trains. By 1939 the Southern Pacific and the Santa Fe abandoned most of these or took them off the mainline railroad financial accounts. Rather, the reason was the simple fact that the long trains of the late 1930s cost much more to operate than the short trains of the 1920s, leaving much less of a margin for management. Railroad managements based their passenger strategy on a false paradigm of railroad economics that adding cars to a train cost them almost nothing.

Had managers wanted to make money from passengers and had they perceived the profitability consequences of their actions, they could have engaged in more fruitful strategies. To begin with, they should have departed from the high 3.6 cent fare as soon as its failure became apparent, about 1922. At that point profit-oriented managers would have lowered the fare and sought means to reduce the excessive cost of passenger operations. If, for example, the public would pay no more than 2.5 cents a mile to ride a train, the onus was on management to find a way of operating the train at a cost of no more than 1.5 cents a passenger mile. The one-cent margin would give managers an adequate return on investment. Restoration of many of the economies that the United States Railroad Administration implemented in World War I would have made a good start toward cost reduction. Railroad managers eliminated these in 1920 in order to solicit freight traffic.

Had managers listened to those who warned them about the falseness of their cost paradigm, they would have done things differently in the 1930s, when they finally decided that carrying nonbusiness travelers was a good idea. By this time managers knew that substantial portions of the public would pay no more than 1.5 cents per mile to ride between larger cities in high-speed trains offering comfortable accommodations. In hindsight, we see that the long, heavy streamliners that they designed to attract this traffic proved too costly to yield substantial profits. An accurate costing method would have shown managers that they needed to reduce substantially the tare weight per passenger while still offering pleasing accommodations. The truly brilliant designs of the first generation streamliners showed that this was possible, but these streamliners failed to excite railroad managers. Informed by the traditional railroad economic paradigm, they saw no compelling reason to maintain a low tare weight per passenger. Blind to the cost consequences of doing so, they gave each passenger more space by making the trains longer, larger, and heavier. Managers also altered the original streamliner designs because they wanted new trains that looked and felt more like how they thought traditional trains ought to look and feel. Small ultra-lightweight trains did not fit in with railroad culture and did not appeal to most railroad managers; long, heavy trains pulled by massive locomotives did.[2] Such considerations motivated managers to offer trains that pleased the public but that ended up costing far more than managers had thought, and too much to make passenger service financially viable.

Pacific Greyhound Lines's impressive financial results during the Depression suggest that California's railroad managers could have done better. The bus company's profits emanated from a managerial consciousness oriented to profits rather than gross revenues. As the market compelled bus managers to lower fares, they compensated with new bus designs and better management to increase the passengers carried per ton of bus. By such means they not only maintained but increased the profit margin on each bus mile, even as the gross revenue per passenger mile fell. In contrast, during the same period the rail deficit per passenger mile increased. Consequently, as bus and rail passenger traffic increased in California after 1933, bus profits mushroomed and rail passenger service sank deeper into the red.

One might protest that bus technology lent itself more to profitable operation than trains. This is perhaps true, but entrepreneurs entering the bus business could not count on profits. The Santa Fe's experience with bus operations showed this. Confidently expecting that it could replicate Pacific Greyhound's 30 percent rate of return, the Santa Fe established a large bus system in Pacific Greyhound's most lucrative territory. The railroad's bus operations succeeded in capturing a significant part of the market, but it failed financially. At the same time, Pacific Greyhound's profits continued undiminished. The Santa Fe's experience suggests that the difference in financial results between buses and trains arose as much if not more from different management methods than from differences in train and bus technology. Railroad managements could please the public, but not in a cost-effective manner.

This is not to suggest that the Southern Pacific and Santa Fe passenger strategies lacked positive results. Both companies received substantial indirect benefits from passenger service. Southern Pacific's management believed that the Santa Fe scored a public relations coup with its *Golden Gates*, which may have helped it gain a greater share of San Joaquin Valley freight revenue as well as unmeasurable but valuable public esteem. Well into the 1950s, the *Daylight* provided a highly visible positive image for the Southern Pacific Company in California. Averell Harriman, board chairman of the Union Pacific, credited streamliners with erasing the negative image of the railroads in the eyes of the public. In a letter to Fred Sargent, president of the Chicago & Northwestern, Harriman commented, "Entirely aside from the stimulation of passenger travel that is resulting, [the streamliner] has been most effective in changing the attitude of the public to the railroad industry."[3] These points likely are true; it is a pity, however, that the railroads did not achieve such secondary benefits through policies that would have carried more passengers at a lower cost and at a profit to the railroads.

Rail managers failed in other ways. The Southern Pacific ignored the development of potentially important markets in the 1930s, primarily because it made its passenger investments in response to competition from other railroads rather than to potential traffic. After opening the Carquinez Straits Bridge in 1930 and dramatically lowering fares in the early 1930s, it did little to develop passenger service between San Francisco and Sacramento. The Santa Fe's experience with its high-speed streamliners between Los Angeles and San Diego showed that such a market contained substantial potential traffic. Had the Southern Pacific implemented high-speed, lightweight motor trains in this market, as its marketing consultant recommended in 1933, passenger traffic would have increased substantially, likely at a profit.

Railroad managers also failed by denying the California business community's legitimate interest in the state's transportation system. This denial led to unnecessary and counterproductive strife, resulting in an overemphasis on highway construction and underinvestment in the state's main rail routes linking northern and southern California. By its promotion of subsidized highways, aqueducts, harbors, and power grids, the business community showed that it was willing to support major infrastructure improvements with tax dollars. Hostility between the state's railroads and its users precluded such investments in railroads.

Investments in better rail routes over mountain passes into the metropolitan areas could have made a major difference. The Bureau of Reclamation's new rail route around Shasta Dam, opened in 1942, showed that modern construction could shorten rail routes and lift passenger train speed limits from around 20 miles an hour to 50 miles an hour in the most difficult mountainous territory. Similar construction over Tejon Pass and Altamont Pass would have removed hours from the rail schedules between Los Angeles and San Francisco. The traffic booms that both the Santa Fe and the Southern Pacific received from high-speed trains in California suggest that new, faster alignments would have resulted in crowds of additional passengers.

The Southern Pacific's and Santa Fe's results with passenger operations mirrored those of other major American railroads, as table 23 confirms. The uniformly dismal passenger operating ratios as shown in the table prompted a thoughtful railroad manager to suggest during World War II that something in railroad passenger management methods was amiss. Charles E. Smith had been in the railroad business since the 1890s and in 1943 was a vice president of the New York, New Haven & Hartford, one of the nation's most important commuter and intercity passenger railroads. During the 1930s he directed the New England Transportation Company, the New Haven's bus subsidiary. In 1943, when Judge R. V. Fletcher, vice president of law for the Association of American Railroads, solicited opinions from railroad executives on postwar passenger policies, Smith eagerly responded.[4]

Smith's reply was a lengthy, pessimistic analysis of American railroad passenger policies predicting a disastrous postwar future if 1930s management policies continued. Evidence as shown in table 23 told Smith that railroads such as the Santa Fe, Southern Pacific, Burlington, or Union Pacific—roads supposedly following the most progressive passenger policies by lowering fares and investing heavily in streamliners—had little financially positive to show for their investments. Much of the blame for this situation Smith placed on his fellow railroad managers:

> I believe there is considerable fallacious, shallow and emotional thinking in connection with the passenger train service problems of the railroads which should be superseded by logical analysis and realistic thinking. . . . In my opinion, there is no phase of railroading that is in more urgent need of study. In discussions of the problem, the investor in the railroads is usually the forgotten man.[5]

Smith wanted the nation's railroad officers to address this situation through the Association of American Railroads, but he later wrote that his suggestions and criticisms so incensed passenger traffic officers that they refused to allow discussion of the matter.[6] Instead they plunged forward blindly with plans to invest almost $1 billion in streamliners that surpassed the inefficiency of those of the late 1930s.

These points suggest that California's rail managers responded less effectively to the automobile than they could have, and most likely rail managers in many other parts of the United States performed as poorly. The concern of California's rail managers with keeping the business community out of the affairs of the railroad resulted in overdeveloped highways and underdeveloped rail routes. It also led management to view passenger service more as a service to the business community than as a source of profit. Combined with the false paradigm of railroad economics, this concern led managements to neglect major nonbusiness markets for about a decade. When managements finally began successfully pursuing such markets after 1933, the prevailing paradigm of railroad economics and a related management culture that preferred massive machines led them into unprofitable passenger investment and operating strategies that persisted into the post–World War II era. The inadequately developed rail routes compounded passenger diseconomies. Such difficulties prevented rail managers from finding profitable niches for passenger trains in the automobile age, although bus (and later air) managers succeeded in operating their public transportation technologies profitably under similar market conditions.

Abbreviations

The following abbreviations appear in the notes and tables:

ACSC   Automobile Club of Southern California library, Los Angeles
BL   Bancroft Library, University of California, Berkeley
CALTRANS   California Department of Transportation library, Sacramento
CRHM   California Railroad History Museum library and archives, Sacramento
CSA   California State Archives, Sacramento
FPC   U.S. Interstate Commerce Commission, *Five Percent Case* (1915), Docket 5860, Record Group 134, Washington National Records Center, Suitland, MD. Decision: 31 ICC 351
HML   Archives of the Hagley Museum and Library, Wilmington, DE. Pennsylvania Railroad Company Records, Accession No. 1807/1810
ICC   U.S. Interstate Commerce Commission, *Decisions,* 1908–41
PFS   U.S. Interstate Commerce Commission, *Passenger Fares and Surcharges* (1936), Docket 26550, Docket Room, ICC, Washington, D.C. Decision: 214 ICC 174
PPS   U.S. Interstate Commerce Commission, *Pullman and Parlor Car Surcharges* (1925), Docket 14785, Record Group 134, Washington National Records Center, Suitland, MD. Decision: 95 ICC 469
RCC   Railroad Commission of California, *Opinions and Orders,* 1915–41
SFC   Collection of William Myers, Anaheim Hills, CA, and James Seal, Santa Monica, CA. Railroad Commission of California, *Santa Fe Case* (1938), Applications 20710 et al. Decision: 41 RCC 239
TWR   Collection of Richard Tower, San Francisco. Southern Pacific Company, selected passenger files from the executive office
VS   Collection of Vernon Sappers, Oakland. Selected passenger files from the Southern Pacific Company executive office; reports prepared for the Oakland, Antioch & Eastern
WMJS   Collection of William Myers, Anaheim Hills, CA, and James Seal, Santa Monica, CA. California Railroad Commission case files

WPF U.S. Interstate Commerce Commission, *Western Passenger Fares* (1915), I&S Docket 600, Record Group 134, Washington National Records Center, Suitland, MD. Decision: 37 ICC 1

Appendix

Determining Passenger Train Profitability, ca. 1911
Notes for Tables 1 and 2

Calculations in table 1 yield average train gross revenues of $3.07 per train mile for limited trains and $1.76 per train mile for local trains. The method is to allocate Southern Pacific 1911 passenger and allied service revenues to the several car types generating them. The table shows car types grouped into typical through and local trains, based on photographs and the knowledge that most through passengers rode in Pullman cars. For example, Lucius Beebe's photographic essay of Southern Pacific was examined for train lengths. Several excellent photographs of premier trains in the 1905–18 period show them to vary in length from six to nine cars, even when running in two sections. See Lucius Beebe, *The Central Pacific & the Southern Pacific Railroads* (Berkeley: Howell-North, 1963), 212–214, 367, 481, 604. In PPS, Santa Fe witnesses also testified that in the early 1920s the company restricted its most prestigious train, the *California Limited,* to six sleeping cars, even though at that time the limited operated in at least two sections every day (PPS, transcript, 1336–1337, 1354–1355). However, some limiteds also carried coach passengers. A special November 1920 study conducted by Santa Fe showed that about a third of its revenues from all of its Chicago–California trains derived from coach travelers. See PPS, exhibit 57.

I based costs on the Western District 1916 cost of $1.16 per passenger train mile (table 2). To account for the 14 percent drop in the consumer price index in 1911 compared to 1916, I adjusted the 1916 cost per Western District passenger train mile downward by 14 percent to $1.00. That figure represents the cost to run a 6-car train one mile. Southern Pacific local trains averaged 5.8 cars and cost proportionately less to operate, about $0.97 per train mile. Southern Pacific through trains averaged 11 cars. (Because through trains rarely operated in lengths greater than 10 cars, the 11-car average indicates that a sizable number of through trains operated in two or more sections.) To account for the longer train length, I increased the cost in proportion to train length and subtracted sleeping car maintenance expenses. These adjustments yield a cost of $1.78 per through train mile and reflect informed railroad thought on costs of later years. Table 2 shows the calculations.

Thus, each through train had an operating ratio of 58 percent and earned $1.29 per mile profit, while each local train had an operating ratio of 55 percent and earned $0.79. The total net revenues that the Southern Pacific received from each class of service was the net revenue per train mile multiplied by the number of train miles. As shown in table 1, through trains operated 6.0 million miles, while locals operated 9.7 million. Thus, the Southern Pacific through trains contributed about $7.7 million in net revenue to company coffers in 1911, while local trains contributed almost the same amount.

Table 1. Analysis of 1911 Southern Pacific Train Earnings (Pacific Lines)

Car mileage (millions)		
Passenger car[a]	(47.5–5.1)	42.4
Dining car[b]		8.5
Sleeping car		37.0
Other[c]	(40.0–8.5)	31.5
Total intercity steam passenger car miles		119.4
Train mileage (millions[a])	(18.9–3.2)	15.7
Average steam train length (cars)		7.6
Revenues ($ millions)		
Passenger[a]	($31.9–$1.3)	$30.6
Allied services		4.7
Net dining car[d]		0.3
Per car mile earnings		
Sleeping car[e]	15.4 passengers @ $.024	$0.3696
Coach[f]		0.4030
Dining		0.0306
Other		0.1492
Gross through train annual earnings ($ millions)		
Through trains—6.0 million miles		
90% of sleeping car miles (33.3 million @ $.3696)		$12.3
90% of dining car miles (7.7 million @ $.0306)		0.2
Coach earnings set to equal 25% of coach and sleeper earnings (10.3 million car miles[g])		4.1
Head end prorated by train mileage: 11.8 @ $.1492		1.8
11.5 cars/scheduled train mile	total earnings	$18.4
	per train mile	$3.07

Table 1. *Continued*

Gross annual local train earnings ($ millions)		
Local trains—9.7 million miles		
10% of sleeping car miles (3.7 million @ $.3696)		$1.4
10% of dining car miles (.85 million @ $.0306)		0.0
Coaches: 42.0–10.3 million car miles @ $.4030		12.8
Head end: 31.5–11.8 million car miles @ $.1492		2.9
5.8 cars/scheduled train miles	total earnings	$17.1
	per train mile	$1.76

Source: U.S. Interstate Commerce Commission, *Statistics of Railways in the United States* (Washington, DC: Government Printing Office, 1911), 240–243; and (1916), 214–221. I factored 1911 Southern Pacific train miles into through and local categories based on my analysis of 1915 schedules as presented in chapter 1.

[a] Ferry suburban trains were factored out. The estimate of 3.2 million annual train miles is calculated for 1919 from information presented in Robert S. Ford, *Red Trains in the East Bay* (Glendale, CA: Interurbans Press, 1977), 151, 327–332. Ford provides headways and the number of cars per train for different times of day. He also provides route lengths. The revenue of $1.3 million comes from Ford, *Red Trains,* 142.

[b] Dining car miles are estimated. The FY1916 *Statistics of Railways* shows 9.8 million dining car miles produced by 94 dining cars, or 104,000 miles per car. The 1911 report shows 82 dining cars, suggesting 8.5 million miles.

[c] It is assumed that dining car miles are grouped in the other car category.

[d] This figure is the difference between dining and buffet costs and revenues per car mile for 1916, multiplied by the 1911 estimate for dining car miles.

[e] CSA: Pullman Company, *Annual Report to the California Railroad Commission* (1912). This report shows an average of 14 passengers per car day for 1912. I factored this upward to 15.4 by using the ratio of Pullman passenger miles per car mile to Pullman passengers per day for those years when both figures were available. The revenue figure comes from the Pullman Company annual report for 1912. There was little variation in revenue yields before World War I.

[f] Sleeping car revenues per car mile multiplied by sleeping car miles yields total revenue generated in sleeping cars. This is subtracted from adjusted passenger revenue to yield revenue generated in coaches. The result is divided by coach miles.

[g] Most long distance passengers traveled in sleeping cars, but before the fare increase of 1920 many used coaches. A Santa Fe survey in 1920 (presented in PPS, exhibit 57) showed that a third of the company's revenues from through Chicago–Los Angeles trains derived from coach passengers. The 25% figure here partly reflects the Santa Fe survey, but I adjusted it downward somewhat to reflect general statements about passenger travel of the period that most long distance passengers used sleeping cars. The 10.3 million car miles comes from the $4.1 million estimate of coach revenue divided by the coach revenue per coach mile of $.4030.

Table 2. Passenger Costs and Revenues for Class 1 Carriers, FY1916

		Expenses and revenues ($1,000s)			
Row	Item	Eastern District	Southern District	Western District	United States
1	Total operating expenses	1,023,985	322,644	860,933	2,207,562
2	Solely related freight expenses	526,727	158,197	347,862	1,032,786
3	Solely related passenger expenses	168,866	49,105	149,083	367,054
4	Solely related freight expenses as % of rows 2 and 3	75.7%	76.3%	70.0%	73.8%
5	Solely related passenger expenses as % of rows 2 and 3	24.3%	23.7%	30.0%	26.2%
6	Apportioned freight expenses	115,800	41,250	129,223	286,273
7	Apportioned passenger expenses	43,199	13,296	56,362	112,857
8	Expenses not apportioned	165,992	60,472	178,004	404,468
9	Taxes	57,723	20,622	67,172	145,517
10	Rows 8 and 9 allocated to freight per row 4	169,405	61,885	171,623	402,913
11	Rows 8 and 9 allocated to passenger per row 5	54,310	19,209	73,553	147,072
12	Total freight expenses (rows 2+6+10)	811,932	261,332	648,708	1,721,972
13	Total passenger expenses (rows 3+7+11)	266,375	81,610	278,998	626,983
14	Freight revenue	1,095,656	361,874	944,682	2,402,212
15	Passenger and allied service revenue	373,427	112,709	360,400	846,536
16	Operating ratio, freight	74.1%	72.2%	68.7%	71.7%
17	Operating ratio, passenger	71.3%	72.4%	77.4%	74.1%
18	Passenger train miles, revenue (100s)	239,519	88,340	241,347	569,206

Table 2. *Continued*

		Expenses and revenues ($1,000s)			
Row	*Item*	*Eastern District*	*Southern District*	*Western District*	*United States*
19	Passenger car miles (1,000s)	1,384,968	478,164	1,447,688	3,310,820
20	Average train length	5.78	5.41	6.00	5.82
21	Passenger-related revenue/train mile	$1.56	$1.28	$1.49	$1.49
22	Passenger expenses per train mile	$1.11	$0.92	$1.16	$1.10

Source: U.S. Interstate Commerce Commission, *Statistics of Railways in the United States* (FY 1916)

Table 3. California Auto Ownership, 1906–1933

Year	California population (1,000s)	Registered autos	Autos per 1,000 people
1906	1,976	6,428	3
1907	2,054		
1908	2,161	17,015	8
1909	2,282		
1910	2,406	36,146	15
1911	2,534		
1912	2,668	76,669	29
1913	2,811		
1914	2,934	123,516	42
1915	3,008	164,795	55
1916	3,071	232,440	76
1917	3,171	306,916	97
1918	3,262	364,800	112
1919	3,339	477,450	143
1920	3,554	532,934	150
1921	3,795	645,522	170
1922	3,991	822,394	206
1923	4,270	1,056,756	247
1924	4,541	1,125,201	248
1925	4,730	1,224,831	259
1926	4,929	1,383,097	281
1927	5,147	1,479,411	287
1928	5,344	1,582,477	296
1929	5,531	1,885,308	341
1930	5,711	1,941,969	340
1931	5,824	1,938,068	333
1933	5,863	1,850,608	316

Source: SFC, exhibit 40.

Table 4. California State and County Highway Expenditures, 1914–1933

Year (1)	Population (1,000s) (2)	Highway expenditures ($ millions)			Per capita expenditures (dollars per capita)		
		State (3)	County (4)	Total (5)	Current (6)	Cost index (1967=100) (7)	Real (1967 $) (8)
1914	2,934	$6.9	$10.4	$17.3	$5.90	34	$17.34
1915	3,008	4.5	13.4	17.9	5.95	34	17.50
1916	3,071	5.8	17.0	22.8	7.42	36	20.62
1917	3,171	1.6	16.2	17.8	5.61	41	13.69
1918	3,262	6.8	15.8	22.6	6.93	49	14.14
1919	3,339	7.6	14.5	22.1	6.62	55	12.03
1920	3,554	9.2	16.9	26.1	7.34	71	10.34
1921	3,795	10.5	28.0	38.5	10.14	59	17.19
1922	3,991	27.7	26.8	54.5	13.66	54	25.29
1923	4,270	16.2	24.4	40.6	9.51	60	15.85
1924	4,541	18.8	24.2	43.0	9.47	57	16.61
1925	4,730	18.6	26.7	45.3	9.58	54	17.74
1926	4,929	19.9	27.2	47.1	9.56	52	18.38
1927	5,147	18.6	27.3	45.9	8.92	52	17.15
1928	5,344	16.7	31.3	48.0	8.98	48	18.71
1929	5,531	31.4	29.4	60.8	10.99	47	23.39
1930	5,711	32.5	29.5	62.0	10.86	43	25.25
1931	5,824	34.0	33.3	67.3	11.56	39	29.63
1932	5,894	39.8	30.9	70.7	12.00	31	38.69
1933	5,863	32.9	24.2	57.1	9.74	39	24.97

Source:
Columns 3, 4, 5: SFC, exhibit 44.
Column 7: U.S. Bureau of the Census, *Historical Statistics of the United States, Colonial Times to 1970* (Washington, DC: Government Printing Office, 1975), series N1356; Consumer Price Index.

Table 5. Southern Pacific Company, Pacific Lines, Indices of Usage and Profitability, 1899–1941

| | Usage index (1913–1914=100) | | | |
| | Ton miles | Passenger miles | Composite | Operating ratio |
Year	(1)	(2)	(3)	(4)
1899	49	38	45	55.47
1900	55	46	51	55.88
1901	68	53	62	54.86
1902	69	61	66	56.68
1903	69	67	68	58.89
1904	74	72	73	58.64
1905	na	na	na	na
1906	86	79	83	55.63
1907	96	90	94	55.38
1908	90	93	91	59.24
1909	85	87	86	54.25
1910	92	102	96	53.19
1911	86	102	92	55.29
1912	91	102	95	68.15
1913	100	103	101	57.40
1914	100	97	99	57.35
1915	91	99	94	59.75
1916	133	117	127	63.49
1917	195	114	163	61.82
1918	190	127	165	64.21
1919	181	137	163	73.83
1920	187	149	172	76.22
1921	149	115	135	82.82
1922	158	115	141	74.30
1923	194	123	166	70.65
1924	193	117	163	68.68
1925	223	119	181	71.99
1926	231	116	185	69.46
1927	235	116	187	70.52
1928	246	112	192	70.26
1929	255	115	199	69.64
1930	212	104	169	71.76
1931	170	96	140	75.09
1932	130	71	106	78.76
1933	129	65	103	77.46
1934	161	75	127	74.08

Table 5. *Continued*

	Usage index (1913–1914=100)			Operating ratio (4)
Year	Ton miles (1)	Passenger miles (2)	Composite (3)	
1935	178	86	141	74.47
1936	na	na	na	na
1937	na	na	na	na
1938	220	101	172	78.78
1939	250	107	193	73.15
1940	288	100	213	72.71
1941	397	131	291	69.20

Source: Figures are derived from U.S. Interstate Commerce Commission, *Statistics of Railways in the United States,* except for 1899–1910, which are taken from CRHM: Southern Pacific Company, annual reports.

Notes: To calculate column 3 I weighted freight gross ton miles by .6 and passenger miles by .4, borrowing the method used by Albro Martin, *Enterprise Denied: Origins of the Decline of American Railroads, 1897–1917* (New York: Columbia University Press, 1971), 374–375. This procedure yields an indicator of usage, whose average for 1913–14 I used as the base of the index of composite usage. Passenger miles and ton miles between 1899 and 1910 are for the entire system. They are indexed to their 1911 value, and that index is set to the 1911 value for the Pacific Lines. The operating ratio between 1899 and 1910 is for the entire system rather than for the Pacific Lines. Between 1911 and 1914, when operating ratios are available for both, the operating ratio for the Pacific Lines was .86 as large as that for the system. This factor was used to diminish the size of the operating ratio for the system between 1899 and 1910.

Table 6. Santa Fe and Southern Pacific Passenger Train Use in California, 1911–1919

		Annual California passenger miles (millions)							
		Intrastate				Interstate			
Year	California population (1,000)	AT&SF	SP	Total	Miles/ capita	AT&SF	SP	Total	Miles/ capita
1911	2,534	112	519	631	249	94	282	376	148
1912	2,668	137	521	658	247	104	271	375	141
1913	2,811	159	552	711	253	119	328	447	159
1914	2,934	159	513	672	229	110	283	393	134
1915	3,008	146	456	602	200	128	279	407	135
1916	3,071	143	470	613	200	174	339	513	167
1917	3,171	131	453	584	184	117	326	443	140
1918	3,262	111	504	615	189	146	373	519	159
1919	3,339	88	562	650	195	161	404	565	169

Source: SFC, exhibits 45, 76, and 629.

Table 7. California Interurban Electric Railway Traffic Trends, 1911–1920

	Annual passengers (millions)		
Year	Visalia Electric	Tidewater Southern	Oakland, Antioch & Eastern
1911	0.14		
1912	0.17		
1913	0.15		
1914	0.16	0.08	
1915	0.13	0.13	0.40
1916	0.11	0.15	0.70
1917	0.12	0.16	0.70
1918	0.09	0.12	0.80
1919	0.07	0.07	1.10
1920	0.07	0.07	1.10

Source: Railroad Commission of California, *Annual Report of the Railroad Commission of the State of California* (San Francisco: annual).
Note: Commuters are excluded for the Oakland, Antioch & Eastern.

Table 8. Class 1 Steam Railroad Passenger Trends, 1920 and 1929

	1920	1929
Passengers (millions)	1,235	780
Pullman and parlor car	39	29
Commuter	447	457
Intercity coach	749	294
Passenger miles (millions)	46,800	31,100
Pullman and parlor car	14,300	14,100
Commuter	6,000	6,900
Intercity coach	26,500	10,100
Average trip length (miles)	38	40
Pullman and parlor car	367	486
Commuter	13	15
Intercity coach	35	34

Source: U.S. Interstate Commerce Commission, *Statistics of Railways in the United States.* The ICC first began reporting commuters separately in 1923. I used the 1923 commuter figures for 1920.

Appendix

Table 9. Comparison of Bus and Rail Revenue and Traffic, West Coast, 1933

Market		Distance (miles)			Average daily passengers		Fare per mile based on air distance	
Between	And	Air	Rail	Bus	Rail	Bus	Rail	Bus
San Francisco	San Jose	41	47	51	293	113	$0.018	$0.021
Sacramento	Stockton	43	48	47	17	41	0.022	0.022
San Jose	Stockton	54	81	77	4	7	0.028	0.024
San Francisco	Stockton	62	91	80	140	64	0.020	0.023
Sacramento	San Francisco	74	92	101	857	27	0.017	0.025
Los Angeles	Santa Barbara	86	104	99	56	37	0.021	0.021
Sacramento	San Jose	87	139	124	4	4	0.022	0.026
Bakersfield	Los Angeles	99	171	122	12	28	0.031	0.029
Bakersfield	Fresno	99	107	105	6	6	0.017	0.020
Average fare per mile for markets between 40 and 99 miles:							$0.018	$0.023
Phoenix	Tucson	105	121	137	22	7	$0.021	$0.023
Los Angeles	San Diego	110	126	129	213	146	0.021	0.019
Sacramento	Reno	110	154	144	20	5	0.028	0.025
Fresno	Stockton	117	122	124	5	4	0.018	0.020
Fresno	San Jose	123	253	174	1	2	0.025	0.037
Stockton	Reno	132	202	191	1	0	0.029	0.028
Riverside	Santa Barbara	136	162	157	0	0	0.036	0.022
Portland	Seattle	147	183	194	195	101	0.018	0.015
Average fare per mile for markets between 100 and 149 miles:							$0.020	$0.018
Fresno	Sacramento	158	170	171	7	4	$0.018	$0.023
Fresno	San Francisco	161	206	184	93	21	0.018	0.020
San Francisco	Reno	182	243	244	72	7	0.022	0.024
San Jose	Reno	186	290	292	1	0	0.026	0.028
San Diego	Santa Barbara	186	230	228	1	1	0.016	0.023
Fresno	Reno	192	324	315	1	0	0.032	0.030
Average fare per mile for markets between 150 and 199 miles:							$0.020	$0.022
Fresno	Los Angeles	200	278	229	26	17	$0.024	$0.024
Bakersfield	Stockton	216	229	229	1	1	0.018	0.019
Fresno	Riverside	225	336	275	0	0	0.028	0.026
San Jose	Santa Barbara	232	320	297	2	1	0.026	0.021
Bakersfield	San Francisco	249	313	289	17	3	0.021	0.021
Average fare per mile for markets between 200 and 249 miles:							$0.023	$0.023

Table 9. *Continued*

Market		Distance (miles)			Average daily passengers		Fare per mile based on air distance	
Between	And	Air	Rail	Bus	Rail	Bus	Rail	Bus
San Francisco	Santa Barbara	274	367	348	19	5	$0.025	$0.021
San Diego	Phoenix	298	391	383	3	3	0.030	0.019
Average fare per mile for markets between 250 and 299 miles:							$0.026	$0.021
Sacramento	Santa Barbara	300	451	413	0	0	$0.026	$0.023
Los Angeles	San Jose	301	424	396	13	9	0.024	0.016
Riverside	Phoenix	306	368	424	1	1	0.023	0.017
Fresno	San Diego	312	407	458	0	1	0.033	0.020
Los Angeles	Stockton	318	400	362	10	6	0.025	0.019
Los Angeles	San Francisco	343	471	447	434	116	0.025	0.027
Los Angeles	Sacramento	355	448	389	37	11	0.025	0.019
Los Angeles	Phoenix	356	426	481	38	53	0.023	0.013
San Diego	Tucson	364	468	417	1	1	0.030	0.019
Riverside	San Francisco	377	529	505	2	1	0.024	0.022
Los Angeles	Reno	382	602	540	4	2	0.031	0.024
Riverside	Sacramento	383	506	458	0	0	0.024	0.021
Riverside	Tucson	387	445	469	0	0	0.021	0.019
Average fare per mile for markets between 300 and 399 miles:							$0.025	$0.025
San Diego	San Jose	414	550	525	0	1	$0.025	$0.020
Los Angeles	Tucson	434	503	527	22	4	0.022	0.015
Santa Barbara	Phoenix	438	530	582	0	0	0.027	0.017
Reno	Portland	438	637	800	1	0	0.030	0.030
San Diego	San Francisco	454	597	576	9	9	0.026	0.020
Sacramento	San Diego	468	574	530	1	1	0.023	0.018
Sacramento	Portland	486	682	656	5	2	0.024	0.017
Fresno	Phoenix	487	704	699	0	0	0.020	0.017
Average fare per mile for markets between 400 and 499 miles:							$0.023	$0.017
Stockton	Portland	524	730	703	2	0	$0.021	$0.019
San Francisco	Portland	530	771	728	80	29	0.023	0.016
San Jose	Portland	558	818	776	1	1	0.022	0.014
Reno	Seattle	573	820	1000	0	0	0.046	0.023
Average fare per mile for markets between 500 and 599 miles:							$0.023	$0.016
Fresno	Portland	617	906	827	1	0	$0.022	$0.019
Sacramento	Phoenix	627	874	893	0	0	0.022	0.019

Table 9. *Continued*

Market		Distance (miles)			Average daily passengers		Fare per mile based on air distance	
Between	And	Air	Rail	Bus	Rail	Bus	Rail	Bus
Sacramento	Seattle	629	865	856	0	2	0.031	0.016
San Francisco	Phoenix	644	897	933	4	1	0.021	0.017
Stockton	Seattle	665	913	903	0	1	0.010	0.017
San Francisco	Seattle	677	954	928	33	33	0.027	0.014
Bakersfield	Portland	725	959	932	0	0	0.023	0.017
San Francisco	Tucson	748	974	991	2	0	0.033	0.023
Fresno	Seattle	759	1089	1027	0	0	0.020	0.018
Santa Barbara	Portland	781	1210	1076	0	0	0.024	0.016
Average fare per mile for markets between 600 and 799 miles:							$0.027	$0.015
Los Angeles	Portland	833	1130	1056	37	13	$0.023	$0.027
San Diego	Portland	916	1256	1181	3	1	0.019	0.017
Los Angeles	Seattle	964	1313	1256	16	17	0.022	0.017
San Diego	Seattle	1048	1439	1382	1	2	0.018	0.017
Average fare per mile for markets between 800 and 1,500 miles:							$0.022	$0.023

Source: U.S. Office of the Federal Coordinator of Transportation, *Passenger Traffic Report* (Washington, DC: 1935), appendix 1. Traffic between San Francisco and Sacramento includes 212,000 trips reported by the Federal Coordinator for the Southern Pacific, plus an estimated 100,000 trips using the Sacramento Northern, the 1933 name of the electric interurban between those points. Distances are from atlases and timetables.

Note: The average fare per mile is a weighted average based on rail traffic.

Table 10. Comparison of Bus and Rail Revenue and Traffic, East Coast, 1933

Market		Distance (miles)			Average daily passengers		Fare per mile based on air distance	
Between	And	Air	Rail	Bus	Rail	Bus	Rail	Bus
Bridgeport	New Haven	17	17	19	126	0	$0.034	$0.069
Wilmington	Philadelphia	25	27	30	879	35	0.026	0.029
Hartford	Springfield	25	25	29	68	102	0.035	0.029
Trenton	Philadelphia	28	33	34	173	121	0.035	0.023
Hartford	New Haven	32	37	38	192	26	0.036	0.037
Worcester	Providence	36	43	43	3	131	0.041	0.024
Boston	Worcester	37	44	42	424	6	0.028	0.030
Boston	Providence	42	44	45	310	477	0.032	0.021
Springfield	Worcester	42	54	50	47	4	0.042	0.027
Newark	Trenton	46	47	48	181	11	0.034	0.026
Bridgeport	Hartford	48	53	57	67	2	0.034	0.035
Average fare per mile in markets between 17 and 49 miles:							$0.030	$0.030
Bridgeport	New York	52	56	58	927	65	$0.028	$0.026
Trenton	New York	52	58	58	431	123	0.033	0.023
Wilmington	Trenton	52	58	64	9	1	0.034	0.025
New Haven	Springfield	58	62	63	39	9	0.033	0.029
Hartford	Worcester	59	79	75	10	5	0.047	0.033
Bridgeport	Newark	60	66	65	2	2	0.053	0.028
Springfield	Providence	62	124	102	1	8	0.067	0.033
Hartford	Providence	65	99	73	1	30	0.058	0.028
Wilmington	Baltimore	67	69	73	81	13	0.031	0.026
New Haven	New York	70	72	73	1,292	78	0.026	0.023
Bridgeport	Springfield	70	79	82	12	6	0.035	0.027
Newark	Philadelphia	73	81	82	498	88	0.032	0.022
New Haven	Newark	77	82	83	3	1	0.050	0.023
Boston	Springfield	78	98	92	268	6	0.027	0.026
New York	Philadelphia	80	91	92	4,132	584	0.031	0.025
New Haven	Providence	85	113	113	37	14	0.042	0.023
New Haven	Worcester	89	116	110	6	4	0.047	0.024
Baltimore	Philadelphia	90	95	103	564	76	0.029	0.025
Hartford	Boston	91	123	118	63	48	0.045	0.022
Washington	Wilmington	98	109	114	58	6	0.030	0.026
Wilmington	Newark	98	108	112	28	3	0.033	0.024
Hartford	New York	98	109	108	694	123	0.026	0.020
Average fare per mile in markets between 50 and 99 miles:							$0.030	$0.024

180   Appendix

Table 10. *Continued*

Market		Distance (miles)			Average daily passengers		Fare per mile based on air distance	
Between	And	Air	Rail	Bus	Rail	Bus	Rail	Bus
Bridgeport	Providence	101	130	132	10	11	$0.042	$0.021
Bridgeport	Trenton	104	115	113	1	0	0.044	0.030
Hartford	Newark	104	119	118	1	3	0.060	0.021
Bridgeport	Worcester	104	133	130	3	4	0.043	0.022
Wilmington	New York	105	117	122	168	14	0.031	0.024
Baltimore	Trenton	117	127	137	16	2	0.033	0.024
New Haven	Boston	118	157	158	88	28	0.041	0.020
Springfield	New York	120	134	133	521	95	0.021	0.017
Washington	Philadelphia	121	135	144	613	58	0.027	0.024
New Haven	Trenton	122	131	131	2	0	0.041	0.024
Springfield	Newark	126	144	143	1	2	0.033	0.019
Bridgeport	Philadelphia	132	146	147	7	4	0.040	0.023
Bridgeport	Boston	135	174	177	23	19	0.042	0.019
Average fare per mile in markets between 100 and 149 miles:							$0.027	$0.021
New Haven	Philadelphia	150	162	165	19	4	$0.037	$0.019
Washington	Trenton	150	167	178	29	2	0.028	0.022
Hartford	Trenton	150	167	166	1	0	0.039	0.023
Providence	New York	153	185	166	385	236	0.039	0.018
Worcester	New York	156	188	183	124	119	0.041	0.017
Bridgeport	Wilmington	158	173	177	1	0	0.038	0.024
Baltimore	Newark	162	175	185	71	6	0.031	0.024
Worcester	Newark	162	198	193	0	2	0.041	0.016
Providence	Newark	165	195	176	3	4	0.046	0.017
Baltimore	New York	170	185	195	753	61	0.030	0.022
Springfield	Trenton	172	194	191	0	0	0.039	0.020
New Haven	Wilmington	174	189	195	1	0	0.040	0.020
Hartford	Philadelphia	177	200	200	7	4	0.039	0.019
Boston	New York	188	229	235	1,495	582	0.035	0.018
Washington	Newark	195	215	226	159	5	0.022	0.023
Boston	Newark	195	239	221	8	12	0.047	0.017
Springfield	Philadelphia	199	225	225	6	4	0.040	0.018
Average fare per mile in markets between 150 and 199 miles:							$0.034	$0.019
Hartford	Wilmington	203	227	230	0	0	$0.038	$0.021
Washington	New York	203	225	236	1,585	75	0.026	0.021
Providence	Trenton	205	245	224	1	0	0.043	0.019
Worcester	Trenton	208	248	241	0	0	0.042	0.019

Table 10. *Continued*

Market		Distance (miles)			Average daily passengers		Fare per mile based on air distance	
Between	And	Air	Rail	Bus	Rail	Bus	Rail	Bus
Bridgeport	Baltimore	223	242	250	2	0	0.037	0.023
Springfield	Wilmington	225	252	255	0	0	0.039	0.020
Providence	Philadelphia	233	276	258	18	10	0.041	0.018
Worcester	Philadelphia	235	279	275	2	3	0.039	0.017
New Haven	Baltimore	239	258	268	4	0	0.038	0.023
Boston	Trenton	240	289	269	3	1	0.043	0.018
Average fare per mile in markets between 200 and 249 miles:							$0.026	$0.021
Washington	Bridgeport	255	282	291	5	1	$0.039	$0.025
Providence	Wilmington	256	303	288	1	0	0.041	0.019
Worcester	Wilmington	260	306	305	0	0	0.040	0.016
Hartford	Baltimore	265	297	303	3	1	0.040	0.023
Boston	Philadelphia	269	320	303	78	34	0.040	0.016
Washington	New Haven	271	298	309	13	1	0.036	0.023
Springfield	Baltimore	288	321	328	2	1	0.039	0.021
Boston	Wilmington	292	347	333	5	2	0.041	0.017
Average fare per mile in markets between 250 and 299 miles:							$0.040	$0.018
Washington	Hartford	300	336	336	7	1	$0.037	$0.022
Washington	Springfield	319	361	369	6	1	0.038	0.020
Providence	Baltimore	323	372	361	4	1	0.041	0.020
Worcester	Baltimore	324	375	378	1	1	0.035	0.019
Washington	Providence	354	412	402	16	2	0.039	0.021
Washington	Worcester	357	415	419	2	1	0.036	0.019
Boston	Baltimore	358	416	406	22	6	0.039	0.019
Washington	Boston	390	456	447	94	10	0.034	0.021
Average fare per mile in markets between 300 and 399 miles:							$0.035	$0.021

Source: U.S. Office of the Federal Coordinator of Transportation, *Passenger Traffic Report* (Washington, DC: 1935), appendix 1. Distances are from atlases and timetables.
Note: Average fares for each market group are weighted by rail passengers.

Table 11. Three Passenger Service Indicators for the Southern Pacific, Pacific Lines, 1920–1930

Year	Passenger train miles (1,000s)	Revenue per train mile	Trip length in miles
1920	22,542	$2.44	39.4
1921	21,294	2.26	33.9
1922	20,662	2.15	36.1
1923	21,762	2.15	37.8
1924	21,099	2.01	38.6
1925	22,682	1.88	39.6
1926	22,127	1.89	40.4
1927	22,156	1.84	42.7
1928	21,065	1.84	43.7
1929	20,846	1.88	45.5
1930	20,089	1.71	44.1

Source: U.S. Interstate Commerce Commission, *Statistics of Railways in the United States.*

Table 12. Southern Pacific Speed Comparisons, ca. 1920 vs. ca. 1930

Between	Circa 1921–23		Circa 1930	
	Average speed in miles per hour	Number of trains	Average speed in miles per hour	Number of trains
Oakland–Port Costa or Martinez	28.5	18	31.6	24
Port Costa or Martinez–Tracy	32.8	6	34.8	6
Tracy–Fresno or Lathrop	30.5	6	35.8	5
Fresno–Bakersfield	34.8	4	39.0	4
Bakersfield–Mojave	24.4	7	26.4	6
Mojave–Saugus	26.3	5	27.3	4
Saugus–Burbank Junction	30.2	7		
San Francisco–San Jose (limited trains)	39.7	5	44.4	5
San Francisco–San Jose (local trains)	28.0	13	33.1	30
San Jose–Watsonville Junction	33.7	7	36.9	9
Watsonville–San Ardo or King City	36.1	5	42.8	6
San Ardo or King City–San Luis Obispo	30.4	5	31.9	6
Santa Barbara–Burbank Junction	31.5	6	35.3	7
Oakland–Sacramento	31.2	15		

Source: Derived from CRHM: Southern Pacific Company, employee timetables for various years and divisions.

Table 13. Pacific Greyhound Lines and Predecessors, Operating Results per Bus Mile

Year	In current dollars			In constant 1926 dollars		
	Operating expenses	Operating revenues	Net	Operating expenses	Operating revenues	Net
1927	$0.286	$0.330	$0.044	$0.304	$0.351	$0.047
1928	0.283	0.320	0.037	0.305	0.344	0.039
1929	0.284	0.318	0.034	0.310	0.347	0.037
1930						
1931	0.260	0.276	0.016	0.347	0.368	0.021
1932	0.231	0.254	0.023	0.329	0.362	0.033
1933	0.215	0.243	0.028	0.302	0.342	0.040
1934	0.206	0.271	0.065	0.263	0.346	0.083
1935	0.196	0.276	0.080	0.257	0.354	0.097

Source: SFC, exhibit 361.

Notes: Predecessor companies operated in 1927 and 1928; the transition to Pacific Greyhound Lines took place during 1929 and 1930. 1931 was Pacific Greyhound's first full year of operation. I deflated the constant dollar columns with the wholesale price index, all commodities other than farm products and food. See U.S. Bureau of the Census, *Historical Statistics of the United States,* series E41.

Table 14. Pacific Greyhound Lines Distribution of Profitability by Route, Partial 1936

Intrastate routes	Revenue	Cost	Net	Percent
San Francisco–Los Angeles (coast)	$502,718	$322,122	$180,596	16.32%
San Francisco–Los Angeles (valley)	448,329	287,133	161,196	14.57
Sacramento–Los Angeles (valley)	216,380	131,934	84,446	7.63
Los Angeles–San Diego (total)	240,344	180,467	59,877	5.41
Los Angeles–San Diego (via Long Beach)	193,166	140,822	52,344	4.73
San Francisco–Ukiah	87,730	60,046	27,684	2.50
Oakland–Vallejo–Napa	45,981	28,365	17,616	1.59
San Francisco–Stockton	55,740	41,472	14,268	1.29
San Francisco–Sacramento	39,692	28,384	11,308	1.02
Sacramento–Modesto	39,549	28,351	11,198	1.01
San Francisco–Santa Rosa–Monte Rio	28,902	18,818	10,084	0.91
San Francisco–Reno	29,764	19,737	10,027	0.91
San Francisco–Santa Cruz	31,147	21,633	9,514	0.86
Los Angeles–San Diego (via Santa Ana)	47,177	39,646	7,531	0.68
Lake County	30,516	24,054	6,462	0.58
Los Angeles–Santa Barbara	22,127	16,398	5,729	0.52
San Francisco–Auburn	14,261	10,040	4,221	0.38
San Diego–El Centro	14,126	10,221	3,905	0.35
Sonoma Valley	17,803	15,337	2,466	0.22
San Jose–Monterey	19,269	17,095	2,174	0.20
Sacramento Junction–Calistoga–Santa Rosa	5,020	3,885	1,135	0.10
Stockton–Sonora	15,177	14,085	1,092	0.10
Sacramento–Winters	160	390	(230)	−0.02
Napa–Sacramento Junction	1,961	2,424	(463)	−0.04
Truckee–Tahoe	248	1,024	(776)	−0.07
Davis–Sacramento	3,573	4,819	(1,246)	−0.11
Santa Paula Valley	9,993	12,091	(2,098)	−0.19
Livermore–San Jose	7,865	10,031	(2,166)	−0.20
Monterey Locals	4,783	8,017	(3,234)	−0.29
Los Angeles–Calexico–El Centro	17,058	20,386	(3,328)	−0.30

Table 14. *Continued*

Intrastate routes	Revenue	Cost	Net	Percent
Selma–Dinuba–Visalia	2,223	5,927	(3,704)	−0.33
San Jose–Hollister	4,569	8,442	(3,873)	−0.35
Sacramento–Redding	6,347	12,818	(6,471)	−0.58
Oakland–Martinez–Stockton	5,877	14,968	(9,091)	−0.82
California intrastate subtotal	$2,209,575	$1,561,382	$648,193	58.59%

Interstate routes	Revenue	Cost	Net	Percent
San Francisco–Portland	$480,127	$334,425	$145,702	13.17%
Los Angeles–El Paso	492,284	366,275	126,009	11.39
San Francisco–Salt Lake	268,696	209,360	59,336	5.36
San Francisco–Portland (Redwood Highway)	211,306	152,505	58,801	5.31
Los Angeles–Albuquerque	267,925	214,071	53,854	4.87
Los Angeles–San Diego–Phoenix	42,678	37,321	5,357	0.48
Medford–Eureka	14,052	11,049	3,003	0.27
Klamath Falls–Weed	4,211	6,325	(2,114)	−0.19
Tucson–Lordsburg	251	2,722	(2,471)	−0.22
Interstate subtotal	$1,781,530	$1,334,053	$447,477	40.45%
Other operations	$379,038	$368,369	$10,669	0.96%
Grand total	$4,370,143	$3,263,804	$1,106,339	100.00%

Source: SFC, exhibit 381.
Note: These revenues are from 14 days of March, 21 days of April, and all of May, June, July, August, and September of 1936. I based costs on the number of bus miles for each route multiplied by Pacific Greyhound's cost per bus mile for 1936.

Table 15. Pacific Greyhound Lines and Predecessors, Evaporation of Rural Traffic, 1924–1934

	Sales		
Agency	For year 1924	For 12 months prior to abandonment	Percent decline
Fowler	$6,313	$1,644	74.0%
Parlier	1,753	298	83.0
Reedley	4,815	952	80.2
Dinuba	6,532	2,379	63.6
Visalia	21,989	11,069	49.7
Exeter	3,822	1,551	59.4
Lindsay	5,232	2,022	61.4
Porterville	8,413	4,518	46.3
Total	$58,869	$24,432	58.5

Source: SFC, exhibit 386.

Table 16. Comparison of Bus and Rail Fare Yields for Trips of Different Lengths, West and East Coasts, 1933

	Fare in cents per mile			
Distance in miles	West Coast		East Coast	
	Rail	Bus	Rail	Bus
17–49	1.8	2.1	3.0	3.0
50–99	1.8	2.5	3.0	2.4
100–149	2.0	1.8	2.7	2.1
150–199	2.0	2.2	3.4	1.9
200–249	2.3	2.2	2.6	2.1
250–299	2.5	2.1	4.0	1.8
300–399	2.5	2.5	3.5	2.1
400–499	2.3	1.7	no samples taken	
500–599	2.3	1.6	no samples taken	
600–799	2.7	1.5	no samples taken	
800–850	2.2	2.3	no samples taken	

Source: Tables 9 and 10.

Table 17. Bus and Rail Fares and Traffic in Important West Coast Markets, 1933

Market	Distance in miles		Average fare		Average daily passengers	
	Rail	Bus	Rail	Bus	Rail	Bus
Bus markets monopolized by Pacific Greyhound:						
San Francisco–Stockton	91	80	$1.26	$1.42	140	64
San Francisco–Sacramento	92	101	1.23	1.82	857	27
Los Angeles–Bakersfield	171	122	3.12	2.87	12	28
Los Angeles–Santa Barbara	104	99	1.82	1.78	56	37
Los Angeles–San Diego[a]	128	129	2.35	2.13	213	146
San Francisco–Fresno	206	184	2.93	3.23	93	21
Los Angeles–Fresno	278	229	4.78	4.72	26	17
San Francisco–Bakersfield	313	289	5.34	5.13	17	3
Los Angeles–San Francisco	471	447	8.43	9.36	434	116
Los Angeles–Sacramento	448	389	8.79	6.80	37	11
Bus markets with railroad-owned bus competition:						
San Francisco–Reno	243	244	$4.81	$5.16	72	7
Bus competition status unclear:						
Los Angeles–Portland	1,130	1,056	$18.88	$22.08	37	13
Cut-rate bus competition:						
Los Angeles–Phoenix	426	481	$8.34	$4.56	38	53
San Francisco–Portland	771	728	12.21	8.35	80	29
San Francisco–Seattle	954	909	18.33	9.50	33	33

Sources: Traffic and fare figures are from table 9. The status of bus competition is from SFC, *Abstract of Evidence of Santa Fe Transportation Company and The Atchison, Topeka & Santa Fe Railway Company,* 1364–1392. Markets are shown where the rail plus bus traffic was 50 passengers or greater, or where service connected important California cities.

[a] The Santa Fe Railway provided rail service in this market.

Table 18. Passenger Service Discontinued in Lieu of Substitute Bus Service, Southern Pacific, Pacific Lines, 1927–1935

Route	Date of change	Company providing bus service	Trains off	Buses on
Santa Cruz–Felton	05/29/27	S.P. Motor Transport	2	6
Felton–Boulder Creek	05/29/27	S.P. Motor Transport	8	10
Portland–Roseburg	09/20/27	S.P. Motor Transport	0	2
Portland–Eugene	09/20/27	S.P. Motor Transport	2	6
Portland–Salem	09/20/27	S.P. Motor Transport	0	4
Portland–McMinnville	09/20/27	S.P. Motor Transport	2	3
Portland–Forest Grove	09/20/27	S.P. Motor Transport	4	4
Portland–Hillsboro	09/20/27	S.P. Motor Transport	2	4
Portland–Corvallis	09/20/27	S.P. Motor Transport	2	2
Portland–Cook	09/20/27	S.P. Motor Transport	10	10
Truckee–Tahoe	05/01/28	S.P. Motor Transport	6	6
Roseburg–Marshfield	07/22/28	S.P. Motor Transport	2	2
Marshfield–Powers	07/22/28	S.P. Motor Transport	2	4
Dallas–Derry	07/22/28	S.P. Motor Transport	10	20
Albany–Newport	08/21/28	S.P. Motor Transport	2	6
Albany–Lebanon	08/21/28	S.P. Motor Transport	12	10
Santa Rosa–Napa	12/06/28	S.P. Motor Transport	4	6
Santa Cruz–Watsonville Junction	01/15/29	S.P. Motor Transport	4	6
Santa Cruz–Davenport	01/15/29	S.P. Motor Transport	2	2
Pacific Grove–Del Monte Junction	01/15/29	S.P. Motor Transport	6	8
Del Monte Junction–Salinas	01/15/29	S.P. Motor Transport	5	5
Gilroy–Tres Pinos	03/28/29	S.P. Motor Transport	4	6
Alamogordo–Cloudcroft	06/01/29	S.P. Motor Transport	4	4
Vallejo–Crockett	06/16/29	S.P. Motor Transport	12[a]	12
Vallejo–Calistoga	07/14/29	S.P. Motor Transport	2	2
Vallejo–Suisun/Fairfield	07/14/29	S.P. Motor Transport	4	4
Surf–Lompoc	07/17/29	S.P. Motor Transport	6	6
Tracy–Los Banos	12/15/29	California Transit	2	2
Exeter–Coalinga	12/15/29	California Transit	6[b]	6
Benicia–Crockett	10/15/30	Pacific Greyhound	0[c]	12
Benicia–Martinez	01/04/32	Pacific Greyhound	0[d]	12
Manor–Point Reyes	02/01/33	Pacific Greyhound	8[e]	10
San Francisco–Palo Alto	02/01/33	Pacific Greyhound	1	1
Sausalito–Belvedere–Tiburon	02/01/34	Pacific Greyhound	30[f]	30

Table 18. *Continued*

Route	Date of change	Company providing bus service	Trains off	Buses on
Los Angeles–Santa Paula	01/13/35	Pacific Greyhound	2	2

Source: SFC, exhibit 396.
[a] Ferry service replaced.
[b] Two of these trips operated only between Exeter and Hanford.
[c] Trains werererouted over new bridge, bypassing Benicia.
[d] Buses were rerouted to train connections at Martinez rather than Benicia.
[e] Northwestern Pacific trains (a wholly owned Southern Pacific subsidiary).
[f] Northwestern Pacific ferries.

Table 19. Passenger Train Traffic in the Vicinity of Santa Cruz and Salinas, August 1927

Train number	Route	Average daily passengers
29	Del Monte–Salinas	0.8
30	Del Monte–Salinas	2.0
31	Del Monte–Salinas	14.5
32	Del Monte–Salinas	1.5
106	Del Monte–Salinas	12.3
401	Santa Cruz–Davenport	28.2
406	Santa Cruz–Davenport	19.6
207	Del Monte Junction–Pacific Grove	7.1
209	Del Monte Junction–Pacific Grove	19.8
210	Del Monte Junction–Pacific Grove	50.4
212	Del Monte Junction–Pacific Grove	18.1
213	Del Monte Junction–Pacific Grove	37.7
214	Del Monte Junction–Pacific Grove	16.7
121	Santa Cruz–Watsonville	29.0
122	Santa Cruz–Watsonville	11.0
124	Santa Cruz–Watsonville	16.1
125	Santa Cruz–Watsonville	10.7
126	Santa Cruz–Watsonville	15.8
127	Santa Cruz–Watsonville	9.3

Source: 32 RCC 332

Table 20. California Intrastate and Interstate Rail Passenger Revenue Trends, Absolute and as a Percentage of State Income, 1911–1941

	Estimated state income			Intrastate		Interstate	
Year	Gross national product per capita (1)	California population in millions (2)	California income in millions (3)	Revenue in millions (4)	Revenue as % of income (5)	Revenue in millions (6)	Revenue as % of income (7)
1911	$382	2.5	$955	$15.30	1.58%	$8.6	0.89%
1912	413	2.7	1,115	15.80	1.43	8.5	0.77
1913	407	2.8	1,140	16.50	1.44	8.9	0.78
1914	389	2.9	1,128	15.30	1.34	8.4	0.74
1915	398	3.0	1,194	13.60	1.14	8.6	0.72
1916	473	3.1	1,466	14.10	0.97	11.0	0.76
1917	585	3.2	1,872	13.80	0.74	10.5	0.57
1918	740	3.3	2,442	15.50	0.64	12.9	0.53
1919	804	3.3	2,653	16.90	0.63	14.7	0.55
1920	860	3.6	3,096	20.80	0.68	19.2	0.63
1921	641	3.8	2,436	18.30	0.75	16.7	0.69
1922	673	4.0	2,692	16.80	0.63	15.7	0.58
1923	760	4.3	3,268	17.10	0.53	17.2	0.53
1924	742	4.5	3,339	15.10	0.45	15.5	0.46
1925	804	4.7	3,779	14.20	0.37	15.0	0.39
1926	826	4.9	4,047	13.60	0.33	14.7	0.36
1927	797	5.1	4,065	13.00	0.32	14.7	0.36
1928	805	5.3	4,267	12.00	0.28	14.0	0.33
1929	847	5.5	4,659	11.80	0.25	14.4	0.31
1930	734	5.7	4,184	10.20	0.24	12.3	0.29
1931	611	5.8	3,544	8.10	0.23	9.3	0.26
1932	465	5.9	2,744	5.40	0.20	6.0	0.22
1933	442	5.9	2,608	4.20	0.16	4.6	0.18
1934	514	6.1	3,135	4.30	0.14	5.0	0.16
1935	567	6.2	3,515	4.70	0.13	6.1	0.17
1936	643	6.3	4,051	5.30	0.13	7.5	0.18
1937	701	6.5	4,557	5.70	0.12	8.8	0.19
1938	651	6.7	4,362	5.40	0.12	8.3	0.19
1939	691	6.8	4,699	na	na	na	na
1940	754	7.0	5,278	na	na	na	na
1941	934	7.2	6,725	7.90	0.12	11.6	0.17

Sources: Column 1 is from U.S. Bureau of the Census, *Historical Statistics of the United States,* series F1–5. Column 2 is from California Department of Finance,

Table 20. *Continued*

California Statistical Abstract (Sacramento: 1961), 4. Column 3 is a conservative estimate of California state income. It is the U.S. gross national product per capita multiplied by California population. This assumes that California per capita income was the same as national income, but in 1929 California per capita personal income was 41% higher than that for the nation. See U.S. Bureau of the Census, *Historical Statistics of the United States,* series F297–348. Thus, the column likely understates California income while reflecting its growth trend. Columns 4 and 6 are from SFC, exhibit 629, and include statistics only for the Southern Pacific and the Santa Fe. I continued the series through 1941 by consulting CSA: Southern Pacific and Santa Fe annual reports to the California Railroad Commission. "Na" means that CSA did not have reports for those years.

Table 21. Southern Pacific Speed Comparisons, ca. 1930 vs. ca. 1940

	Ca. 1930		Ca. 1940	
Between	Average speed in miles per hour	Number of trains	Average speed in miles per hour	Number of trains
Oakland–Port Costa or Martinez	31.6	24		
Port Costa or Martinez–Tracy	34.8	6	43.4	4
Tracy or Lathrop–Fresno	35.8	5	40.4	4
Fresno–Bakersfield	39.0	4	44.8	4
Bakersfield–Mojave	26.4	6	30.6	6
Mojave–Saugus	27.3	4	33.1	4
Saugus–Burbank Junction			28.4	4
San Francisco–San Jose (limited trains)	44.4	5	48.0	6
San Francisco–San Jose (local trains)	33.1	30	33.4	12
San Jose–Watsonville Junction	36.9	9	47.7	8
Watsonville–San Ardo or King City	42.8	6	47.6	7
San Ardo or King City–San Luis Obispo	31.9	6	41.9	6
Santa Barbara–Burbank Junction	35.3	7	38.6	4
Oakland–Sacramento			41.7	14

Source: Derived from CRHM: Southern Pacific Company, employee timetables for various years and divisions.

Table 22. Productivity Consequences of Passenger Strategy of the Southern Pacific Company, Pacific Lines

Year	Train miles in 1,000s	Cars per train	Cost per train mile (deflated)	Average cost per car mile (deflated)	Revenue per car mile (deflated)	Resources needed to earn a dollar in revenue	Deflator
1927	22,156	7.5	$2.31	$0.31	$0.35	$0.89	0.982
1928							
1929	20,846	8.1	2.37	0.29	0.34	0.85	1.005
1930							
1931							
1932							
1933	12,462	7.8	2.62	0.34	0.30	1.10	0.811
1934							
1935	13,266	8.8	2.50	0.28	0.25	1.13	0.917
1936	16,458	8.9	2.20	0.25	0.22	1.12	0.957
1937	17,540	9.1	2.36	0.26	0.22	1.18	0.997
1938							
1939	14,133	10.5	2.54	0.24	0.22	1.09	1.024
1940							
1941	14,898	11.4	2.54	0.22	0.21	1.05	1.108

Sources: Costs are fully allocated passenger costs that I found in CSA and Southern Pacific Company: Annual Reports to the Interstate Commerce Commission. I divided them by train miles and car miles, found in the same sources. Revenues include passenger, passenger-related, and dining car revenues from the same sources. I adjusted these figures for changes in railroad wages, fuel, and materials, as shown in table 26.

Table 23. Ratio of Passenger Expenses to Passenger Revenues as Calculated by the ICC

Railroad	1932	1933	1934	1935	1936	1937	1938	1939	1940	1941
Major western lines										
Southern Pacific	109	110	107	112	112	118	119	109	117	105
Santa Fe	124	139	143	145	136	138	129	128	123	110
Union Pacific	116	107	115	126	129	128	126	132	128	128
Burlington	127	127	129	134	130	125	126	128	130	121
Northern Pacific	183	196	191	189	155	164	170	172	167	146
Great Northern	159	147	151	147	144	135	144	146	151	151
Major eastern lines										
Pennsylvania	100	104	104	106	102	103	98	101	104	99
New York Central	84	85	93	100	95	95	96	98	105	106
New Haven	77	84	85	87	80	82	86	82	85	84
Long Island	68	67	73	81	81	85	81	80	82	83

Source: HML: Records of the Pennsylvania Railroad, VP Operations, file 521.31, Post War Passenger Train Problems, 1943, Charles E. Smith to R. V. Fletcher, 1 September 1943. Ratios are taken from the ICC in a report that appears to have been published by the Association of American Railroads.

Table 24. Comparison of Fare Yield Trends by Region, 1922–1934 (Commuter Traffic Excluded)

	Regional fare yields (dollars per passenger mile)				
Year	Group 1	East	South	West	Intra-California
1922	$0.0355	$0.0349	$0.0347	$0.0334	$0.0300
1923	0.0355	0.0348	0.0349	0.0330	0.0290
1924	0.0355	0.0347	0.0347	0.0325	0.0280
1925	0.0358	0.0346	0.0344	0.0315	0.0280
1926	0.0356	0.0345	0.0348	0.0316	0.0270
1927	0.0358	0.0346	0.0340	0.0314	0.0260
1928	0.0358	0.0345	0.0337	0.0310	0.0260
1929	0.0358	0.0347	0.0332	0.0304	0.0250
1930	0.0359	0.0346	0.0329	0.0296	0.0240
1931	0.0346	0.0331	0.0308	0.0270	0.0200
1932	0.0317	0.0297	0.0243	0.0238	0.0180
1933	0.0286	0.0265	0.0192	0.0206	0.0170
1934	0.0280	0.0257	0.0176	0.0178	0.0150

Sources: PFS, exhibit 29; SFC, exhibits 67 and 568. Group 1 was a subset of eastern railroads, including the Pennsylvania, the New York Central, and the New York, New Haven & Hartford. These were the most important noncommuter passenger carriers in the region.

Table 25. Revenue per Train Mile of Principal Trains between Los Angeles and San Francisco, 1934–1941

		Year							
Row	Train	1934	1935	1936	1937	1938	1939	1940	1941
1	Daylight	$1.97	$2.34	$2.69	$4.61	$4.88	$5.40	$3.80	$3.98
2	Numbers 77–78	nt	nt	$0.74	$0.74	$0.74	$0.74	$0.74	$0.74
3	Noon Daylight	nt	nt	nt	nt	nt	nt	$3.11	$3.03
4	Lark	$3.31	$3.51	$3.52	$3.27	$3.52	$3.76	$3.22	$3.44
5	Sunset Limited	$2.90	$2.90	$2.90	$2.90	$2.90	$2.90	$2.90	$2.90
6	Owl	$1.48	$1.48	$1.48	$1.48	$1.48	$1.48	$1.48	$1.48
7	San Joaquin	$1.39	$1.56	$1.67	$1.52	$1.40	$1.33	$1.48	$2.54
8	Golden Gate	nt	nt	nt	nt	$0.88	$1.46	$1.49	$1.74
9	Golden Gate	nt	nt	nt	nt	$0.88	$1.46	$1.49	$1.74
10	Total	$11.05	$11.79	$13.00	$14.52	$16.68	$18.53	$19.71	$21.59
	(index, 1934=100)	100	107	118	131	151	168	178	195
11	LA-SF population (millions)	3.0	3.1	3.2	3.2	3.3	3.3	3.4	3.5
	(index, 1934=100)	100	103	107	107	110	110	113	117
12	Gross national product per capita	$514	$567	$643	$701	$651	$691	$754	$934
13	Regional income (billions)	$1.5	$1.8	$2.1	$2.2	$2.1	$2.3	$2.6	$3.3
	(index, 1934=100)	100	114	133	145	139	148	166	212

Sources: Rows 1, 3, 4, and 7 are from TWR, File 521-3, undated early post–World War II analysis of possible investment in new equipment for the *Sunset Limited*. The 1941 earnings for the *San Joaquin* reflect the last half of the year after streamlining. Those for the *Lark* represent the entire year, as streamlining had little effect on revenues. Rows 2, 5, and 6 represent averages of train mile earnings for 1936 and

Table 25. *Continued*

April 1938. The 1936 figures are presented in SFC, exhibits 816 and 839. The 1938 figures are from TWR, April 1938 train earnings for the Southern Pacific, Pacific Lines. The 1936 and 1938 earnings for the applicable trains are respectively: *77/78* $0.74 and $0.74; *Sunset Limited* (LA–SF only), $3.05 and $2.74; *Owl* $1.50 and $1.45. Row 9 is calculated from incremental intra-California Santa Fe passenger revenues and train miles for each year compared to 1937, with the assumption that San Joaquin Valley revenues were 70% of those for the Los Angeles to San Diego route. Revenues are derived from the CSA: Atchison, Topeka & Santa Fe Railway, *Annual Reports to the Railroad Commission*. Row 13, the estimated regional income of Los Angeles and San Francisco, is the combined populations multiplied by the U.S. gross national product per capita.
Note: "Nt" means no train.

Appendix

Table 26. Construction of Railroad Operating Cost Index, 1923–1941 (1926 = 1.00)

Year	Rail labor		Fuel		Iron steel		All other		Weighted price index (9)
	Price index (1)	Ratio of output (2)	Price index (3)	Ratio of output (4)	Price index (5)	Ratio of output (6)	Price index (7)	Ratio of output (8)	
1923	0.977	61.3	0.973	12.4	1.093	9.3	1.043	17.0	0.999
1924	0.975	62.6	0.920	10.2	1.063	7.9	0.997	19.3	0.981
1925	0.991	62.9	0.965	9.9	1.032	9.0	1.026	18.2	0.998
1926	1.000	63.0	1.000	9.9	1.000	10.6	1.000	16.5	1.000
1927	1.012	63.0	0.883	9.4	0.963	8.7	0.940	18.9	0.982
1928	1.031	63.7	0.843	8.5	0.970	8.3	0.929	19.5	0.990
1929	1.053	64.2	0.830	7.9	1.005	8.9	0.916	19.0	1.005
1930	1.036	64.8	0.785	7.7	0.921	7.6	0.852	19.9	0.971
1931	1.005	64.9	0.675	7.5	0.845	5.8	0.750	21.8	0.915
1932	0.885	62.9	0.703	7.3	0.802	3.9	0.702	25.9	0.821
1933	0.871	62.3	0.663	7.9	0.798	4.6	0.712	25.2	0.811
1934	0.910	62.1	0.733	8.8	0.864	6.1	0.784	23.0	0.863
1935	0.997	63.3	0.735	8.9	0.864	5.1	0.779	22.7	0.917
1936	1.047	63.0	0.762	9.1	0.870	8.0	0.796	19.9	0.957
1937	1.075	63.6	0.776	9.3	0.957	9.8	0.853	17.3	0.997
1938	1.122	64.1	0.765	8.8	0.957	4.6	0.817	22.5	1.014
1939	1.138	63.8	0.731	8.7	0.944	8.0	0.813	19.5	1.024
1940	1.157	63.6	0.717	8.7	0.958	8.4	0.830	19.3	1.039
1941	1.235	63.6	0.762	9.4	0.994	10.2	0.890	16.8	1.108

Sources: Column 1 is from table 28. Columns 2, 4, 6, and 8 are from table 27. Column 3 is from U.S. Bureau of the Census, *Historical Statistics of the United States*, series E46 and E29. Column 5 is from *Ibid.*, series E47. Column 7 is from *Ibid.*, series E41 and E23. Column 9 is an average of the indexes in the other columns, weighted by their respective contributions to output.

Table 27. Factor Inputs to Railroad Operating Expenses

Year	Total expenses, millions (1)	Labor amount, millions (2)	% (3)	Fuel amount, millions (4)	% (5)	Iron & steel amount, millions (6)	% (7)	Other % (8)
1923	$4,999	$3,062	61.3	$618	12.4	$465	9.3	17.0
1924	4,609	2,883	62.6	472	10.2	366	7.9	19.3
1925	4,633	2,916	62.9	459	9.9	419	9.0	18.2
1926	4,766	3,002	63.0	473	9.9	507	10.6	16.5
1927	4,663	2,963	63.0	439	9.4	407	8.7	18.9
1928	4,509	2,874	63.7	385	8.5	375	8.3	19.5
1929	4,579	2,940	64.2	364	7.9	407	8.9	19.0
1930	3,994	2,589	64.8	307	7.7	305	7.6	19.9
1931	3,274	2,125	64.9	245	7.5	189	5.8	21.8
1932	2,442	1,535	62.9	178	7.3	95	3.9	25.9
1933	2,285	1,424	62.3	181	7.9	104	4.6	25.2
1934	2,480	1,541	62.1	217	8.8	151	6.1	23.0
1935	2,630	1,666	63.3	233	8.9	135	5.1	22.7
1936	2,973	1,874	63.0	272	9.1	239	8.0	19.9
1937	3,165	2,014	63.6	294	9.3	311	9.8	17.3
1938	2,763	1,771	64.1	244	8.8	127	4.6	22.5
1939	2,959	1,889	63.8	257	8.7	236	8.0	19.5
1940	3,132	1,991	63.6	274	8.7	264	8.4	19.3
1941	3,710	2,360	63.6	350	9.4	380	10.2	16.8

Sources: Columns 1 and 2 are from U.S. Bureau of the Census, *Historical Statistics of the United States,* series Q367 and Q399. Columns 4 and 6 are from *Ibid.,* series Q395 and Q397.

Note: The values in column 8 are 100% minus the values in columns 3, 5, and 7.

Table 28. Computation of Railroad Labor Price Index

Year	Rail workers, 1,000s (1)	Total wages, millions (2)	Wage per worker (3)	Index based on 1926 (4)
1923	1,902	$3,062	$1,610	0.977
1924	1,795	2,883	1,606	0.975
1925	1,786	2,916	1,633	0.991
1926	1,822	3,002	1,648	1.000
1927	1,776	2,963	1,668	1.012
1928	1,692	2,874	1,699	1.031
1929	1,694	2,940	1,736	1.053
1930	1,517	2,589	1,707	1.036
1931	1,283	2,125	1,656	1.005
1932	1,052	1,535	1,459	0.885
1933	991	1,424	1,436	0.871
1934	1,027	1,541	1,500	0.910
1935	1,014	1,666	1,643	0.997
1936	1,086	1,874	1,726	1.047
1937	1,137	2,014	1,771	1.075
1938	958	1,771	1,849	1.122
1939	1,007	1,889	1,876	1.138
1940	1,046	1,991	1,903	1.157
1941	1,159	2,360	2,036	1.235

Sources: Columns 1 and 2 are from U.S. Bureau of the Census, *Historical Statistics of the United States,* series Q398 and Q399. Column 3 figures are those from column 2 divided by those from column 1. The index is the wage for a given year divided by the wage for 1926.

Notes

Preface

1. This view prevails among scholars of transportation policy. See Alan Altshuler, *The Urban Transportation System: Politics and Policy Innovation* (Cambridge, MA: MIT Press, 1979); James A. Dunn, Jr., *Miles to Go: European and American Transportation Policies* (Cambridge, MA: MIT Press, 1981); John Pucher, "Urban Travel Behavior as the Outcome of Public Policy: The Example of Modal-Split in Western Europe and North America," *Journal of the American Planning Association* 54 (1988), 509–520.

2. Leonard Rapport, "No Grandfather Clause: Reappraising Accessioned Records," *American Archivist* 44 (Spring 1981), 143–150; Rapport, "The Interstate Commerce Commission Formal Case Files: A Source for Local History," *American Archivist* 15 (Winter 1983), 229–242; Rapport, "In the Valley of Decision: What to Do about the Multitude of Files of Quasi Cases," *American Archivist* 48 (Spring 1985), 173–189. For a rebuttal, see Karen Benedict, "Invitation to a Bonfire: Reappraisal and Deaccessioning of Records as Collection Management Tools in an Archives—A Reply to Leonard Rapport," *American Archivist* 47 (Winter 1984), 43–49. See also page 3 of the same issue for the editor's comment, "Leonard Rapport truly broke new ground in his article." I also spoke with Mr. Rapport on these topics in August 1983 and on 13 February and 28 February 1988. I gratefully acknowledge his willingness to share his perspective with me on case files.

3. Rapport, "Interstate Commerce Commission Case Files," 229–231; Rapport, "In the Valley of Decision," 176–178. The structure of the case file comes from my own reading of four ICC and three California Railroad Commission case files.

4. SFC. The public and some railroad executives referred to the Atchison, Topeka & Santa Fe Railway as the "Santa Fe," although some railroaders referred to it as the "Atchison." I follow the popular convention and use "Santa Fe" or "Santa Fe Railway."

5. Clyde H. Freed, *The Story of Railroad Passenger Fares* (Washington, DC: Clyde H. Freed, 1942). The Interstate Commerce Commission case files that I researched, some only in part, include FPC, PFS, PPS, and WPF.

Introduction

1. Alfred D. Chandler, Jr., *The Visible Hand: The Managerial Revolution in American Business* (Cambridge, MA: Harvard University Press, 1977), chapter 3.

2. For an overview of the historiography of the rise of big business see Glenn Porter, *The Rise of Big Business, 1860–1910* (Arlington Heights, IL: Harlan Davidson, 1973), 102–111, and specifically on the new synthesis, pages 109–111.

3. George W. Hilton, *Amtrak: The National Railroad Passenger Corporation* (Washington, DC: American Enterprise Institute for Public Policy Research, 1980),

1–14; John R. Meyer and Clinton V. Oster, Jr., *Deregulation and the Future of Intercity Passenger Travel* (Cambridge, MA: MIT Press, 1987), 161–166.

4. Thomas C. Cochran, *Railroad Leaders, 1845–1890* (New York: Russell & Russell, 1966), chapter 6 and pages 126, 135, 147, 150. See also Cochran, *Business in American Life: A History* (New York: McGraw-Hill, 1972); Cochran, *200 Years of American Business* (New York: Dell, 1977), in particular pages xiii-xvi. For an example of subsequent histories centered on this concept, see James J. Flink, *The Automobile Age* (Cambridge, MA: MIT Press, 1988).

5. Stephen Salsbury, *No Way to Run a Railroad: The Untold Story of the Penn Central Crisis* (New York: McGraw-Hill, 1982), 10–11, 13, 35, 50–54, 189; Flink, *The Automobile Age*.

6. Jack Simmons, *The Railway in England and Wales, 1830–1914: Vol. 1, The System and Its Working* (Leicester: Leicester University Press, 1978), 111.

7. Albro Martin, *Enterprise Denied: Origins of the Decline of American Railroads, 1897–1917* (New York: Columbia University Press, 1971).

8. Bradford Snell, *American Ground Transport: Testimony to Subcommittee on Anti-Trust and Monopoly of the Committee on Judiciary, United States Senate* (Washington, DC: Government Printing Office, 1974), 29.

Chapter 1

1. U.S. Department of Commerce, Bureau of the Census, *Census of Manufacturers* (Washington, DC: Government Printing Office, 1914), 79–85.

2. Fred Matthews, *Northern California Railroads: The Silver Age*, vol. 1 (Denver: Sundance Books, 1983), 9.

3. Albro Martin, *Enterprise Denied: Origins of the Decline of American Railroads, 1897–1917* (New York: Columbia University Press, 1971). See also Maury Klein, *Union Pacific: The Rebirth, 1894–1969* (New York: Doubleday, 1989), 48–68.

4. Jack Simmons, *The Railway in England and Wales, 1830–1914: Vol. 1, The System and Its Working* (Leicester: Leicester University Press, 1978), 56, 58, 91. Simmons observes that after knowledge of the potential accessibility benefits of railways became widespread, communities and individuals believed they had a right to such advantages. However, because of profitability considerations, private railroads could not serve all areas and individuals equally, which gave rise to a tension between the demands of the public and the abilities of railways to serve those demands. The tension could produce extreme geographically based hatred toward particular railroads, notably the hatred shown by Hull toward North Eastern.

5. Edmund S. Morgan, *American Slavery, American Freedom* (New York: W. W. Norton, 1975), 218–220, 278–279, 361; Merritt Roe Smith, *Harper's Ferry Armory and the New Technology: The Challenge of Change* (Ithaca: Cornell University Press, 1977), 26–33. See also Thomas C. Cochran, *Business in American Life: A History* (New York: McGraw-Hill, 1972), 14, 21, 26.

6. Sam Bass Warner, Jr., *The Urban Wilderness* (New York: Harper & Row, 1972), 15–34, 46–66; Thomas C. Cochran, *200 Years of American Business* (New York: Dell, 1977), 29.

7. Cochran, *200 Years*, 91, 95, 128, 200; Cochran, *Business in American Life*, 67; Robert R. Dykstra, *The Cattle Towns* (Lincoln: University of Nebraska Press, 1968), 3–5.

8. John R. Logan and Harvey L. Molotch, *Urban Fortunes: The Political Economy of Place* (Berkeley: University of California Press, 1987), 50–98.

9. Stuart Daggett, *Chapters on the History of the Southern Pacific* (New York: Augustus M. Kelley, 1966; first published 1922), 1–49; Ward McAfee, *California's Railroad Era, 1850–1911* (San Marino, CA: Golden West Books, 1973), 1–68.

10. Michael W. Donley, Stuart Allan, Patricia Caro, Clyde P. Patton, *Atlas of California* (Culver City: Pacific Book Center, 1979), 17–27; John L. Andriot, *Population Abstract of the United States*, vol. 1 (McLean, VA: Andriot Associates, 1983), 59–72; California Department of Finance, *California Statistical Abstract, 1961*, table F-2.

11. McAfee, *California's Railroad Era*, 67–108; Daggett, *Chapters on the History of the Southern Pacific*, 49, 83–103.

12. The discussion over the next several paragraphs on management views of their cost structures and the impact of these views on rate practices is summarized from Gregory L. Thompson, "Misused Product Costing in the American Railroad Industry: Southern Pacific Passenger Service between the Wars," *Business History Review* 63 (1989), 510–554, and Thompson, "Myth and Rationality in Management Decision-Making: The Evolution of American Railroad Product Costing, 1870–1970," *Journal of Transport History* 12 (1991), 1–10.

13. Alfred D. Chandler, Jr., *Henry Varnum Poor* (Cambridge, MA: Harvard University Press, 1956), 118–119; J. Shirley Eaton, *Railroad Operations: How to Know Them from a Study of the Accounts and Statistics* (New York: Railroad Gazette, 1900), 282–284; Emory R. Johnson, *American Railway Transportation* (New York: D. Appleton, 1912), 222; Isaiah Leo Sharfman, *The Interstate Commerce Commission: A Study in Administrative Law and Procedure* (New York: Commonwealth Fund, 1931–1937), vol. 3B, 316–317.

14. Alfred D. Chandler, Jr., *The Visible Hand: The Managerial Revolution in American Business* (Cambridge, MA: Harvard University Press, 1977), 134.

15. Stephen Salsbury, *The State, the Investor and the Railroad* (Cambridge, MA: Harvard University Press, 1967), 64–68 and chapter 10; Thomas C. Cochran, *Railroad Leaders, 1845–1890* (New York: Russell & Russell, 1965), 152–161. A respected contemporary source on the workings of the rate system ca. 1900 is provided by Henry Carter Adams, the economist and statistician of the Interstate Commerce Commission, whose analysis is summarized in Martin, *Enterprise Denied*, 38–45.

16. Daggett, *Chapters on the History of the Southern Pacific*, 222, 236–250. Chapter 15 offers a detailed analysis of the workings of such a system in California.

17. McAfee, *California's Railroad Era*, 104; McAfee, "Local Interests and Railroad Regulation in California during the Granger Decade," *Pacific Historical Review* 37 (1968), 51–66; Daggett, *Chapters on the History of the Southern Pacific*, 273, 277, 281.

18. The Associates built many of their extensions under different corporate organizations, one being the Southern Pacific Railroad.

19. Daggett, *Chapters on the History of the Southern Pacific*, 40–44, 182.

20. The Central Pacific rails extended to Goshen Junction near Visalia; Southern Pacific rails extended from there to the south.

21. Carey McWilliams, *Southern California: An Island on the Land* (Santa Barbara: Peregrine Smith, 1979), 113–118.

22. McAfee, *California's Railroad Era*, 121–127, 181–183; McAfee, "Local Interests and Railroad Regulation in California"; Daggett, *Chapters on the History*

of the Southern Pacific, 237–292. The population of Los Angeles County stood at 3,530 in 1850 and 11,333 in 1860. It grew to 15,309 in 1870 and 33,381 in 1880. McWilliams implies that the more heady growth rate of the 1870s was well established before the Southern Pacific arrived in 1876. McWilliams, *Southern California*, 113–118. For the population figures, see Andriot, *Population Abstract of the United States*, 59–72.

23. William L. Preston, *Vanishing Landscapes: Land and Life in the Tulare Lake Basin* (Berkeley: University of California Press, 1981), 90–136. For population growth of individual counties and towns, see Andriot, *Population Abstract of the United States*, 59–72. All of the San Joaquin Valley counties contained 22,109 people in 1860 and 44,150 people in 1870. The population grew to 65,116 by 1880, less than half the growth rate of the previous decade.

24. The combined populations of San Francisco, Alameda, and Contra Costa counties stood at 71,057, 182,171, and 309,478 people in 1860, 1870, and 1880, respectively. Andriot, *Population Abstract of the United States*, 59–72.

25. Daggett, *Chapters on the History of the Southern Pacific*, 27, 271–272; quote is on page 290.

26. Ward M. McAfee, "A Constitutional History of Railroad Rate Regulation in California, 1879–1911," *Pacific Historical Review* 37 (1968); McAfee, *California's Railroad Era*, 197–207; McAfee, "Local Interests and Railroad Regulation in California," 51–66.

27. Mansel S. Blackford, *The Politics of Business in California, 1890–1920* (Columbus: Ohio State University Press, 1977), 78–95.

28. McAfee, "Constitutional History of Railroad Rate Regulation," 265–279; Daggett, *Chapters on the History of the Southern Pacific*, 181–198.

29. Keith L. Bryant, Jr., *History of the Atchison, Topeka and Santa Fe Railway* (New York: Macmillan, 1974), 100–105, 173–181; Daggert, *Chapters on the History of the Southern Pacific*, 273. The Atchison, Topeka & Santa Fe Railroad was reorganized as the Atchison, Topeka & Santa Fe Railway in the 1890s.

30. The population of Los Angeles County increased from 33,381 in 1880 to 101,454 in 1890. See Andriot, *Population Abstract of the United States*, 59–72. McWilliams implies that most of the growth took place between 1887 and 1890. McWilliams, *Southern California*, 118–128, 147, 150–154.

31. William F. Deverell, "The Los Angeles 'Free Harbor Fight,' " *California History* 70 (Spring 1991), 12–29. Maury Klein, *Union Pacific*, 113–118; John R. Signor, *The Los Angeles and Salt Lake Railroad Company* (San Marino: Golden West Books, 1988), 11–35.

32. Ibid.

33. McWilliams, *Southern California*, 122–128, 134, 187–204, 274; William A. Myers, *Iron Men and Copper Wires* (Glendale, CA: Trans-Anglo Books, 1983), 22–30, 38–39, 47, 79, 110, 140–149.

34. McWilliams, *Southern California*, 128, 134, 274.

35. Daggett, *Chapters on the History of the Southern Pacific*, 281, 283, 300.

36. CRHM: Passenger times are from *Official Guide*, June 1915. The freight time is from Southern Pacific Company, *Employees Timetable, San Joaquin Division*, 12 February 1922. Passenger and freight times in 1893 would have been no shorter than these times, and almost certainly considerably longer. McAfee, *California's Railroad Era*, 202; Daggett, *Chapters on the History of the Southern Pacific*, 324.

37. McAfee, *California's Railroad Era,* 197–207; Daggett, *Chapters on the History of the Southern Pacific,* 340–346.

38. After the Santa Fe took control of the Santa Fe & San Joaquin, it agreed with the Southern Pacific to restore local valley rates to their old levels. See Daggett, *Chapters on the History of the Southern Pacific,* 340–346; McAfee, "Constitutional History of Railroad Rate Regulation," 265–279. However, lower rates remained in effect to Los Angeles and to eastern points. See Blackford, *Politics of Business in California,* 3–12.

39. Daggett, *Chapters on the History of the Southern Pacific,* 238, 270–286; Carey McWilliams, *Factories in the Field* (Santa Barbara: Peregrine Smith, 1978), 3–10, 48–65; Blackford, *Politics of Business in California,* 3–12; Preston, *Vanishing Landscapes,* 133–135, 146–150, 159, 162–163, and particularly page 167. The population of the valley counties grew from 113,000 in 1890 to 143,000 in 1900. In 1910 the population of the same counties stood at 262,000. See Andriot, *Population Abstract of the United States,* 59–72.

40. The 36 percent rural figure was emphasized in U.S. Bureau of Public Roads, *Study of California Highway System* (Washington, DC: 1920), 120. U.S. Department of Commerce, Bureau of the Census, *Special Reports of the U.S. Census: Manufacturers, Part 2, States and Territories, 1905* (Washington, DC: Government Printing Office, 1907), 56–65; Bureau of Census, *Census of Manufacturers, 1914,* 79–80. In 1914 railroad and streetcar repair shops were included in the top ten industrial employers. Using 1910 census data showing employment by category for both the United States and California, I performed a location quotient analysis of California's employment. Bureau of the Census, *Historical Statistics of the United States, Colonial Times to 1970* (Washington, DC: Government Printing Office, 1975), series F297–348. Only three areas had higher incomes: the District of Columbia at $1,292, New York at $1,164, and Delaware at $1,037.

41. CRHM: Annual Reports of the Southern Pacific Company and Proprietary Companies, 1899–1914. See the "Forty-Third Annual Report of the Southern Pacific Lines and Affiliated Companies, Year Ended 31 December 1926," 31, for a summary of passenger trends between 1885 and 1926. In 1899, Southern Pacific carried 540 million passenger miles and 3.5 billion ton miles; this increased to 1,640 million passenger miles and 6.6 billion ton miles in 1910. The average trip length of nonsuburban passengers was seventy-one miles in both 1899 and 1914. The high point was eighty-six miles in 1906.

42. National figures are from the U.S. Office of the Federal Coordinator of Transportation, *Passenger Traffic Report* (Washington, DC: 1935), 111. State figures are from SFC, exhibits 629 and 630; transcript, 11600–11603. In 1911 the average Californian spent $6.02 for intrastate travel on just Southern Pacific and Santa Fe. There was another significant intrastate rail passenger carrier, the Northwestern Pacific. I do not know what its noncommute revenues were, but they could have been as high as $1.00 per capita in 1911. In addition, one must estimate expenditures Californians made for interstate rail travel. While this figure was not reported to the California Railroad Commission, railroads did report a suitable proxy. This was total rail passenger revenue from California stations less intrastate revenue, which in 1911 for the Southern Pacific and Santa Fe amounted to about $3.41 per capita. Many non-Californians would have contributed to these revenues. On the other hand, many Californians returning from out of state would have bought tickets at non-California stations, and these revenues are not included. I assume that the two errors roughly cancel each other. Thus, we have known expenditures per capita for intercity rail in California in 1911 in the amount of $9.43, plus an unknown amount for the Northwestern Pacific. In addition there are unknown intercity revenues from Californians riding the other two interstate carriers, the Union Pacific and Western Pacific.

43. Klein, *Union Pacific,* 122.

44. Klein, *Union Pacific,* 87–88, 121–132. See George Kennan, *E. H. Harriman,* vol. I (Boston: Houghton Mifflin, 1922), 234, for a figure in 1900 of about 2 million shares of Southern Pacific stock outstanding with a market value of about $100 million. On page 242 Kennan states that the Southern Pacific's funded debt was nearly $350 million in 1900. See pages 257–258 for investment summary.

45. Blackford, *Politics of Business in California,* 1–12.

46. Electric train miles are derived from 1919 headways given for each route for different times of the day, and the route lengths as found in Robert S. Ford, *Red Trains in the East Bay* (Glendale, CA: Interurbans Press, 1977), 151, 327–332. All other figures are derived from the 1915 Southern Pacific system timetable (in author's collection) by multiplying the annual runs of each train by the distance that it traveled on each run. I classified through trains as those traveling more than three hundred miles without local stops.

47. SFC, exhibit 112.

48. The schematic actually understates the volume of local service, for it leaves out service on the Santa Fe, whose network of branch lines in the valley by this time, while not as extensive as the Southern Pacific's, still provided intense competition. It also neglects electric interurban trains of the Visalia Electric, the Tidewater Southern between Modesto and Stockton, and the Central California Traction between Stockton and Sacramento.

49. Tulare County Library: "Visalia Electric Railroad Modernized By Removal Of Overhead Lines, Replaced By Diesel-Electric Engines After 40 Years," Exeter *Sun,* 23 November 1944.

50. The January–February 1915 Southern Pacific system timetable (in author's collection) is the basis of this analysis. I calculated the average speed of every steam train operated by the Southern Pacific Company, Pacific System.

51. Daggett, *Chapters on the History of the Southern Pacific,* 347–354; see also Klein, *Union Pacific,* 122–123.

52. Blackford, *Politics of Business in California,* 78–95; McAfee, *California's Railroad Era,* 197–207.

53. "Incomplete Returns Show Johnson Carrying Entire State Ticket and Control of Legislature," *New York Times,* 18 August 1910, 3:3; Gerald D. Nash, *State Government and Economic Development: A History of Administrative Policies in California, 1849–1933* (Berkeley: University of California, Institute of Governmental Studies, 1964), 254–255; Spencer C. Olin, Jr., *California's Prodigal Sons: Hiram Johnson and the Progressives, 1911–1917* (Berkeley: University of California Press, 1968), 22–29.

54. Franklin Hichborn, *Story of the Session of the California Legislature of 1911* (San Francisco: James H. Barry, 1911). Hichborn's account of the 1911 legislature gloats over the defeat of the Southern Pacific forces, commenting from time to time how previous leaders of the legislature who were known as railroad men could be seen lurking around the halls at times of crucial votes, but how they did not appear to utilize their remaining influence.

55. Hichborn, *Story of the 1911 Legislature,* 147–151; Nash, *State Government*

and Economic Development, 256–259; McAfee, *California's Railroad Era*, 221–228; California Railroad Commission, *Annual Report of the Railroad Commission of the State of California*, 1 January 1911 to 30 June 1912 (San Francisco: California Railroad Commission, 1912), 6–17.

56. Martin, *Enterprise Denied;* this view also is contained in Stephen Skowronek, *Building a New American State: The Expansion of National Administrative Capacities, 1877–1920* (Cambridge: Cambridge University Press, 1982), 248–284. This was considered the railroad argument during the Progressive period, but by the early 1920s it was generally accepted by those critical of private railroad management. See William J. Cunningham, *American Railroads: Government Control and Reconstruction Policies* (New York: A. W. Shaw, 1922), 9–22; William G. McAdoo, *Crowded Years: The Reminiscences of William G. McAdoo* (Boston: Houghton Mifflin, 1931), 111, 223, 303, 455–462; Ari and Olive Hoogenboom, *A History of the ICC: From Panacea to Palliative* (New York: W. W. Norton, 1976), 91; Claude Moore Fuess, *Joseph B. Eastman: Servant of the People* (New York: Columbia University Press, 1952), 84, 87–88, 312–313; Earl Latham, *The Politics of Railroad Coordination, 1933–1936* (Cambridge, MA: Harvard University Press, 1959), vii–viii.

57. Daggett, *Chapters on the History of the Southern Pacific*, 347–354; Klein, *Union Pacific*, 122.

58. Blackford, *Politics of Business in California*, 78–95.

59. Ford, *Red Trains in the East Bay*, 142–143.

60. Hichborn, *Story of the 1911 Legislature*, 230–231; CRHM: Southern Pacific Company, "Annual Report to Stockholders, Year Ended 30 June 1912," 9.

61. Ford, *Red Trains in the East Bay*, 144–146.

62. Don L. Hofsommer, *The Southern Pacific, 1901–1985* (College Station: Texas A&M University Press, 1986), chapter 6. See also Klein, *Union Pacific*, 247–249; Portland Public Library: Arthur C. Spencer, *Address: The Southern Pacific–Central Pacific Dissolution Case, and Its Bearing on Oregon Transportation*, 5 July 1922, 2, 7; Kennan, *Harriman*, 280–281, 292–294; Daggett, *Chapters on the History of the Southern Pacific*, 430–436.

63. George W. Hilton and John F. Due, *The Electric Interurban Railways in America* (Stanford, CA: Stanford University Press, 1960), 398–406.

64. Giles T. Brown, *Ships That Sail No More: Maritime Transportation from San Diego to Puget Sound, 1910–1940* (Lexington: University of Kentucky Press, 1966). Brown's sources are reports on Section 4 ICC cases, opinions and orders from the California Railroad Commission, and quoted railroad officer statements from West Coast newspapers.

65. Klein, *Union Pacific*, 259–260.

66. 165 ICC 379; Brown, *Ships That Sail No More*, 8–11, 226–227.

67. Nash, *State Government and Economic Development*, 221–223; CALTRANS: William H. Boudier, *The Paths of Humanity: A Chronicle of California Highway Development* (Sacramento: California Division of Highways, 1966), 3; U.S. Bureau of Public Roads, *Study of California Highway System*, 13–15, 143.

68. This was the Savage Act of 1907. See Nash, *State Government and Economic Development*, 328–329; Boudier, *Paths of Humanity*, 3–4.

69. Nash, *State Government and Economic Development*, 329; U.S. Bureau of Public Roads, *Study of California Highway System*, 14.

70. U.S. Bureau of Public Roads, *Study of California Highway System*, 143; Boudier, *Paths of Humanity*, 8.

71. California Secretary of State, *Statement of Vote, 1910* (Sacramento: 1910), 26.

72. James J. Flink, *America Adopts the Automobile, 1895–1910* (Cambridge, MA: MIT Press, 1970), 212.

73. Bruce E. Seely, *Building the American Highway System: Engineers as Policy Makers* (Philadelphia: Temple University Press, 1987), 18, 96, 102, 131. Seely claims that initial interest in roads centered on connecting farms with local markets. Interest in through roads did not develop until the 1920s. This assessment is wrong for the California state highway system, where the main emphasis of the 1909 plan was on intercity roads paralleling the railroads. Counties may have championed farm-to-market roads, however.

74. California Highway Commission, *Biennial Report of the Highway Commission, 1917–18* (Sacramento, n.d.), 9, 70; ACSC: *Touring Topics* 7/3 (1919), 20–21; CALTRANS: *California Highways and Public Works* 8 (1924), 3–4; ACSC: *Joint Review of Detailed Engineering Reports of the Automobile Club of Southern California and California State Automobile Association on the California State Highways*, part 1 (Los Angeles: 1921),16; *California Blue Book* (1911), 459.

75. ACSC: *Joint Engineering Report*, part 1, 19, 21, 24; Part 2, 18, 99–100.

76. CALTRANS: "Controversies over Highway Routes Reviewed," *California Highway Bulletin* 1 (1913), 7–11.

77. ACSC: *Touring Topics* 11 (1915), 7–9; California Senate and Assembly, "Report of the Department of Engineering, 1914–1916: Part 3, Roads and Highways," *Appendix to Journals of Senate and Assembly, Forty-Second Session, 1917*, vol. 5 (Sacramento: State Printing Office, 1917), 198; Myers, *Iron Men and Copper Wires*, 46.

78. U.S. Bureau of Public Roads, *Study of California Highway System*, 56, 143; CALTRANS: *California Highways and Public Works* 8 (1924), 3–4.

79. Ibid.

80. ACSC: *Touring Topics* 6 (1914), 8.

81. Letter from Peggy Wickman Bogan of Glenview, IL, to Gregory L. Thompson, 1 August 1985, covering two short histories of the Greyhound Corporation. Neither histories were dated; one appears to be from the late 1930s and was written by Carl L. Colreg or Correg (the name is not clear); the other is unsigned and appears to be from the early 1950s. For incorporation of the story into histories of the Greyhound Corporation, see Carlton Jackson, *Hounds of the Road: A History of the Greyhound Bus Company* (Bowling Green, Ohio: Bowling Green University Press, 1984), 7–10; Oscar Schisgall, *The Greyhound Story: From Hibbing to Everywhere* (Chicago: J. G. Ferguson, 1985), 3–5.

82. Albert E. Meier and John P. Hoschek, *Over the Road: A History of Intercity Bus Transportation in the United States* (Upper Montclair, NJ: Motor Bus Society, 1975).

83. SFC, transcript, 6753; exhibit 328.

84. SFC, transcript, 423.

85. Burton B. Crandall, *The Growth of the Intercity Bus Industry* (Syracuse, NY: Syracuse University, College of Business Administration, 1954), 11–15.

86. SFC, transcript, 6755. Even as late as the early 1920s, timetable folders of the larger systems, such as Pickwick, showed service on almost every important state and county road.

87. 8 RCC 190, 220.

88. SFC, transcript, 6753; exhibit 328.
89. Nash, *State Government and Economic Development*, 267.
90. Crandall, *Growth of the Intercity Bus Industry*, 14–15, 43; SFC, transcript, 6750–6765, 6808–6809.
91. Crandall, *Growth of the Intercity Bus Industry*, 14–15, 38–39, 93–94, 267; SFC, transcript, 6750–6765, 6808–6809. The decision was "Buck v. Kuykendall," 267 U.S. 307, 1925.
92. Buck Travis testified on the industry's transformation. He did not place a date on the beginning of the loss of traffic, but he testified that the initial merger movement began as a consequence of the traffic decline. That movement started about 1917. The earliest large system to form was Pickwick Stages, which began to take shape in 1917 (SFC, transcript, 6758–6759; exhibit 325).
93. SFC, transcript, 6760–6767, 6803–6804, 6808–6809, 6850; SFC, *Brief of Applicant and of the Atchison, Topeka & Santa Fe Railway*, 11–12; Crandall, *Growth of the Intercity Bus Industry*, 91, 135, 150, 267.
94. SFC, transcript, 6751. See also 6846–6849.
95. SFC, transcript, 6571, 6752–6755; Kimball, interviews with Thompson and Seal, St. Helena, CA, 29 September 1984, and with Thompson, 19 May 1985. Kimball, who was a protege of Fred Ackerman, Travis's closest associate, described Travis's youth in Nevada. He said that Travis was sent to Harvard to knock off the rough edges, but the effort was generally considered to have been a failure. Travis distinguished himself in football while at school, according to Kimball. See also Meier and Hoschek, *Over the Road*, 11–12.
96. These included Pickwick Stages operating in two divisions, the Star Auto Stage Association (soon to be incorporated as the California Transit Company), Valley Transit, United Stages, Motor Transit, West Coast Transit, and Western Motor Transportation Company.
97. U.S. Bureau of Public Roads, *Study of California Highway System*, 129–133.

Chapter 2

1. Thomas C. Cochran, *Railroad Leaders, 1845–1890* (New York: Russell & Russell, 1965); Alfred D. Chandler, Jr., *The Visible Hand: The Managerial Revolution in American Business* (Cambridge, MA: Harvard University Press, 1977).
2. Glenn Porter, "The Corporate Culture of the Pennsylvania Railroad, 1846–1896," paper presented at the Coloquio Internacional Sobre Transporte E Industrializacion, Siglos XIX y XX, Fundacion de los Ferrocarriles Espanoles, Palacio de Fernan Nunez, Madrid, Spain, 18–20 January 1990.
3. Seminar given at the Hagley Museum and Library by Maury Klein, January 1987.
4. CRHM: Southern Pacific *Bulletin* (April 1921), 3.
5. SFC, transcript, 627, 2295, 11126–11127, 14834–14841.
6. CRHM: Southern Pacific *Bulletin* (April 1921), 6.
7. CRHM: Southern Pacific *Bulletin* (April 1921), 6; (December 1921), 13–14; (April 1924), 8–10, 22; (October 1935), 10–11.
8. TWR: see, for example, Shasta Route file, memorandum from M. J. Wise to A. D. McDonald, 8 August 1935.

9. Chandler, *The Visible Hand,* chapter 3 and in particular pages 94–109. See also Chandler, *Henry Varnum Poor* (Cambridge, MA: Harvard University Press, 1956); Emory R. Johnson, *American Railway Transportation* (New York: D. Appleton, 1912), 184–193.

10. Chandler, *The Visible Hand,* 109, 115–117, 267–268, 277–279, 464–465.

11. Harold Livesay, "Entrepreneurial Persistence through the Bureaucratic Age," in Richard S. Tedlow and Richard R. John, eds., *Managing Big Business* (Boston: Harvard Business School Press, 1987), 116.

12. Chandler, *The Visible Hand,* 115–117.

13. Ibid.

14. HML: Pennsylvania Railroad Collection, Organization of Transportation Officers, Report No. 547, H. M. Carson and R. N. Durborow, "Confidential Report of a Trip over the Union Pacific Railroad," 6–21 November 1908, 12–15.

15. BL: Southern Pacific Company, *Student Course in Railroading* (San Francisco, 1914).

16. Chandler, *The Visible Hand,* 386, 431–450.

17. Dwight R. Ladd, *Cost Data for the Management of Railroad Passenger Service* (Boston: Harvard University, Graduate School of Business Administration, Division of Research, 1957), 9. Ladd's study pertains to the 1950s, but he indicates that the structures he described had been in place for decades.

18. CRHM: Southern Pacific *Bulletin* (April 1921), 3–6, 13; BL: Southern Pacific Company, *Student Course in Railroading,* 27; SFC, transcript, 2640, 2644, 2652, 2655, 2660.

19. Revenue and train mile data for each train on the Southern Pacific were listed in a regular report compiled monthly by the accounting department based upon a seven-day sample. See SFC, transcript, 16931–16933. Both the Southern Pacific and the Santa Fe cited revenues per train mile for particular trains from before World War I, indicating such figures were kept at that time. In the early 1930s origin-destination traffic and revenue data in the U.S. Office of the Federal Coordinator of Transportation, *Passenger Traffic Report* (Washington, DC, 1935), were compiled from records of one-way and round-trip ticket sales. For the method used, see PFS, testimony of report statistician Arthur White, transcript, 1568–1604.

20. SFC, transcript, 627, 2295, 11126–11127, 14834–14841.

21. *Who's Who in America* 23 (Chicago: Marquis, 1944–45), 1410; CRHM: Southern Pacific *Bulletin* (April 1921), 6.

22. PPS, transcript, 1112, 1212, 1833–1883, 1949–1954, 2178.

23. According to Pullman Company records, the four largest users of its sleeping cars in 1923 were the Pennsylvania Railroad, the New York Central, the Southern Pacific, and the Santa Fe, assigned 838, 821, 455, and 378 cars, respectively. In addition, the El Paso & Southwestern, which was absorbed into the Southern Pacific the next year, was assigned another 18 cars. See PPS, unmarked exhibit titled "The Pullman Company, Response to Request of Commissioner J. B. Campbell. Statement Showing By Specified Geographic Regions and Individual Railroads: (1) Average Number of Pullman Cars Operated; (2) Pullman Contract Revenue Due Railroads; (3) Average Contract Revenue Per Car Operated; (4) Number of Pullman Car Miles Run; (5) Average Mileage Per Car; (6) Average Contract Revenue Per Car Mile. For the Calendar Year 1923," 1–4.

24. Albert Fishlow, "Productivity and Technological Change in the Railroad Sector, 1840–1910," in Conference on Research in Income and Wealth, *Output,*

Employment and Productivity in the United States after 1800 (New York: National Bureau of Economic Research, 1966), 626–630. For sources of productivity improvement, see pages 634–641.

25. Albro Martin, *Enterprise Denied: Origins of the Decline of American Railroads, 1897–1917* (New York: Columbia University Press, 1971). See the appendix and passim for a summary of the argument on railroad investments declining in relation to need over the decade. By the early 1920s, this argument was generally accepted, even by influential people critical of private railroad management, including William Cunningham, William McAdoo, and Joseph Eastman. Cunningham, a Harvard economics professor, took a leave of absence to work as an officer in the United States Railroad Administration and believed that on the whole, government operation of the railroads was beneficial. McAdoo, secretary of the treasury under President Woodrow Wilson as well as Wilson's son-in-law, served as the first director general of the railroads. Eastman, a protege of Louis Brandeis, served on the Interstate Commerce Commission from 1919 until his death in 1944. He was regarded as one of the two most influential members during the history of the commission, was critical of railroad management, and believed the railroad industry should be nationalized. He was the only member of the commission to favor continued federal control of the railroads. See William J. Cunningham, *American Railroads: Government Control and Reconstruction Policies* (New York: A. W. Shaw, 1922), 9–22; William G. McAdoo, *Crowded Years: The Reminiscences of William G. McAdoo* (Boston: Houghton Mifflin, 1931), 111, 223, 303, 455–462; Ari and Olive Hoogenboom, *A History of the ICC: From Panacea to Palliative* (New York: W. W. Norton, 1976), 91; Claude Moore Fuess, *Joseph B. Eastman: Servant of the People* (New York: Columbia University Press, 1952), 84, 87–88, 312–313; Earl Latham, *The Politics of Railroad Coordination, 1933–1936* (Cambridge, MA: Harvard University Press, 1959), vii–viii.

26. Chandler, *The Visible Hand*, 116–119; T. M. R. Talcott, *Transportation by Rail: An Analysis of the Maintenance and Operation of Railroads* (Richmond, VA: Whittet & Shepperson, 1904), 22–23, 51–52.

27. Talcott, *Transportation by Rail*, 17.

28. Lorenz joined the commission in 1911 and became statistician in 1917, a position he held until 1944. See *National Cyclopedia of American Biography*, vol. 47 (New York: James T. White, 1965), 490. M. O. Lorenz, "Constant and Variable Railroad Expenditures and the Distance Tariff," *Quarterly Journal of Economics* 21 (1907), 283–298.

29. M. O. Lorenz, "Cost and Value of Service in Railroad Rate-Making," *Quarterly Journal of Economics* 30 (1916), 205–232.

30. FPC: *Brief of Louis Brandeis*, 1914, 103–105.

31. In the *Five Percent Case* (1914) O. E. Butterfield, representing the Eastern carriers, quoted from ICC Docket No. 4606, the *Youngstown Sheet & Tube Company Case:* "In [the Commission's] opinion each branch of the service should contribute its proper share of the cost of operation and of return upon the property devoted to the use of the public." See FPC, transcript, 22395. See also PPS, transcript, 1574–1576, referring to the *North Dakota Coal Case,* which appears to have been decided in 1910, and in which the commission decided that the carriers were entitled to a compensatory rate on coal, that should not burden other commodities. Also beginning in 1910 the commission decided a series of cases allowing railroads to collect more than a single fare for certain types of Pullman accommodations on the grounds that they were more expensive to the railroad. See, for example, 18 ICC 135 (1910), 25 ICC 207 (1912), the *Nevada Drawing Room Case* 36 ICC 351 (1915), 33 ICC 521 (1915), and 43 ICC 51 (1917).

32. FPC, 1915, transcript, 22585–22588.

33. 30 ICC 676, 680.

34. See *In the Matter of the Separation of Operating Expenses* 30 ICC 676 (1914), 677, which stated that separation between freight and passenger service was a necessary first step toward finding costs of particular classes of traffic. The *Five Percent Case* 31 ICC 351 (1914), 392, states: "We know of no provision of law under which we should be justified in increasing freight rates to provide a return upon property used exclusively in the passenger service, much less to take care of losses incurred in such service. In our opinion each branch of the service should contribute its proper share of the cost of operation and of return upon the property devoted to the use of the public." Earlier decisions stated that railroads were entitled to a fair return on each and every investment made, and not only on the aggregate investment. See 22 ICC 604; 29 ICC 428, 436.

35. 30 ICC 676; 37 ICC 1, 13.

36. For earlier opposition to cost separation on the grounds that it could not be done, see 29 ICC 428, 434–435. In 37 ICC 1 (1915), 13–19, forty-six roads proposed six methods for separating passenger and freight costs. Results ranged from a high of allocating 33.38 percent of total operating expenses to passenger service to a low of 31.74 percent. Most of the fuss surrounded maintenance of way and structures (MWS) expenses. Here the range was from 45.11 percent of MWS expenses on the high side to 36.88 percent on the low side. The report states that there was no serious difference of opinion among industry leaders on cost separation except in maintenance of way and structures.

Union Pacific correspondence in Maury Klein collection (University of Rhode Island), R. S. Lovett to H. W. Clark, Esq., counsel, Union Pacific System, 10 May 1915. In this letter Lovett states that many joint costs should not be assigned and objects to the ICC's promulgating uniform rules for cost separation.

37. William J. Cunningham, "Transportation: Part 1.—Railways," in Herbert Hoover, ed., *Recent Economic Changes: Report of the Committee on Recent Economic Changes of the President's Conference on Unemployment,* vol. 1 (New York: McGraw-Hill, 1929), 255–308.

38. From 1913 until 1930 the California Railroad Commission published statistics of California's electric lines in its annual reports. See California Railroad Commission, *Annual Report of the Railroad Commission of the State of California* (San Francisco). Lines with streetcar service must be disregarded, because electric railways statistics include passenger boardings rather than passenger miles, and the statistics combine streetcar and interurban boardings. Typically, streetcar boardings were many times greater than interurban boardings, completely masking trends in the latter for companies that carried both categories of passengers. In order to decipher interurban trends, it is necessary to examine passenger traffic for only those systems that did not operate streetcars.

39. 31 RCC 457.

40. Its trains carried commuters between eastern Contra Costa County and Oakland and San Francisco, through passengers between the Bay Area and Sacramento, and connecting passengers from the Bay Area to points north of Sacramento via the Northern Electric. Of the 1.1 million passengers using the system in 1920,

approximately 300,000 were commuters and suburban passengers, while approximately 30,000 were connecting passengers. Thus, about 770,000 were passengers between the Bay Area and Sacramento. The commuter and suburban passenger numbers come directly from company records for the year 1929 and my assumption that they were about equal for 1920. For the nation as a whole, commuter traffic did not change much over the decade. The figure can also be arrived at from a 1914 report written for owners of the electric line. The report noted that suburban patronage accounted for 28 percent of total patronage, the balance of which was through traffic to and from Sacramento. Connecting passengers can be counted directly from dispatchers' sheets for the railroad. The Bay Area Electric Railway Museum at Rio Vista, California, contains a collection of these sheets. I tabulated connecting passengers for February and August 1923 and February and June 1927. Annual averages based on each of the four months were 25,039, 35,405, 27,959, and 31,163 passengers, respectively. See WMJS: California Railroad Commission, "In the Matter of the Application of the Sacramento Northern Railway for an Order Authorizing the Discontinuance of Passenger Train Operations between the City and County of San Francisco and the City of Pittsburgh, Contra Costa County, and intermediate points," Application 24127 (1941), transcript, 11.5–12. VS: Bion J. Arnold, "Report to Hirsch, Lilienthal & Company on the Oakland, Antioch & Eastern Railway Line Extending from Oakland to Sacramento" 26 June 1914, 8–9.

41. Stephen Salsbury, *The State, the Investor and the Railroad* (Cambridge, MA: Harvard University Press, 1967), chapter 10; Chandler, *The Visible Hand*, 98.

42. U.S. Interstate Commerce Commission, *Annual Report on the Statistics of Railways in the United States* (Washington, DC: Government Printing Office, 1916).

43. Edwin A. Pratt, *American Railways, Reprinted (With Additions) from the Times* (London: Macmillan, 1903), 70.

44. Walter E. Weyl, *The Passenger Traffic of Railways* (Philadelphia: Ginn & Co., 1901), chapter 1.

45. "Gilded Stairs and Marble Halls," *Railway Age Gazette* 57 (23 October 1914), 724, as cited in WPF: transcript, 960–962, 977.

46. John A. Droege, *Passenger Terminals and Trains* (New York: McGraw-Hill, 1916; rpt. Kalmbach Publishing, Milwaukee, 1969), 3–4.

47. WPF (1914): several western state commissions (not California) ordered railroads about 1907 to reduce intrastate rates from the prevailing rate of about 2.5 cents per mile to 2.0 cents per mile. In *Western Passenger Fares* the western lines petitioned the ICC to overturn the state orders.

48. For a description of the protracted efforts of the carriers to obtain such freight rate increases, see Martin, *Enterprise Denied*.

49. Maury Klein, *Union Pacific: The Rebirth, 1894–1969* (New York: Doubleday, 1989), 190, 200.

50. McGanny, interview with Thompson, Hillsborough, CA, 18 May 1985.

51. CRHM: Southern Pacific *Bulletin* (20 November 1913), 1; (29 November 1913), 1.

52. Ibid.; San Francisco *Chronicle* article opposing the Central Pacific unmerger is quoted in Southern Pacific *Bulletin* (15 January 1916); Stuart Daggett, *Chapters on the History of the Southern Pacific* (New York: Augustus M. Kelley, 1966; first published 1922), 436–440; Don L. Hofsommer, *The Southern Pacific, 1901–1985* (College Station: Texas A&M University Press, 1986), 116.

53. CRHM: Southern Pacific Company, *Annual Report, Year Ended June 30,*

1914, 18. See also *Annual Report, Year Ended June 30, 1915*, 18, for the same message. In 1916 and 1917 it was reported that local passenger demand continued to fall because of the automobile, but those declines were more than compensated for by growth in longer distance traffic. See *Annual Report, Year Ended June 30, 1916*, 19; *Annual Report, Year Ended December 31, 1917*.

54. CRHM: Southern Pacific *Bulletin* (15 April 1916), 8. The article is cited from the 31 March 1916 issue of the Redding *Courier Free Press*.

55. Author's collection, Southern Pacific Company, System Timetable, January–February 1915, 8; BL: Southern Pacific Lines, "Trips Around San Francisco" (1917).

56. CRHM: Southern Pacific *Bulletin* (1 September 1916), 2; (October 1916); (1 December 1916), 8; (1 March 1917).

57. Spencer Crump, *Ride the Big Red Cars: How Trolleys Helped Build Southern California* (Los Angeles: Crest, 1962), 57, 234–235; George W. Hilton and John F. Due, *The Electric Interurban Railways in America* (Stanford, CA: Stanford University Press, 1960), 404–405; Robert S. Ford, *Red Trains in the East Bay* (Glendale, CA: Interurbans Press, 1977), 142–144. Ford presents Southern Pacific testimony that in FY 1913, the deficit of the East Bay lines, based on out-of-pocket costs, was $384,000 on gross revenues of $1,340,000. Southern Pacific at the time valued the electric services at $26.6 million, part of which was attributable to the steam lines existing prior to 1911, and part of which was attributable to the reconstruction of the lines and purchase of new rolling stock associated with electrification. See also CRHM: Southern Pacific *Bulletin* (15 June 1917), 1; (15 August 1917), 1; (August 1920), 15.

58. Martin, *Enterprise Denied*, 32.

59. PPS, exhibit 65. For costs and weights, see John H. White, Jr., *The American Railroad Passenger Car* (Baltimore: Johns Hopkins, 1978), 107–144, 187. For the Pullman Company's converting its fleet to steel, see page 275. It released its first production model in 1910; by 1913 twenty-one hundred all-steel sleeping cars were in operation—one-third of the fleet.

Southern Pacific wooden coaches built around 1908 weighed about 41 tons and seated about seventy passengers. By the middle 1920s Southern Pacific steel coaches weighed about 70 tons and seated about ninety passengers. An eight-car wood coach train (one baggage car and seven coaches) pulled by a large 4-6-0 steamer offering .036 pounds of tractive effort per pound of train weighed 1,725 pounds per seat. The cars for such a train weighed 328 tons, while the locomotive weighed another 95 tons. An eight-car steel train of the the late 1920s (one baggage car and eight coaches) pulled by a large 4-8-2 steamer offering .036 pounds of tractive effort per pound of train weighed 2,495 pounds per seat, a 45 percent increase in tare weight per seat. The cars for such a train weighed 530 tons, while the locomotive weighed another 256 tons.

According to White, Pullman sleeping cars typically weighed between 50 and 60 tons at the end of the wood era. Steel Pullman cars weighed about 70 tons. See pages 268, 273–275.

60. CRHM: Southern Pacific *Bulletin,* (20 December 1913), 1–2, contains Sproule's warning.

61. The San Francisco *Chronicle* for 8 August 1912, 7/6, reported a Southern Pacific capital program of $32 million for 1913. The major projects were a new, more direct line between California and Oregon called the Natron Cut-Off; double tracking of the mainline east from Sacramento over the Sierra; and double tracking

of the line between Bakersfield and Mojave over Tehachapi Pass. The story also reported a $22 million capital budget for the Santa Fe, which included funds to be spent on the Tehachapi project.

62. 31 ICC 351, as quoted in Clyde H. Freed, *The Story of Railroad Passenger Fares* (Washington, DC: Clyde H. Freed, 1942), 28–29.

63. SFC, exhibit 112, showing intra- and inter-California train mileage of Santa Fe.

64. Cunningham, *American Railroads*, 9–22; McAdoo, *Crowded Years*, 111, 223, 303, 455–462; Hoogenboom, *History of the ICC*, 91; Fuess, *Joseph B. Eastman*, 84, 87–88, 312–313; Latham, *Politics of Railroad Coordination*, vii-viii.

65. Cunningham, *American Railroads*, 33–43; Stephen Skowronek, *Building a New American State: The Expansion of National Administrative Capacities, 1877–1920* (Cambridge: Cambridge University Press, 1982), 277–279; K. Austin Kerr, *American Railroad Politics, 1914–1920: Rates, Wages and Efficiency* (Pittsburgh, PA: University of Pittsburgh Press, 1968), 72–100.

66. Cunningham, *American Railroads*, 87–88.

67. California services operated in different years are shown in SFC, exhibits 106, 112.

68. CRHM: *Official Guide of the Railways*, July 1915, 979 and 815; SFC, transcript, 641–643, 660–661; exhibit 137. Exhibit 137 shows passenger revenue per train mile for trains 15 and 16, respectively the *Saint* and the *Angel*, by month between 1914 and 1917. For 1914, 1915, 1916, and 1917 the *Saint* grossed $1.09, $1.58, $0.91, and $1.25 per train mile, respectively, while the *Angel* grossed $1.35, $1.76, $1.06, and $1.49. At the time Santa Fe's California fare yield was about 2.4 cents per passenger mile, indicating a range of thirty-eight to seventy-three passengers on each train.

69. SFC, transcript, 1680–1681. See also 1672–1673 and exhibit 112. Despite the presence of the Pacific Electric, all three of the major steam railroads serving Los Angeles still operated extensive local service in that area in 1915, but all abandoned most such service by 1920. Comparisons of timetables between 1915 and 1919 show that in the former year the Southern Pacific still operated three local trains daily on its Colton Line and four on its Santa Ana line. By 1919 most of this service was gone. In 1915 the Santa Fe operated seven daily trains on its Redlands loop and extensive local service on both of its mainlines between Los Angeles and San Bernardino, as well as on its San Diego route. Again, by 1919 most of this service was gone. The Salt Lake Route operated substantial local service in 1915. In 1919 it still operated several daily trains to Long Beach and on to the shipyards. By 1921 most of its local service was gone, except as extensions of mainline trains.

70. Giles T. Brown, *Ships That Sail No More: Maritime Transportation from San Diego to Puget Sound, 1910–1940* (Lexington: University of Kentucky Press, 1966), 43–49.

71. Cunningham, *American Railroads*, 95–100.

72. Ibid., 137–139; Skowronek, *Building a New American State*, 278–279; Kerr, *American Railroad Politics*, 101–127.

73. Cunningham, *American Railroads*, 135–140, 171–173, 219–234; Skowronek, *Building a New American State*, 278–279; Kerr, *American Railroad Politics*, 101–127.

74. Cunningham, *American Railroads*, 171–196; Skowronek, *Building a New American State*, 278–279.

75. Cunningham, *American Railroads*, 199–204.

Chapter 3

1. The operating ratios for CY 1920 are cited in *Reduced Rates* 68 ICC 728 (1922). For the eastern region the ratios were 103 and 90 for freight and passenger service, respectively. For the southern region they were 97 and 83. For the western region they were 91 and 83. See also William J. Cunningham, *American Railroads: Government Control and Reconstruction Policies* (New York: A. W. Shaw, 1922), 249.
2. Ari and Olive Hoogenboom, *A History of the ICC: From Panacea to Palliative* (New York: W. W. Norton, 1976), 71, 84–108.
3. Ibid.
4. In PPS, Brief and Argument for Western Carriers, 4–8, there is a long quotation from Dayton–Goose Creek Railway Co. v. United States et al. 68 L. Ed. 216 (decided 7 January 1924). The opinion states that the ICC is required under the Transportation Act of 1920 to set rates giving the railroad an adequate return. However, even if a railroad has an adequate return, the commission may allow railroads to raise rates on classes of traffic whose revenues are noncompensatory: "The [Transportation Act of 1920] does not require that the net return from all the rates shall affect the reasonableness of a particular rate or class of rates. In such an inquiry, the Commission may have regard to the service done, its intrinsic cost, or a comparison of it with other rates, and need not consider the total net return at all. Paragraph 17 of Section 15a makes this clear."

For a discussion of ICC policy regarding cross subsidizing grain movements, see Ann F. Friedlaender, *The Dilemma of Freight Transport Regulation* (Washington, DC: Brookings, 1969), 16–19.

5. On the restoration of competitive passenger service, see *Increased Rates*, 58 ICC 220 (1920), 227, 239–240. See also Cunningham, *American Railroads*, 210–211. Railroads implemented only two pooling agreements for passenger service during the 1920s. See Hoogenboom, *History of the ICC*, 109. By the mid-1930s only a few more pools had been created. See SFC, Southern Pacific Brief, 219–222. Cases cited in the brief on the formation of pools, all of which the ICC readily approved, were Montreal to Kennebunk and Portland, ME: 201 ICC 699; Duluth and Milwaukee: 194 ICC 430, 220 ICC 659; Duluth and Twin Cities: 107 ICC 493, 112 ICC 403, 132 ICC 413, 161 ICC 659; Portland and Seattle: 96 ICC 116, 128 ICC 149, 167 ICC 308, 169 ICC 244, 194 ICC 426, 218 ICC 239.
6. *Increased Rates* 58 ICC 220 (1920); *Reduced Rates* 68 ICC 728 (1922).
7. 58 ICC 220; PPS, transcript, 539–549. PPS is reported in *Pullman and Parlor Car Surcharges* 95 ICC 469 (1923). The carriers commented extensively in qualitative terms on how Pullman operations caused terminals to become more complex and more expensive to operate. Condit more explicitly explained this phenomenon. See Carl W. Condit, *The Port of New York: Vol. 1, A History of the Rail and Terminal System from the Beginnings to Pennsylvania Station* (Chicago: University of Chicago Press, 1980), 113, 118–119, 126, 152–153, 162, 274, 276–279, 300, 308, 391n. 58; Condit, *The Port of New York: Vol. 2, A History of the Rail and Terminal System from the Grand Central Electrification to the Present* (Chicago: University of Chicago Press, 1981), 76, 153–154, 178–182, 267; Condit, *The Railroad and the City: A Technological and Urbanistic History of Cincinnati* (Columbus: Ohio State University Press, 1977), 120–121, 150, 179, 195, 228, 269–270.
8. PPS, transcript, 776.

9. 58 ICC 220; PPS, transcript, 539–549.
10. 68 ICC 728, 95 ICC 469.
11. James J. Flink, *The Car Culture* (Cambridge, MA: MIT Press, 1972), 70, 81, 85, 88, 140.
12. There is a large literature on the alteration of American social and economic life as a consequence of the adoption of the automobile. In particular, see James J. Flink, *The Automobile Age* (Cambridge, MA: MIT Press, 1988); John B. Rae, *The Road and Car in American Life* (Cambridge, MA: MIT Press, 1971); Howard L. Preston, *Automobile Age Atlanta: The Making of a Southern Metropolis, 1900–1935* (Athens: University of Georgia Press, 1979); Norman T. Moline, *Mobility and the Small Town, 1900–1930: Transportation Change in Oregon, Illinois* (Chicago: University of Chicago, Department of Geography, Research Paper No. 132, 1971); Warren James Belasco, *Americans on the Road: From Autocamp to Motel, 1910–1945* (Cambridge, MA: MIT Press, 1979). Moline's work is particularly important for its description of the role of steam railroad and electric interurban passenger service in the small town before the automobile and the subsequent complete change in travel patterns as a consequence of the automobile. Belasco's work is important for the effect of the automobile on mainline railroad leisure and business travel, while Rae stresses the point, also made in all of the other works, that the automobile's main effect was not to merely absorb the traffic of public modes but to vastly expand the base of travel. Preston's work examines the effect of the auto on intrametropolitan travel and pays close attention to its effect on Atlanta's transit system.
13. U.S. Office of the Federal Coordinator of Transportation, *Passenger Traffic Report* (Washington, DC: 1935), 14, 20–21, 111–112.
14. Michael W. Donley, Stuart Allan, Patricia Caro, Clyde P. Patton, *Atlas of California* (Culver City, CA: Pacific Book Center, 1979), 17–27; John L. Andriot, *Population Abstract of the United States*, vol. 1 (McLean, VA: Andriot Associates, 1983), passim.
15. CALTRANS: *California Highways and Public Works* 1 (January 1924), 3; 1 (March 1924), 5; 5 (January 1928), 9.
16. CALTRANS: *California Highways and Public Works* 1 (January 1924), 5; 1 (March 1924), 5; 1 (July 1924), 4; 2 (December 1925), 4–7; 3 (October 1926), 4.
17. CALTRANS: *California Highways and Public Works* 4 (August 1927), 10.
18. CALTRANS: *California Highways and Public Works* 1 (January 1924), 3, 6.
19. CALTRANS: *California Highways and Public Works* 7 (January 1930), 9–10; 9 (February 1932), 3, 29. The first article describes the new Ridge Route, the second the California ten-year highway plan.
20. CALTRANS: "Toll Roads and Bond Issues Are Discussed," *California Highways and Public Works* 5 (February–March 1928), 13; "Highway Policies in California," *California Highways and Public Works* 5 (April 1928), 18–19; *California Highways and Public Works* 6 (May–June 1929), 15–16; *California Highways and Public Works* 7 (May 1930), 8–9; (December 1930), 8, 20; "Governor Rolph Outlines Policies Governing Public Works Program," *California Highways and Public Works* 9 (January 1931), 17–18; "Relation of Laws to Highway Work," *California Highways and Public Works* 9 (May 1931), 6; (June 1931), 15–16, 20; *California Highways and Public Works* 18 (June 1940), 1; (September 1940), 1–6.
21. SFC, transcript, 6760; exhibit 325. Exhibit 325, prepared by Earl Bagby,

Pacific Greyhound's lawyer and a longtime Travis associate, presents in its eighty-one pages the legal history of bus consolidations in California from 1917 to 1930. See also Eli Bail, *From Railway to Freeway: Pacific Electric and the Motor Coach* (Glendale, CA: Interurbans Press, 1984), 11–58; Burton B. Crandall, *The Growth of the Intercity Bus Industry* (Syracuse, NY: Syracuse University, College of Business Administration, 1954), 10.

22. SFC, exhibit 647; transcript, 6766, 7074–7075.

23. Giles T. Brown, *Ships That Sail No More: Maritime Transportation from San Diego to Puget Sound, 1910–1940* (Lexington: University of Kentucky Press, 1966), 159–160. Brown reports that the Los Angeles Steamship Company carried 92,000 passengers in 1923 and 155,000 passengers in 1929. About 30 percent of the passengers traveled to or from Hawaii.

24. Brown, *Ships That Sail No More*, 61–184.

25. HML: Records of the Pennsylvania Railroad, VP Operations, file 521.31, Post War Passenger Train Problems, 1943, Charles E. Smith to R. V. Fletcher, 1 September 1943; Keith L. Bryant, Jr., *History of the Atchison, Topeka and Santa Fe Railway* (New York: Macmillan, 1974), 332; Herbert Hoover, ed., *Recent Economic Changes: Report of the Committee on Recent Economic Changes of the President's Conference on Unemployment*, vol. 1 (New York: McGraw-Hill, 1929), 269–273; President's Research Committee on Social Trends, *Recent Social Trends in the United States* (New York: McGraw-Hill, 1933), 170–171.

26. This statistic was derived from a November 1920 Santa Fe survey of the patronage characteristics of its passenger trains. See PPS, exhibit 57.

27. SFC, exhibit 629 shows revenue trends individually for the two railroads.

28. U.S. Federal Coordinator of Transportation, *Passenger Traffic Report*, appendix 1. Tables 9 and 10 of this book summarize results for western and eastern cities.

29. For the Southern Pacific position and reports of railroad workers' views see CRHM: Paul Shoup, "Are Railroads of the Country Passing?" Southern Pacific *Bulletin* (September 1921), 29–30; (October 1921), 9; (November 1921); (December 1921), 16; (January 1922), 9; (February 1922), 11, 15, 16, 18; (March 1922), 7; (January 1923), 26. The Vallejo demonstration is reported in "SP Men Present Views on Motor Competition," *Bulletin* (April 1922), 7. Paul Shoup, in "Commercial Auto Lines Cost Train Service," *Bulletin* (May 1922), 14, asserts, "There is among owners of private machines a feeling growing stronger and stronger against the highways being turned into roadbeds for public utility purposes." At the time Shoup, a vice president, headed the company's subsidiary electric operations. He served as company president from 1929 to 1933.

30. SFC, exhibit 325; transcript, 6760. In this testimony, Travis stated that the Motor Carriers Association was formed in 1921, but he amended his testimony later to state that it was formed at an earlier date.

31. PPS, exhibit 28.

32. Cost figures are reported only for scattered abandonment cases. From the mid-1920s, these include 23 RCC 750 on the discontinuance of two daily Southern Pacific gas-electric round trips between Anaheim and Los Angeles, 1923. Out-of-pocket costs of $0.47 and $0.42 per car mile were shown, not including track or roadway maintenance, station expenses, superintendence or general expenses, depreciation, taxes, or interest. Revenue was $0.13 to $0.15 a car mile. 32 RCC 419 on the discontinuance of two daily trains on the Santa Rosa branch shows direct

train expenses of $0.58 per train mile, defined as train and engine crews, fuel oil, locomotive repairs, locomotive and train supplies, and expenses. To these are added taxes and passenger car repairs to yield what is called total out-of-pocket expenses of $0.64 a train mile. To this figure is added an allowance for maintenance of way and indirect expenses, for total expenses per train mile of $0.72. In 34 RCC 874, discontinuance of the Sacramento–Colfax locals in 1930, expenses are shown as $1.05 per train mile for the steam train and $0.60 per mile for the motor train.

In 1935 Southern Pacific's president, Angus D. McDonald, asked a staff assistant to prepare operating cost estimates of a new train he was contemplating. Marion J. Wise responded with a memo showing that the average out-of-pocket cost for a nine-car air-conditioned coach train of standard cars pulled by a 4-8-2 locomotive would be $1.00 per train mile. See TWR: Shasta Route file, memorandum from M. J. Wise to A. D. McDonald, 8 August 1935, untitled.

When the Santa Fe prepared its case for operating buses and streamlined trains through the San Joaquin Valley, it included estimated costs for operating the *Saint* and the *Angel* prior to World War I, as well as cost comparisons between steam local trains and buses. Again, train mile costs averaged about $0.79 in pre–World War I dollars for the all-Pullman *Saint* and *Angel* and between $1.04 and $1.18 in 1935 dollars for what the Santa Fe considered typical steam coach trains operating in California in 1935. See SFC, exhibits 105 and 136.

33. SFC, transcript, 8267–8273.
34. SFC, transcript, 8267.
35. Ibid. For a brief history of the company, see R. Patrick Stanford, "New England Transportation Company," *Motor Coach Age* 21 (1969), 8–18.
36. SFC, transcript, 8267; George W. Hilton and John F. Due, *The Electric Interurban Railways in America* (Stanford, CA: Stanford University Press, 1960), 395–396. The Southern Pacific electrified lines to Corvallis, eighty miles from Portland, but most suburban service operated within ten miles of Portland.
37. SFC, transcript, 8267.
38. SFC, transcript, 6797–6798, 7089, 8267–8268, 8273.
39. SFC, exhibit 325; transcript, 6797–6798, 7089, 8287, 8489–8490. The Santa Cruz–Watsonville decision was decided on 28 October 1928 and reported in 32 RCC 332.
40. TWR: Shasta Route file, Wise to McDonald, 8 August 1935.
41. SFC, transcript, 10936.
42. *Who's Who in America* 23 (Chicago: Marquis, 1944–45), 1410; CRHM: Southern Pacific *Bulletin* (April 1921), 6; McGanny, interview with Thompson, Hillsborough, CA, 18 May 1985. McGanny worked in Southern Pacific's executive offices during the 1930s and 1940s and later became vice president of research for the company.
43. SFC, transcript, 11400. See also 8608 for Pacific Greyhound general manager Lee D. Jones subscribing to cut-off fare view. See also PFS, transcript, 254, 299–310.
44. See SFC, transcript, 10848, 10994–10995. Santa Fe president Samuel Bledsoe also subscribed to this view: SFC, transcript, 250. So did Pacific Greyhound general manager Lee D. Jones: SFC, transcript, 8540–8542.
45. CRHM: Southern Pacific Company, *Annual Reports*, 1931, 1932, 1933; *Bulletin* (May–June 1931), 11–12; Passenger Train Earnings Show Improvement (September 1929), 6.

46. TWR: Shasta Route file, Wise to McDonald, 8 August 1935.

47. Brown, *Ships That Sail No More*, 167–168, 181, 188–200. SFC, exhibit 613, shows the following traffic figures for all water carriers in California: 1930— 386,065 passengers; 1931—323,546; 1932—222,494; 1933—204,871; 1934— 150,524; 1935—132,825. In 1935 California steam railroads carried 30 million passengers (about half of these were commuters), while intercity buses carried 9 million. SFC, *Abstract of Evidence of Santa Fe Transportation Company and The Atchison, Topeka and Santa Fe Railway Company*, 2005–2011, shows that all coastal water carriers operated only for part of the year in 1935 and 1936 and incurred heavy losses. For example, the Los Angeles Steamship Company's *Yale* ran between Los Angeles and San Francisco from 1 January through 30 September 1935 and lost $77,762. It next provided service between these ports from 16 May through 6 July 1936, during which it lost $57,775. Regardless of volume it could not make money on the low fares it had to offer to attract passengers. Other remaining carriers (with vessels having accommodations for fifteen or sixteen passengers each) also temporarily suspended service in 1936. They hoped to resume service in 1938 or 1939, but I do not believe that any did.

48. CRHM: Southern Pacific *Bulletin* (December 1920); (December 1926); (March 1928); (June 1929); (May 1930), 4.

49. Belasco, *Americans on the Road*, 7, 90–96; President's Research Committee, *Recent Social Trends*, 170–171; see also Richard C. Overton, *Burlington Route* (New York: Alfred A. Knopf, 1965), 319, 352–353.

50. Union Pacific correspondence in the Maury Klein collection (University of Rhode Island). See W. Sproule, Southern Pacific president, to A. L. Mohler, Union Pacific president, 18 March 1914, re reducing trains and amenities on the Overland Route, claiming luxury trains were losing a dollar a mile, including everything. Similar arguments are in R. S. Lovett to B. L. Winchell, 3 May 1915; J. D. Farrell to B. L. Winchell, 19 June 1916. The argument of similar time between all major West Coast cities and Chicago is in E. P. Ripley, Santa Fe president, to W. Hill, Great Northern president, 9 November 1917, with copies to J. M. Hannaford, R. S. Lovett, H. E. Byram. Ripley protests that his past speed-ups were necessitated by Florida competition and that he sees no reason for other West Coast routes to match his times. He obviously was under pressure to slow his trains. This type of concern is still evident in 1930. See Carl R. Gray, Union Pacific president, to C. B. Seger, chairman of the executive committee, 26 April 1930, stating, "The nut we will have to crack is with respect to the California schedules. I do not believe that San Francisco and Los Angeles, the former particularly, will stand for an hour and 15 minutes longer schedule than obtains to the North Coast." In C. R. Gray to F. W. Charske, vice chairman of the executive committee, 13 January 1932, Gray complains about the Santa Fe unilaterally installing air conditioning on dining cars on its premier *Chief* between Los Angeles and Chicago. This would compel the Union Pacific to respond by air conditioning its dining cars on its *Los Angeles Limited* between Los Angeles and Chicago. It would also necessitate air conditioning on Chicago to San Francisco and Chicago to Portland trains: "We are under [Central Pacific] contract to afford the same character of service between Omaha and San Francisco that we do at all times between Omaha and Los Angeles or Portland."

51. PFS, transcript, 361–364; SFC, transcript, 10698; TWR: Shasta Route file, Wise to McDonald, 8 August 1935.

52. CRHM: Southern Pacific *Bulletin* (September 1925), 9–10.

53. CRHM: Southern Pacific *Bulletin* (July 1928), 3–5.
54. SFC, transcript, 11608–11611.
55. CRHM: Southern Pacific *Bulletin* (October 1930), 7–8.
56. John R. Signor, *Tehachapi* (San Marino: Golden West Books, 1983), 58–59.
57. There is no reference to this proposal in testimony of the *Santa Fe Case*. I have found no cost estimates. I made this estimate based on unit costs for Southern Pacific's line relocation around Shasta Dam in the late 1930s, when price levels were about the same as in the mid-1920s. The construction difficulties of both lines appears about equal. See the discussion of this line in chapter 5.
58. CRHM: Southern Pacific *Bulletin* (September 1923), 3–4; (July 1924); (November 1925); (April 1928), 4; (July 1928), 3–5; (April 1929), 17–24; (December 1929), 8. See also Don L. Hofsommer, *The Southern Pacific, 1901–1985* (College Station: Texas A&M University Press, 1986), 78–89.
59. Hofsommer, *The Southern Pacific*, 98–102; 37 RCC 77.
60. CRHM: Southern Pacific *Bulletin* (January 1926), 14; (December 1926), 4.
61. In August 1920, the company ordered fifty passenger cars. CRHM: Southern Pacific *Bulletin* (August 1920), 7. In 1923, it ordered sixty suburban cars, eleven buffet-baggage cars, thirty-five mail-baggage cars, and ten baggage cars at a cost of $3.5 million ([January 1923], 5). In May 1924, it purchased ten dining cars ([May 1924]). The order of suburban cars was evidently increased to seventy costing $1.7 million ([September 1925], 9). The *Bulletin* of December 1929 reported on page 8 the purchase of another forty-seven passenger cars, "such as dining, lounge and baggage cars."
62. CRHM: Southern Pacific *Bulletin* (March 1922), 3; (November 1923), 15.
63. Hofsommer, *The Southern Pacific*, 117.
64. William J. Cunningham, "Transportation, Part I.—Railways," in Hoover, *Recent Economic Changes*, 255–308.
65. Albert Fishlow, "Productivity and Technological Change in the Railroad Sector, 1840–1910," in *Output, Employment and Productivity in the United States after 1800* (New York: National Bureau of Economic Research, 1966), 626–630.
66. SFC, exhibit 629.
67. U.S. Federal Coordinator of Transportation, *Passenger Traffic Report*, 109. Passenger revenues in Analysis 2 are slightly underreported by failure to include dining revenues, whereas costs include dining costs. See PFS, transcript, 1548, which comments on Analysis 2.
68. SFC, transcript, 11806–11808; PFS, transcript, 1417–1418, 1424, 1891. CSA: Southern Pacific Company, *Form A Annual Report to the ICC*, 1927 and 1929.
69. SFC, transcript, 1681.
70. PPS, transcript, 1504, 1515; SFC, transcript of Quirk testimony, 1672, 1680–1682; exhibit 112.
71. SFC, transcript, 641–643, 660–661.
72. SFC, exhibit 45.
73. SFC, transcript, 10796–10797; Southern Pacific Brief, 91–96.
74. SFC, exhibit 612 is a photostat of the ad with the inscription, which McGinnis also read into the record on page 10976 of the transcript.
75. SFC, transcript 10975–10977; Southern Pacific Brief, 87–88. See also 2344–2346, 10881–10882.
76. SFC, Pacific Greyhound Lines Digest of Transcript of Santa Fe Witnesses

Up to June 25, 1936, vol 1, 176. The Santa Fe's James B. Duffy testified almost identically on 13 May 1936. See SFC, transcript, 2344–2346.

77. SFC, exhibit 112; Bryant, *History of the Atchison, Topeka and Santa Fe Railway*, 332–335.
78. SFC, exhibits 45 and 76.
79. SFC, exhibit 45.

Chapter 4

1. SFC, exhibit 647; transcript, 6766, 7074–7075, 7088, 7091–7092.
2. SFC, transcript, 6782, 7088–7093.
3. 32 RCC 332. The case was decided 28 October 1928.
4. SFC, transcript, 6787–6788, 6797, 7093–7094.
5. SFC, Southern Pacific Brief, 223–225; transcript, 6791, 6793, 10672–10673. The Southern Pacific approached the Santa Fe a second time in 1933 to buy into Pacific Greyhound, when the bus company purchased a bus route between Los Angeles and Albuquerque that ran along the Santa Fe mainline. The Santa Fe again refused.
6. SFC, transcript, 6787–6788, 6797, 7093–7094.
7. *Motor Coach Age* 27 (February 1975), 23; Eli Bail, *From Railway to Freeway: Pacific Electric and the Motor Coach* (Glendale, CA: Interurbans Press, 1984), 11–58; Burton B. Crandall, *The Growth of the Intercity Bus Industry* (Syracuse, NY: Syracuse University, College of Business Administration, 1954), 10.
8. SFC, transcript, 8288; Santa Fe Abstract, 1326.
9. SFC, transcript, 8622–8623.
10. SFC, transcript, 7120–7123.
11. SFC, transcript, 7616.
12. SFC, transcript, 7120–7123.
13. SFC, transcript, 6782, 7123–7124; exhibit 333. For comments on Wren (who Pacific Greyhound's management rarely mentioned in Santa Fe Case testimony), see *Motor Coach Age* 31/12 (December 1979), 11; 24/10 (October 1972), 16.
14. Bradford Snell, *American Ground Transport: Testimony to Subcommittee on Anti-Trust and Monopoly of the Committee on Judiciary, United States Senate, 27–540 0* (Washington, DC: 26 February 1974), 29.
15. SFC, exhibits 329, 330, 331.
16. SFC, transcript, 6782, 7123–7124; exhibit 333.
17. Kimball, interview with Thompson, St. Helena, CA, 19 May 1985.
18. SFC, transcript, 7125.
19. Kimball, interview with Thompson, St. Helena, CA, 19 May 1985.
20. SFC, transcript, 8418–8419.
21. SFC, transcript, 8628–8630; see 8631 for quote.
22. SFC, transcript, 11817–11818.
23. SFC, exhibit 367.
24. SFC, exhibits 385 and 645a–c; transcript, 6818, 6822, 11817–11818.
25. SFC, transcript, 6810–6817, 8426.
26. SFC, transcript, 6818–6822.
27. SFC, transcript, 8424.
28. SFC, transcript, 8425–8426.

29. Kimball, interview with Thompson and Seal, St. Helena, CA, 29 September 1984; SFC, testimony of Travis, transcript, 6818–6819, 6887.

30. SFC, exhibits 369, 381, 382. During the period March to September 1936 the load factors for the Valley and Coast routes were 54 and 63 percent respectively. For the entire year of 1935, Pacific Greyhound's average load factor measured as passenger miles divided by seat miles was 54 percent. That for the Coast Route was 58 percent, while that for the Valley Route was 53 percent.

31. Pacific Greyhound computed the average one-way fare per mile between approximately fifty principal points in California for the years 1929–1936. The same points were used each year. SFC, exhibit 337.

32. Gordon J. Fielding, *Managing Public Transit Strategically* (San Francisco: Jossey-Bass, 1988), 59–63.

33. SFC, exhibits 359–360.

34. SFC, exhibit 340; transcript, 11174.

35. SFC, transcript, 1198–1199.

36. SFC, transcript, 6838–6839; Albert E. Meier and John P. Hoschek, *Over the Road: A History of Intercity Bus Transportation in the United States* (Upper Montclair, NJ: Motor Bus Society, 1975), 81–83, 101.

37. Meier and Hoschek, *Over the Road*, 81–83, 101; *Motor Coach Age* 24 (October 1972), 13–14; SFC, transcript, 6842; see exhibit 338 for price comparisons.

38. SFC, transcript, 6838–6839; Meier and Hoschek, *Over the Road*, 81–83, 101.

39. SFC, transcript, 6840–6841.

40. SFC, transcript, 6836–6837.

41. Pacific Greyhound bought buses from Yellow Coach, Pioneer, White, Fageol, Twin Coach, C. H. Will, and Pickwick. It bought engines from Cadillac, Knight, Hall-Scott, Waukesha, GMC, Sterling, and Pickwick.

42. SFC, exhibit 338, which presents a detailed roster of Pacific Greyhound Lines bus equipment and purchases between 1929 and 1936.

43. SFC, exhibit 359 shows annual passenger revenue. The average fare per passenger mile described earlier in this chapter, divided into this amount each year, yields annual passenger miles. Based on revenue results for the first nine months of 1936 compared to those of 1935, together with an estimated fare yield of 1.6 cents per passenger mile after 1 July 1936, Pacific Greyhound is estimated to have carried approximately 455 million passenger miles in 1936. SFC, exhibit 385 shows that the $2.21 million in revenue earned between January and June of 1936 was 13 percent higher than that earned during the same period of 1935 at the same fare level. Fares were reduced from a base of 2.0 cents per mile to a base of 1.5 cents per mile on 1 July 1936. Revenue for July, August, and September of 1936 was 14 percent over that for the same period of 1935. From this exhibit, we know the revenue for the first six months of 1935 was $2.0 million. From exhibit 359 we know that passenger revenue for all of 1935 was $6.9 million. Thus, revenue for the last half of 1935 must have been $4.9 million, and other exhibits verify the substantial seasonal peaking implied. Assuming a growth of 13 percent in 1936, which seems reasonable based on the first three months' experience following the fare decrease, we have an estimated revenue for the last half of 1936 of $5.5 million. At an average yield of 1.6 cents per passenger mile, this level produces 344 million passenger miles during the last six months. At an average yield of 2.0 cents

per passenger mile, the $2.21 million revenue during the first six months produces 111 million passenger miles, or 455 million for the year.

44. SFC, exhibit 381.

45. The highway commission also completed other projects on this route between 1932 and 1934, including a new high-speed bypass around Saugus and a new high-speed road descending from the summit of Tejon Pass to the valley floor.

46. ACSC: *Touring Topics* 25 (January 1933), 26. Kimball, interview with Thompson and Seal, St. Helena, CA, 29 September 1984, and with Thompson, St. Helena, 19 May 1985. Kimball graduated from a transportation economics course at the University of Southern California in 1935 and then joined a trucking line that specialized in attracting volume traffic at low fares away from the Southern Pacific. He attributed the existence of the truck carrier to the opening of the new Ridge Route, which he said doomed the Southern Pacific as a profitable carrier of intra-California freight.

47. See, for example, CALTRANS: *California Highways and Public Works* 14 (September 1938), 4, 10, on the opening of the new four-lane divided Altamont Pass realignment, which had two-thousand-foot minimum radius curves and cut 8.5 miles from the old route. The previous route was characterized by narrow winding turns and lengthy traffic congestion delays.

48. CALTRANS: *California Highways and Public Works* 7 (December 1930), 5–7, 20, describes the first braided junction, while *California Highways* 12 (February 1935), 6–7, 20, 24, describes the first grade separated urban arterial, Ramona Boulevard, which ran east from Los Angeles for six miles without a grade crossing. The Arroyo Seco and Cahuenga Pass routes, whose first parts opened in July 1940, are typically called California's first freeways, but the earlier Ramona Boulevard, if not a freeway, was something radically different from roads that preceded it.

49. CALTRANS: *California Highways and Public Works* 13 (July 1936), 2–3; 14 (December 1938), 6–10.

50. Felix S. McGinnis, Southern Pacific's vice president of passenger traffic, observed in February 1937, "I think practically all travelers on the highway claim they do it in 10, some of them do it in less." He was referring to driving between San Francisco and Los Angeles. See SFC, transcript, 11247.

51. SFC, Pacific Greyhound Timetable, October–November 1936; transcript, 8665–8667, 9035; Answering Brief, 276–277.

52. Technically, this is twenty-seven and seventeen bus miles per route mile for each of the two routes. SFC, exhibit 364.

53. SFC, Pacific Greyhound and Southern Pacific system timetables for October–November, 1936.

54. SFC, transcript, 8451–8452, 8543–8546, 11150–11152; Santa Fe Brief, 307.

55. U.S. Federal Coordinator of Transportation, *Passenger Traffic Report*, appendix 1, presents results from the 1933 traffic survey, which yields both the annual number of passengers traveling between selected points and the annual revenue generated by that traffic. A division of passengers into revenue yields the average fare actually paid between each pair of points.

56. Derived from SFC, exhibit 348.

57. Wildcat sedans occasionally operated between Los Angeles and either Stockton or Sacramento. Even more rarely they dropped off or picked up intermediate passengers between Los Angeles and San Francisco.

58. SFC, transcript, 425–593, 15062–15090; RCC Decision 34924, decided 12 January 1942.
59. SFC, transcript, 8514–8515.
60. SFC, transcript, 6802.
61. SFC, transcript, 10901–10905.
62. PFS, transcript, 219–220.
63. SFC, transcript, 8404–8406.
64. SFC, exhibit 421; transcript 8409–8410.
65. SFC, exhibit 340.
66. SFC, transcript, 11174.
67. SFC, exhibits 730, 818.
68. SFC, exhibit 818.
69. Nos. 51–52, the *San Joaquin*.
70. SFC, exhibit 816.
71. SFC, transcript, 8384–8389.
72. SFC, transcript, 8276–8278; exhibit 396 lists substituted services; exhibit 404.
73. SFC, exhibit 400.
74. SFC, transcript, 8469–8472; exhibit 407.
75. SFC, Santa Fe Brief, 5–14.
76. SFC, transcript, 8469–8472; exhibit 407.
77. SFC, transcript, 8469–8472; exhibits 406, 407, 599 and 600.
78. Fred A. Stindt, *The Northwestern Pacific Railroad* (Kelseyville, CA: Fred A. Stindt, 1964), 54; CRHM: *Official Guide of the Railways*, June 1933, 839.
79. SFC, exhibits 396, 411.
80. SFC, transcript, 8341, 11264; SFC, exhibit 358, Agreements 8, 9, 10. The pooling agreement did not take effect until the California Railroad Commission approved the train discontinuances and the pooling agreement itself, 39 RCC 880; see also SFC, Southern Pacific Brief, 220.

The agreement did not cover special Pacific Greyhound bus services for which Northwestern Pacific had specifically contracted in 1933 in order to replace trains operating between Fairfax and Point Reyes and similar contracted service established in 1934 to replace a ferry between Tiburon, Belvedere, and Sausalito.

81. SFC, exhibit 601.
82. Meier and Hoschek, *Over the Road*, 35, 48; SFC, exhibit 334; transcript, 6787–6788. The Great Northern held 45 percent of Northland Greyhound Lines; the New York Central and the Pennsylvania each held 50 percent of Central Greyhound and Pennsylvania Greyhound, respectively; the Richmond, Fredericksburg & Potomac held 49 percent of Richmond Greyhound Lines; and the St. Louis Southwestern and the Southern Pacific each held 16.67 percent of Southwestern Greyhound.

Chapter 5

1. CRHM: F. S. McGinnis, "Fine Passenger Service Without Competition," Southern Pacific *Bulletin* (July 1929), 3–4; "Passenger Earnings Show Improvement" (September 1929), 6; "Making Passenger Travel More Attractive" (August 1930), 7–8.

2. SFC, exhibit 643. The California business index—with industrial production weighted 4, car loadings weighted 3, bank debits weighted 2, and department store sales weighted 1—declined from a high of 126 in 1929 to a low of 56 in 1933.

3. U.S. Office of the Federal Coordinator of Transportation, *Passenger Traffic Report* (Washington, DC, 1935), 12, 17, 20, 108, 111, 112. Passenger service revenue, including mail and express, declined from $1.234 billion in 1929 to $0.491 billion in 1933, a 60 percent decline. Passenger-only revenue declined from $872 million in 1929 to $329 million in 1933, a 62 percent decline. Rail passenger miles (including commute) declined from 31 billion in 1929 to 16 billion in 1933, a 48 percent decline.

4. Robert S. and Helen Merrel Lynd, *Middletown in Transition: A Study in Cultural Conflict* (New York: Harcourt, Brace & World, 1937), 10, 26; U.S. Federal Coordinator of Transportation, *Passenger Traffic Report*, 12, 17, 20, 108, 111, 112. Intercity auto passenger miles declined from 208 billion in 1929 to 185 billion in 1933, an 11 percent decline. For California auto registrations see table 3.

5. Warren James Belasco, *Americans on the Road: From Autocamp to Motel, 1910–1945* (Cambridge, MA: MIT Press, 1979), 140–144.

6. U.S. Federal Coordinator of Transportation, *Passenger Traffic Report*, 20.

7. TWR: Shasta Route file, memorandum from M. J. Wise to A. D. McDonald, 8 August 1935.

8. U.S. Interstate Commerce Commission, *Statistics of Railways in the United States* (1929–33). The Southern Pacific slashed its passenger train miles from 20 million in 1929 to 12 million in 1933. SFC, exhibit 112 shows that in 1929 the Santa Fe operated 2.0 million passenger train miles in California with trains that crossed the state line and 1.7 million passenger train miles with trains that did not. By 1933 these two figures both shrank to 1.3 million train miles.

9. SFC, transcript, 11125–11126. See also 2344–2346, 2652, 10881–10882, 10975–10976, 14839–14859; exhibit 612; Southern Pacific Brief, 87–88.

10. HML: Records of the Pennsylvania Railroad, VP Operations, file 521.31, Post-War Passenger Train Problems, 1943, Charles E. Smith to R. V. Fletcher, 1 September 1943. The passenger service operating ratios are from a report that appears to have been prepared by the Association of American Railroads based on ICC figures.

11. SFC, transcript, 2619–2620, 10876–10877.

12. SFC, transcript, 2619–2625, 10807–10808, 11161, 11385–11387, 11422.

13. SFC, exhibit 643.

14. CRHM: Southern Pacific *Bulletin* (October 1935), 10–11.

15. Ibid.

16. SFC, exhibit 629.

17. PFS, transcript, 807–813.

18. PFS, transcript, 813–815, 840; SFC, exhibit 81.

19. Ibid.

20. Ibid.

21. Earl Latham, *The Politics of Railroad Coordination, 1933–1936* (Cambridge, MA: Harvard University Press, 1959); Claude Moore Fuess, *Joseph B. Eastman: Servant of the People* (New York: Columbia University Press, 1952).

22. U.S. Federal Coordinator of Transportation, *Passenger Traffic Report*, 41, 150.

23. Ibid., 38–48, 148; SFC, Santa Fe Brief. The public viewed the cost of

operating a car at 2.8 cents per auto mile. The 1.2 cent figure is based upon an average occupancy of 2.4 passengers.

24. SFC, transcript, 2325–2326, 16980.

25. Ibid. I interpret these figures as the fare reduction increasing gross revenues by 10 percent and later improvements to the economy increasing gross revenues on the San Diego route by another 30 percent.

26. PFS, transcript, 340, 351, Exceptions on Behalf of Lines in Eastern District.

27. SFC, transcript, 2655–2658.

28. Maury Klein, *Union Pacific: The Rebirth, 1894–1969* (New York: Doubleday, 1989), 298–306.

29. SFC, exhibit 140: Coverdale & Colpitts, *Report on High-Speed Trains, Chicago–Twin Cities* (New York: Coverdale & Colpitts, June and July 1935). For discussion of the exhibit, see SFC, transcript, 2820–2845.

30. SFC, Santa Fe Transportation Company Brief, vols. 1 and 2, 58–67, 112, and passim. Answering Brief, passim.

31. SFC, transcript, 901; Santa Fe Brief.

32. SFC, Santa Fe Brief, 5–14. These were Southern Kansas Stage Lines, Cardinal Stage Lines, Rio Grande Stages, and the Central Arizona Transportation Company.

33. Ibid.

34. SFC, Santa Fe Brief, 11–12; 41 RCC 239, 257–260, 286–287.

35. Ibid.

36. SFC, transcript, 10639.

37. SFC, Southern Pacific Brief. The transcript also contains testimony from spokespeople from business and social groups in every community affected by the proposal. Examination and cross examination reveals the heavy lobbying of them conducted by both Southern Pacific and Santa Fe officers.

38. SFC, transcript, 7041–7042, 7069, 7081–7086, 7125.

39. SFC, Santa Fe Brief and Answering Brief.

40. CRHM: Southern Pacific *Bulletin* (February 1936), 5–6; SFC, transcript, 2611–2619.

41. Don L. Hofsommer, *The Southern Pacific, 1901–1985* (College Station: Texas A&M University Press, 1986), 134–137.

42. Richard K. Wright, *Southern Pacific Daylight*, vol. 1 (Thousand Oaks, CA: Wright Enterprises, 1970), 39–45.

43. Wright, *Southern Pacific Daylight*, 39–45; Hofsommer, *The Southern Pacific*, 134–139.

44. Coverdale & Colpitts, *Report on Streamline, Light-Weight, High-Speed Passenger Trains* (New York: Coverdale & Colpitts, 30 June 1939), 26–27.

45. CRHM: Southern Pacific *Bulletin* (January 1938), 3; (April 1938), 9–10.

46. U.S. Federal Coordinator of Transportation, *Passenger Traffic Report*, appendix 2, Analysis of Pullman Services. TWR: Pacific Lines Train Earnings, May 1938.

47. SFC, transcript, 10644–10647.

48. SFC, transcript, vol. 30, 4610–4700. Edwin G. Wilcox, an attorney and manager of the San Francisco Chamber of Commerce transportation department in 1936, described how the department unanimously supported the Santa Fe proposal, how McGinnis as a director of the chamber attempted to influence the board

to repudiate the department's stand, and how he ultimately lost on a seven to six vote, with eight directors abstaining. My reading of public testimony from SFC, transcript, 3297 to 5641, revealed no organization supporting the Southern Pacific, with the type of struggle revealed above occurring time and again.

49. Kimball, interview with Thompson and Seal, St. Helena, CA, 29 September 1984. Kimball stated that Travis remained as president for some time but effectively turned the reins over to Ackerman. Kimball was an Ackerman protege who eventually rose to become vice president of the Greyhound Corporation and president of Eastern Greyhound Lines.

50. CRHM: Southern Pacific *Bulletin* (February 1938), 15.

51. McGanny, interview with Thompson, Hillsborough, CA, 18 May 1985; SFC, transcript, 10655–10657.

52. CRHM: Southern Pacific *Bulletin* (March 1940), 4.

53. SFC, transcript, 10645. McDonald testified on 9 February 1937.

54. California Railroad Commission, *Opinions and Orders*, 1935–1941; TWR: Coast Line file, system train passenger earnings, May 1938.

55. Klein, *Union Pacific*, 363–368.

56. CRHM: Southern Pacific *Bulletin* (May 1938), 3; (September 1938), 7–8; (March 1941), 12–13.

57. For San Joaquin strategies, see TWR: Santa Fe file, draft letter to Hale Holden, 22 July 1938. For *Sunbeam* performance, see CRHM: Southern Pacific *Traffic Gram* 3 (September 1937), 1; 4 (June 1938), 1, which state that double daily service was then in operation, offering a schedule of 265 miles in 265 minutes; TWR: Sunset file, undated analysis of new streamlined equipment for the *Sunset Limited* ca. 1948, showing earnings of the *Sunbeam*, one of the two Dallas–Houston trains, of $1.23 per train mile in 1939, $1.43 in 1940, and $1.63 in 1941; TWR: File on Santa Fe–San Joaquin Valley service, draft letter to Hale Holden dated 22 July 1938, file 081-AT&SF, 5. The letter states that one tactic for counteracting the Santa Fe was to transfer the two *Sunbeam* trains to the San Joaquin Valley. It comments, "Although results from these trains have not been up to expectations, in absence of Mr. McDonald, hesitate to suggest transfer of the SUNBEAM equipment, as understand he has been in favor of keeping them on the T&NO a while longer." The T&NO refers to the Texas & New Orleans, the Southern Pacific subsidiary operating most Southern Pacific–controlled trackage east of El Paso during the 1930s.

58. CRHM: Southern Pacific *Bulletin* (May 1938), 3; (September 1938), 7–8; (March 1941), 12–13; Klein, *Union Pacific*, 363–368. U.S. Federal Coordinator of Transportation, *Passenger Traffic Report*, 19–49.

59. SFC, Santa Fe Brief.

60. SFC, Southern Pacific Brief, 68–74; Coverdale & Colpitts, *Report on Streamline, Light-Weight, High-Speed Passenger Trains* (30 June 1939 and 30 June 1941).

61. CRHM: Southern Pacific *Bulletin* (March 1937), 5.

62. CALTRANS: "Progress on Trail of Padres," *California Highways and Public Works* 13 (October 1937), 8.

63. See previous chapter.

64. CRHM: Southern Pacific *Bulletin* (July 1939), 2–4; Bill Bradley, *The Last of the Great Stations* (Glendale, CA: Interurbans Press, 1979), 80; Carl W. Condit, *The Railroad and the City: A Technological and Urbanistic History of Cincinnati* (Columbus: Ohio State University Press, 1977).

65. The federal coordinator of transportation's terminal unification studies document the number of switch engine hours worked by each railroad in several California cities and towns. Based upon a survey of switch engine hours during the week of 21 January 1934, we can determine that the Southern Pacific had a much more dominant presence in territory than the Santa Fe served with its northern California mainline. This is shown in the following table:

	Switch Engine Hours Worked (weekday average)	
	Southern Pacific	Santa Fe
Bakersfield[1]	49	28
Fresno[2]	87	32
Stockton[3]	63	21
Oakland/Richmond[4]	460	68
Total	659	149

Source: All figures are from the U.S. Office of the Federal Coordinator of Transportation, Files of the Western Regional Office, Reports of Coordination Projects, Record Group 133, National Archives, Washington, DC.
[1] "Proposed Unification of Railroad Facilities at Bakersfield, California, Report of the Local Terminal Committee," 38.
[2] "Proposed Unification of Railroad Facilities at Fresno, California, Report of the Local Terminal Committee," 55.
[3] "Proposed Unification of Railroad Facilities at Stockton, California, Report of the Local Terminal Committee," 86.
[4] "Proposed Unification of Railroad Facilities at Oakland, California, Report of the Local Terminal Committee," 163.

66. VS: Golden Gate Service file, A. D. McDonald to Hale Holden, 15 July 1938.

67. TWR: File 081-AT&SF, draft letter to Hale Holden, 22 July 1938.

68. Coverdale & Colpitts, *Report on Streamline, Light-Weight, High-Speed Passenger Trains.*

69. *Moody's Manual of Investments, American and Foreign, Public Utilities Securities* (New York: Moody's Investor Services, 1933–1941).

70. Kimball, interview with Thompson, St. Helena, CA, 19 May 1985; *Moody's Manual of Investments, American and Foreign, Railroad Securities* (New York: Moody's Investor Services, 1940, 1941). In 1940 the Santa Fe Transportation Company lost $116,000, and it lost $103,000 in 1941. This was the subsidiary that operated Santa Fe's intra-California bus service. The interstate bus subsidiary, the Santa Fe Trail Transportation Company, lost $165,000 in 1940 but made $319,000 in 1941. TWR: Santa Fe file, A. D. McDonald to Hale Holden, 13 July 1938; F. S. McGinnis to A. T. Mercier, 13 July 1938, reporting on a meeting McGinnis had just completed with Buck Travis, president of Pacific Greyhound Lines. VS: Golden Gate file, W. E. Travis to W. A. Worthington, 18 July 1938. Keith L. Bryant, Jr., *History of the Atchison, Topeka and Santa Fe Railway* (New York: Macmillan, 1974), 269–270, 338.

71. U.S. Interstate Commerce Commission, *Statistics of Railways in the United States* (Washington, DC: Government Printing Office, 1927 and 1939). The East Bay suburban service still ran, but beginning in 1939 it operated as a wholly owned subsidiary and its statistics were no longer reflected in Southern Pacific operating statistics.

72. SFC, exhibit 629; CSA: *Annual Report of the Atchison, Topeka and Santa Fe Railway to the Interstate Commerce Commission and the California Railroad Commission* (selected years, 1933–1941).

Chapter 6

1. For an example of the argument that the ICC formula offered a false indicator of passenger losses, see Stanley Berge, "Why Kill the Passenger Train?" *Journal of Marketing* 28 (January 1964), 1–6.

2. George W. Hilton and John F. Due, *The Electric Interurban Railways in America* (Stanford: Stanford University Press, 1960), 246–248.

3. Dwight R. Ladd, *Cost Data for the Management of Railroad Passenger Service* (Boston: Harvard University, Graduate School of Business Administration, Division of Research, 1957), 7–8, 38–39, 74, 93–94, 96–97, 115, 120, 131, 142.

4. SFC, transcript 11584–11586; 129 ICC 15; CRHM: Southern Pacific *Bulletin* (April 1924), 8–10; Stuart Daggett, *Chapters on the History of the Southern Pacific* (New York: Augustus M. Kelley), 285–286, 291–292.

5. 165 ICC 379; Giles T. Brown, *Ships That Sail No More: Maritime Transportation from San Diego to Puget Sound, 1910–1940* (Lexington: University of Kentucky Press, 1966), 226–227.

6. 129 ICC 15–16.

7. 129 ICC 17; 165 ICC 373–379.

8. 165 ICC 373–379; SFC, transcript, 11651–11652; Kimball, interview with Thompson, St. Helena, CA, 19 May 1985.

9. 165 ICC 382, 391–392, 410; SFC, transcript, 11651–11652. See also Ford K. Edwards, *Study of Rail Cost Finding for Rate Making Purposes, Case No. 4402* (San Francisco: California Railroad Commission, Transportation Department, Engineering Division, 1 December 1938), 138–146, 182–185. Edwards summarizes the pioneering work of Day and adopts most of his methods.

10. 129 ICC 17; 165 ICC 373–379; Edwards, *Study of Rail Cost Finding*, 138–146.

11. SFC, transcript, 11687, 11703, 11718–11720.

12. Ibid.

13. Edwards, *Study of Rail Cost Finding*, cover letter of J. G. Hunter, assistant director of transportation and chief Engineer. This letter refers to chapters 223 and 312 of the statutes of 1935, as amended.

14. Kimball, interview with Thompson, St. Helena, CA, 19 May 1985.

15. Edwards, *Study of Rail Cost Finding*, 35–39, 141–143, 171.

16. Edwards, *Study of Rail Cost Finding*, cover letter of Ford K. Edwards, transportation economist.

17. Kimball, interview with Thompson, St. Helena, CA, 19 May 1985.

18. Ibid.

19. Ladd, *Cost Data*, 40–41.

20. Meyer's original work on this subject was conducted for the Aeronautical Research Foundation, which the Association of American Railroads retained to study the railroad passenger deficit in 1956 and 1957. This work was later incorporated into a more general study on transportation competition. See John R. Meyer, Merton J. Peck, John Stenason, Charles Zwick, *The Economics of Competition in the Transportation Industries* (Cambridge, MA: Harvard University Press, 1960).

21. Howard Hosmer, *Report Proposed by Howard Hosmer*, ICC Docket 31954 (1958), 7, 8–10. This report is summarized in George W. Hilton, *Amtrak: The National Railroad Passenger Corporation* (Washington, DC: American Enterprise Institute for Public Policy Research, 1980), 7–10.

22. A summary of such work is given in Theodore Keeler, *Railroads, Freight, and Public Policy* (Washington, DC: Brookings, 1983), 50–53, 153–161. Keeler states that the most sophisticated work is that by Friedlaender and Spady. See Ann F. Friedlaender and Richard H. Spady, *Freight Transport Regulation: Equity, Efficiency, and Competition in the Rail and Trucking Industries* (Cambridge, MA: MIT Press, 1981), 23, 28–35, 217–234.

23. These are Southern Pacific's fully allocated passenger costs per train mile and car miles, respectively, as calculated from the Southern Pacific Company, *Annual Report to the Interstate Commerce Commission* (1937).

24. Ibid.

25. SFC, transcript, 11282–11283.

26. SFC, transcript, 11283–11284.

27. SFC, transcript, 11422–11424, 11687–11691, 11714–11721, 11754–11758.

28. For the Santa Fe probably not having cost analyses of the proposed trains, see SFC, transcript, 1700–1703. For Weidel's work presented a month later, see SFC, exhibit 140: Coverdale & Colpitts, *Report on High-Speed Trains, Chicago–Twin Cities* (New York: Coverdale & Colpitts, June and July 1935); see also SFC exhibits 142 and 143, in which Weidel estimated that the direct costs of a five-car streamliner similar to the Twin Cities *Zephyr* would be $0.71 per train mile, while those for a seven-car streamliner would be $0.97 per mile. For full discussion, see transcript, 2820–2845.

29. SFC, transcript, 11714–11715, 11754–11758.

30. SFC, transcript, 11651–11663, 11678–11682.

31. TWR: accounting department report for *Daylight*, July 1938, in postwar *Noon Daylight* file. The Tower Collection contains monthly statements for the *City of San Francisco*, the *Forty-Niner*, the *Daylight*, and the *Lark*, all after the trains were equipped with streamlined equipment or, in the case of the *Forty-Niner*, a mixture of new and upgraded equipment. The earliest of these statements is for 1937.

32. For a description of Pullman statistics, see PPS, transcript, 1331, 2125, and passim. Pullman statistics also are contained in Pullman Company annual reports, which are summarized in U.S. Interstate Commerce Commission, *Statistics of Railways in the United States*, after the mid-1920s.

33. SFC, transcript, 10772, 10795, 11662, 11688–11690, 11724–11726, 11747; SFC, exhibits 637, 638.

34. SFC, transcript, 10772, 10795, 11662, 11688–11690, 11724–11726, 11747. Two special studies of coach load factors were referred to. One was conducted for the U.S. Office of the Federal Coordinator of Transportation and is reported in the *Passenger Traffic Report* (Washington, DC: 1935), appendix 2. For statistics pertaining to Southern Pacific (which were collected by the Bureau of

Transportation Research on behalf of the Federal Coordinator's Office), see appendix 2, 344–345. The *Daylight* averaged 25 passenger miles per coach mile; the *San Joaquin* averaged 16.6. In the other study, consultants were employed to study the Burlington's pioneering efforts with lightweight diesel streamliners. The consultants documented load factors on these trains. Their study showed that the average occupancy of the *Twin Cities Zephyr* was about 65 percent, while that of the Milwaukee Road's *Hiawatha* was 45 percent and that of the Chicago & Northwestern's *400* was 30 percent. All three of these high-speed day train services competed for through Chicago–Twin Cities business and were commonly reported as being sold out. See SFC, exhibit 140, which is Coverdale & Colpitts, *Report on High-Speed Trains, Chicago–Twin Cities*, made to Ladenburg, Thalmann & Company of New York, page 17. It is possible that the operation of three duplicate high-speed rail services produced more seats than demand justified.

35. PFS, transcript, 1389–1397.

36. Maury Klein, *Union Pacific: The Rebirth, 1894–1969* (New York: Doubleday, 1989), 298–306.

37. Coverdale & Colpitts, *Report on Streamline, Light-Weight, High-Speed Passenger Trains* (New York: Coverdale & Colpitts, 30 June 1939); *Railway Age* 96 (3 February 1934), 184–196; 98 (16 March 1935), 387; 98 (20 April 1935), 600; 98 (27 April 1935), 632; Gregory L. Thompson, "The Passenger Train in the Motor Age," appendix 5 (unpublished Ph.D. dissertation, University of California, Irvine, 1977); John H. White, Jr., *The American Railroad Passenger Car* (Baltimore: Johns Hopkins University Press, 1978), 144, 175–177, 185–186, 282. White presents detailed weight, capacity, and purchase cost information for various types of cars that operated on U.S. railroads during different eras, which I used in part for this analysis. However, White follows the traditional railroad view that tare weights were unimportant in the economics of passenger trains.

38. TWR: Sunset file, undated analysis of new streamlined equipment for the *Sunset Limited* ca. 1948, showing earnings of the *Sunbeam*, one of the two Dallas–Houston trains, of $1.23 per train mile in 1939, $1.43 in 1940, and $1.63 in 1941.

39. U.S. Federal Coordinator of Transportation, *Passenger Traffic Report;* for 1933 air traffic, see appendix 2, table 2. See also SFC, transcript, 10782, 11595.

40. TWR: Sunset file, analysis of new equipment for *Sunset Limited*. This analysis presents histories of the gross train mile earnings for Southern Pacific trains that the company streamlined prior to World War II. Gross train mile revenues for the *Lark* were $3.31 for 1934, $3.51 for 1935, $3.52 for 1936, $3.27 for 1937, $3.52 for 1938, $3.76 for 1939, $3.22 for 1940, $3.44 for 1941, $5.31 for 1942. The Southern Pacific passenger department credited the lightweight equipment for causing the large increase in revenue for 1942 and offered this as a reason for buying streamlined equipment for the *Sunset Limited* in 1948. However, the first streamlined cars entered *Lark* service on 2 March 1941, and the entire two trains were streamlined on 10 July 1941. The 1941 revenue increase of $0.22 over that for 1940 is insignificant. What caused the huge revenue increase in 1942 was the fact that the *Sunset Limited*, a companion overnight train on the same run as the *Lark* and also with revenues of about $3.00 per mile, was discontinued in January 1942, and its passengers were put onto the *Lark*.

41. CRHM: "Operations of 1940 Pass in Review," Southern Pacific *Bulletin* (April 1941), 5–8.

42. U.S. Federal Coordinator of Transportation, *Passenger Traffic Report*,

appendix 1, 1933 traffic survey. Coverdale & Colpitts, *Report on Streamline, Light-Weight, High-Speed Passenger Trains* (New York: Coverdale & Colpitts, 30 June 1941), shows only traffic for diesel trains on route, carrying 32.2 million passenger miles per year. This is equivalent to about 320,000 passengers. Analysis of changes in intra-California revenues suggests that steam trains on the route carried at least 180,000 additional passengers—probably considerably more.

43. U.S. Federal Coordinator of Transportation, *Passenger Traffic Report*, appendix 1, 1933 traffic survey, shows about 220,000 annual Southern Pacific passengers in 1933. I estimate that the Sacramento Northern, a competing electric interurban, carried another 100,000 passengers. By 1939 the interurban traffic declined to about 15,000 passengers (not including commuters or passengers riding to points north of Sacramento), according to a special study conducted by Pacific Greyhound Lines and another study that the railroad commission conducted a year later. Analysis of 1938 Southern Pacific train earnings found in TWR: Coast Line file, shows that Southern Pacific trains still carried about 200,000 passengers per year. Pacific Greyhound Lines remained a minor player in this service.

44. CALTRANS: *California Highways and Public Works* 17 (July 1939), 1–3, 23. The new line had 2,028 degrees of curvature, compared to 7,129 degrees for the old; its maximum curvature was 4 degrees compared to 11 degrees for the old. The comparison of schedules of the *Cascade* before and after the line opened are in CRHM: Southern Pacific Company, Shasta Division Employees Timetables nos. 49 and 50, 28 September 1941 and 7 June 1942.

45. Such improvements would have increased rail passenger traffic by 35 percent over the level achieved by the *Daylight* and would have earned a social return on investment. See Gregory L. Thompson, "Inferring Regional Structure from Partial Transportation Flow Data," *Papers of the Regional Science Association* 67 (1987), 137–155.

Conclusion

1. This number is based on fifty seat coaches at 50 percent occupancy, which was typical of the streamlined *Daylight* before the fare decrease of July 1938. After the fare decrease, the *Daylight* ran with 90 percent or better occupancy during the summer months, but its year-round occupancy was much lower.

2. Klein presents another perspective on this culture in his discussion of the resistance of Union Pacific officers to dieselization and to modernization in general. At the end of World War II the new Union Pacific president criticized railroad executives for always seeking rate increases rather than efficiency improvements, thereby pricing themselves out of the market. See Maury Klein, *Union Pacific: The Rebirth, 1894–1969* (New York: Doubleday, 1989), 437, 441–443, 446–449, 494–497.

3. Maury Klein collection: W. A. Harriman to Fred W. Sargent, 26 June 1936.

4. HML: Records of the Pennsylvania Railroad, VP Operations, file 521.31, Post-War Passenger Train Problems, 1943, Charles E. Smith to R. V. Fletcher, 1 September 1943.

5. Ibid., 2, 3. See also page 6.

6. HML: Records of the Pennsylvania Railroad, VP Operations, file 521.31, Post-War Passenger Train Problems, 1943, Charles E. Smith to J. P. Newell, 9 October 1952.

Index

Abraham Lincoln, 143
Ackerman, Fred W., 35, 92, 94–95, 126, 209n. 95, 228n. 49
Adams, Henry Carter, 203n. 15
Airlines: as competition for railroads, xiii, 147
Allan, Stuart, 203n. 10, 217n. 14
Altamont Pass, 103, 150, 160, 224n. 47, photo 16
Altshuler, Alan, 201n. 1 (preface)
American Motor Transportation Company, 69; formation of, 92
American Toll Bridge Company, 68
Andriot, John L., 203n. 10, 204nn. 22–24, 30, 205n. 39, 217n. 14
Angel, 59, 87; passenger revenue, 215n. 68
Anti-trust: Central Pacific, 30; Union Pacific/Southern Pacific, 30
Arnold, Bion J., 212n. 40
Associates, The, 11, 12–13; opposition to rate regulation, 15; relation with Los Angeles Chamber of Commerce, 17; reorganization into Southern Pacific Company, 22
Association of American Railroads, 161
Association of Western Traffic Officers: fare reductions of 1933, 117
Atchison. *See* Santa Fe
Atchison, Topeka and Santa Fe Railroad. *See* Santa Fe
Atchison, Topeka and Santa Fe Railway. *See* Santa Fe
Austin, Dwight, 98
Auto Truck and Stage Act of 1917, 36
Automobile: competition with railroads, xiii, 1, 35, 151, 152; effect of Depression on, 114; effect on rail passenger demand, 55–56, 66–67, 114, 153; effect on rail schedules in 1920s, 82; ownership growth, 32, 55–56, 63, 66–67, 170 table 3; popularity of, 32–33; rail management response to growth of, 152, 161; traffic increase, 1920–23, 67–68

Bagby, Earl, 142, 217n. 21
Bail, Eli, 217n. 21, 222n. 7
Batters, Frank E., 88
Bay Bridge, 69, 122
Beebe, Lucius, 165
Belasco, Warren James, 82, 114, 217n. 12, 220n. 49, 226n. 5
Benedict, Karen, 201n. 2 (preface)
Bevington, E. L., 66
Blackford, Mansel S., 15, 23, 204n. 27, 205n. 38, 205n. 39, 206nn. 45, 52, 207n. 58
Bledsoe, Samuel, 219n. 44
Boudier, William H., 207nn. 67, 70
Bradley, Bill, 228n. 64
Brandeis, Louis D., 47–48, 89, 211n. 25
Brown, Giles T., 207nn. 64, 66, 215n. 70, 218nn. 23–24, 220n. 47, 230n. 5
Bryant, Keith L., Jr., 70, 204n. 29, 229n. 70
Burckhalter, Frank L., 126
Bureau of Transportation Research, 136
Burlington-Rock Island, 128
Bus: merger of 1929, 92–93; passenger characteristics, 107; regulation of, 36
Bus fares: and passenger trends, 1933, 187 table 17; yields per mile, 1933, 186 table 16
Bus, intercity: photos 5, 7, 10, 11; in California, 35; competition with railroads 1, 37–38; emer-

235

Bus, intercity (*continued*)
gence of, 35. *See also* Jitney, interurban
Bus revenue: East Coast, 1933, 179–81 table 10; West Coast, 1933, 176–78 table 9
Bus route: decline of rural traffic on, 186 table 15; expansion of, 36–37
Bus service: as civic responsibility, 97; by New York, New Haven, and Hartford Railroad, 78. *See also* New England Transportation Company
Bus service, operating costs of: 1927–35, 183 table 13; Southern Pacific, 78–79, 91; transcontinental, 69
Business community: and decline of railroads, 10–11; hostility toward railroads, 7, 14–15, 18, 27, 153; Section 4 waivers, 137
Business interests: role in railroad development, 1890–1920, 23
Butterfield, O. E., 211n. 31
Byram, H. E., 220n. 50
Byrne, John J., 80

Cahuenga Pass, 224n. 48
California Board of Trade, 18–19
California Highway Commission, 150; creation of, 33; objectives of, 33–34
California Limited, 88, 165
California Railroad Commission of 1912, 29
California Toll Bridge Authority, 69
California Transit Company, 37, 69
Campbell, J. B., 210n. 23
Car. *See* Automobile
Cardinal Stage Lines, 227n. 32
Caro, Patricia, 203n. 10 (chap. 1), 217n. 14
Carquinez Straits, 83
Carquinez Straits Bridge, 68, 85, 159
Carson, H. M., 210n. 14

Case file: as data source, xiv; definition of, xiv–xv
Central Arizona Transportation Company, 227n. 32
Central Pacific: anti-trust, 30; business community opposition to, 12; competition from sailing ships, 13; connection with Union Pacific, 11; expansion to Los Angeles, 14; expansion from San Francisco, 14; incorporation of, 11; merger case effect on investment, 58; rate reduction in 1870s, 13
Certificates of convenience and necessity: purchase of, by SPMT, 79
Challenger, 129
Chandler, Alfred D., Jr., 1, 2, 13, 39, 41, 42–43, 153, 201n. 1 (intro.), 203nn. 13–14, 209n. 1, 210nn. 9–10, 12–13, 16, 211n. 26
Chandler Act of 1911, 33
Charske, F. W., 220n. 50
Chicago, Burlington & Quincy, 121, 144
Chicago, North Shore & Milwaukee, 121
Chicago & Northwestern, 159
Chief, 88, 220n. 50
Chief engineer, 41
City of Los Angeles, 128
City of San Francisco, 231n. 31; average speed, 128; introduction of, 128; operating costs, 142
Cochran, Thomas C., 2, 10–11, 39, 153–54, 202nn. 4 (intro.), 5–7 (chap. 1), 203nn. 15, 209n. 1
Collusion hypothesis. *See* Conspiracy theory
Condit, Carl W., 65, 131, 216n. 7, 228n. 64
Conner, F. W., 107
Conspiracy theory, 5–6; agreements between Southern Pacific and Pacific Greyhound, 109–10;

effect on rail decline, 151; fare reduction of 1936, 108; passenger traffic patterns, 105; relations between Southern Pacific, Pacific Greyhound, General Motors, 111–12; role of fares, 104–5, 186 tables 16, 17; and Superbus, 99

Cooley, Thomas M., xiv

Cost: fluctuation, 47; fully allocated 1923, 73; increase due to federal regulation, 60; increase in passenger service, 1920, 65–66; long/heavy vs. short/light trains, 138; out-of-pocket, 73; passenger, 1920s, 77; passenger vs. freight, 141; relation to gross revenue, 45–46

Cost accounting, 41–42; importance of, 1–2

Cost analysis, 62

Cost-based rates, 62

Cost control, 41–42

Cost reduction efforts, 56

Cost separation, 168–69 table 2, 212n. 36; rail management opposition to, 50–51

Cost of service vs. value of service, 49

Cost variability research: rail management rejection of, 139–40; refinement of, 139

Costing methods, 218n. 32; advances in, 138; effect on railroad profitability, 151; failure of rail management, 3, 136–37, 141–42, 151, 152, 153–54; ICC formula, accuracy of, 135–36; improvements in, 1930s, 142–43; marginal costs, 138–39; out-of-pocket, effectiveness of, 135; as pessimistic indicator, 135; Pullman Company, 144; rail management operating statistics used in, 140–42, 165–66, 166–67 table 1, 168–69 table 2; rail management rejection of ICC, 154; regression analysis in, 138, 140; streamliners, 142; as underestimation of passenger costs, 140; unit costs, 140–41; using tare weight, 136

Coverdale & Colpitts, 121, 125, 130, 132, 133, 134, 227nn. 29, 44, 228n. 60, 229n. 68, 231n. 28, 232n. 37, 233n. 42

Crandall, Burton B., 208n. 85, 209nn. 90–91, 93, 218n. 21, 222n. 7

Cross subsidization, 40, 50, 54, 61, 154; discouragement of, 64; opposition to, 48, 65–66; as social obligation of railroad, 48–49

Crump, Spencer, 214n. 57

Cuesta Grade, photos 12, 15, 103, 130

Cunningham, William J., 86, 207n. 56, 211n. 25, 212n. 37, 215nn. 64–66, 71–75, 216n. 5, 221n. 64

Daggett, Stuart, 15, 27, 55, 203nn. 9, 16–17, 19, 22, 204nn. 25, 28–29, 35–36, 205nn. 38–39, 206n. 51, 207nn. 57, 62, 213n. 52, 230n. 4

Darlington, Newell Dyke, 33

Day, Clarence, 138, 142, 144, 230n. 9

Daylight, photos 12, 14, 104, 144, 145, 223n. 45, 231n. 31; as corporate image, 159; cost analysis of, 143–44; decline of, 79; fare reduction, 1929, 81; fare reduction, 1937, 156; load factors, 144, 231n. 34; new, 125, 128; new, average speed, 128; new, revenue increase, 130; schedule improvements, 124; slowing of, 115

Depression: effect on passenger fares, 115, 117–18

Development interests: effect on

Development interests (*continued*)
    transportation competition,
    30–31
Deverell, William F., 204n. 31
Director General of USRA, 59
Donley, Michael W., 203n. 10,
    217n. 14
Droege, John A., 54, 213n. 46
Due, John, 56–57, 135, 207n. 63,
    214n. 57, 219n. 36, 230n. 2
Duffy, James B., 221n. 76
Dunn, James A., Jr., 201n. 1 (preface)
Durborow, R. N., 210n. 14
Dykstra, Robert R., 11, 202n. 7
    (chap. 1)

East Bay Electric, 30, 126
Eastman, Joseph, 211n. 25. *See
    also* Federal Coordinator of
    Transportation
Eaton, Shirley, 203n. 13
Economies of scope, 36
Edwards, Ford K., 139, 203nn.
    9–10, 13, 15–16
El Dorado, 56
Ellery, Nathan, 31, 32
El Paso & Southwestern (EP&SW):
    purchase of, by Southern
    Pacific, 85

Farrell, J. D., 220n. 50
Federal Coordinator of Transportation, 205n. 42, 210n. 19, 217n.
    13, 218n. 28, 221n. 67, 224n.
    55, 226nn. 3, 6, 227n. 46,
    228n. 58, 232n. 39, 232n. 42,
    233n. 43
Fielding, Gordon J., 98, 223n. 32
Filer, W. G., 94
Fink, Albert, 42, 47
Finkbohner, T., 94, 96
Fishlow, Albert, 46, 86, 210n. 24,
    221n. 65
Fletcher, Austin B., 33
Fletcher, R. V., 160, 226n. 10,
    233n. 4

Flink, James J., 3, 33, 202nn. 4–5
    (intro.), 208n. 72, 217nn. 11–12
Ford, Robert S., 206n. 46, 207nn.
    59, 61, 214n. 57
Forty-Niner, 231n. 31
Frailey, M. C., 94
Freed, Clyde H., 201n. 5, 215n. 62
Freight rates: components of, 13; discriminatory, 13–14; and development interests, 14–15; erosion
    of, 18; freeze, 29; increase to
    subsidize passenger service, 54;
    and San Francisco, 15
Freight service: improvements to
    operation of, 1920s, 86
Freight tariffs of 1873, 13
Freight traffic: effect of World War
    I on, 58–59; growth of, 1899–
    1910, 21–22; trends, Southern
    Pacific, 1937, 1938, 125
Friedlaender, Ann F., 140, 216n. 4,
    231n. 22
Fuess, Claude Moore, 207n. 56,
    211n. 25, 215n. 64, 226n. 21
Fully allocated costs, Southern
    Pacific, 1911, 27

General Motors: conspiracy theory,
    role in, 5–6, 111–12, 151; design of Superbus, 98–99
Gillett, James N., 32
Golden Gate, 129, 132, photo 13; as
    corporate image, 159
Goldsboro experiment: results of, 119
Grand Canyon Limited, 88
Great Northern Railway: Southern
    Pacific opposition to, 78
Grey, Carl R., 220n. 50
Greyhound Corporation: conspiracy
    theory, role in, 5–6, 111; cooperation with railroads, 111–12;
    effect of Depression on, 94;
    founding of, 35, 95; takeover
    of Pacific Greyhound, 1930s,
    94–95
Gross revenue, 43, 45–46
Growth machine, 11

Hannaford, J. M., 220n. 50
Harriman, Averell, 159, 233n. 3
Harriman, Edward H., 22–23, 54
Harriman, W. A. *See* Harriman, Averell
Harriman Era, 9
Harvard, 31, 60; return to West Coast, 1921, 69–70
Hepburn Act of 1906, 9–10, 29
Hiawatha: load factors, 231n. 34
Hichborn, Franklin, 206nn. 54–55, 207n. 60
Highway: competition with railroads, 152; expenditures, 1914–33, 171 table 4; freeways, 103–4
Highway development, 31–33; funding of, 31–32, 34; initial interest in, 208n. 73; as rail service competition, 31–32
Highway improvements: 1920s, 67; 1930s, 101, 103–4; cost of, 1920s, 68–69; effect on bus service, 1930s, 101, 103–4; effect on rail passenger service, 1916, 1920s, 83; government policy, 4–5; to mountain highways, 68–69, 103–4; following World War I, 63
Hill, W., 220n. 50
Hilton, George W., 2, 56–57, 135, 201n. 3 (intro.), 207n. 63, 214n. 57, 219n. 36, 230n. 2, 231n. 21
Hines, Walker D., 61
Hoch-Smith Resolution of 1925, 64
Hofsommer, Don L., 30, 86, 124, 207n. 62, 213n. 52, 221nn. 58–59, 63, 227nn. 41, 43
Holden, Hale, 132, 228n. 57, 229nn. 66–67
Hood, William, 22
Hoogenboom, Ari and Olive, 207n. 56, 211n. 25, 215n. 64, 216nn. 2–3, 5
Hoover, Herbert, 212n. 37, 218n. 25, 221n. 64
Hoschek, John P., 35, 208n. 82, 209n. 95, 223nn. 36–38, 225n. 82

Hosmer, Howard, 140, 231n. 21
Hunter, J. G., 230n. 13
Huntington, Collis P., 22
Hupmobile, 35

Imperial Valley, 35, 68
Infrastructure, rail: photos 12, 15; operating costs of, 136; poor development of, 136
Infrastructure, subsidized: effects on development, 18; as railroad competition, 38
Infrastructure improvements, 153, 214n. 61; 1930s, 130–31, 149–50; effect on railroad costs, 149–50; highway improvements compared to, 6
Infrastructure investments: decline of rail, 58
Intercity bus: attack by Southern Pacific, 73; reorganization of, 1920s, 69
Intercity transportation system: role of government in, xiii; role of private enterprise in, xiii
Interstate Commerce Act of 1887, 64
Interstate Commerce Commission (ICC): control of, by shippers, 29; formation of, xiv; jurisdiction over intercity buses, 122; rail rate increase requests, 1910–17, 46–47; rail rate regulation by, 4–5; rail rate regulation policy, 5
Interurban Electric Railway: passenger service elimination, 127; passenger trends, 174 table 7
Interurban railway, electric, 30; construction of, 17–18; passenger trends, 217n. 12, 233n. 43

Jackson, Carlton, 208n. 81
Jitney, interurban, 35, 36
John, Richard R., 210n. 11
Johnson, Emory R., 203n. 13, 210n. 9
Johnson, Hiram, 27, 29

Index

Jones, Lee D., 77–78, 93, 96, 97, 107, 219nn. 43–44
Judah, Theodore, 11

Keeler, Theodore, 140, 231n. 22
Kelley, Augustus M., 203n. 9
Kennan, George, 206n. 44, 207n. 62
Kerr, K. Austin, 215nn. 65, 72–73
Key System, 126
Kimball, Cloyd, 95, 126, 133, 139, 209n. 95, 222nn. 17, 19, 223n. 29, 224n. 46, 228n. 49, 229n. 70, 230nn. 8, 14, 17–18
Klein, Maury, 22, 31, 40, 82, 128, 202n. 3, 204n. 31, 206nn. 43–44, 51, 207nn. 62, 65, 209n. 3, 212n. 36, 213n. 49, 220n. 50, 227n. 28, 228nn. 55, 58, 232n. 36, 233nn. 2–3
Kruttschnitt, Julius, 42, 57

Labor interests and nationalization, 61
Labor relations and rail industry, 60, 61
Labor settlements: effect on railroad losses, 63–64
Ladd, Dwight R., 136, 139, 210n. 17, 230nn. 3, 19
Lark, 59, 104, 128, 231n. 31; cost of operation, 1923, 73, 77; profitability of, 147; streamlined, 232n. 40
Latham, Earl, 207n. 56, 211n. 25, 215n. 64, 226n. 21
Livesay, Harold, 41–42, 210n. 11
Load factor: coach, 144, 231n. 34; defined, 36, 97; Pacific Greyhound Lines, 97, 223n. 30; Pacific Greyhound Line use of, 144–45; rail management failure to manage, 144; streamliners, 145
Locomotive: design improvements, 1920s, 82–83
Logan, John R., 203n. 8
Lorenz, Max O., 47, 138, 139, 140, 211nn. 28–29

Los Angeles Chamber of Commerce: and the Associates, 17; and development interests, 16–17
Los Angeles harbor fight, 17
Los Angeles Limited, 220n. 50
Los Angeles Terminal Railroad, 17
Los Angeles Union Passenger Terminal, 85, 131
Lovett, R. S., 54–55, 212n. 36, 220n. 50
Lynd, Helen Merrel and Robert S., 226n. 4
Lynd study, 114

Mainline densities: relationship to costs, 140
Management, rail, attitudes of, 39–40; passenger service as civic responsibility, 41; passenger service as public relations, 155; siege mentality, 40; toward shippers, 154–55
Management, rail, cross subsidization, 40; nationalization, 61; operating statistics used in, 42–43, 50; passenger policy failure, xiii, 151, 152–53, 157–58, 160–61; resistance to accurate costing, 139–40
Management strategies, Pacific Greyhound: success of, 158–59
Management strategies, rail: vs. bus, 158–59; effect on passenger traffic trends, 56–57; failure of, xiii–xiv, 4–5, 6–7, 151, 152–53; 157–58, 160–61; failure to control costs, 145, 147–49; to increase speed, 121; for operating efficiency, 1920s, 64–65; operating statistics used in, 42–43, 50; rate increase requests, 1910–17, 46–47; Santa Fe, 1930s, 121–22; Southern Pacific, 72–73, 192 table 22
Management structure, rail: 1840–90, 39; criticism of, 45–46; division officers in, 45; division of responsibility in, 43–44; failure

of, 2–3, 153–54; modernization
of, 1–2; in passenger responsibility, 43; Santa Fe, 40–41; Southern Pacific, 40–41; vice president of operations, 41
Manager of passenger traffic, 43–44
Mann-Elkin Act of 1910, 10, 29
Martin, Albro, 4, 9, 46, 152, 173 table 5, 202nn. 7 (intro.), 3 (chap. 1), 203n. 15, 207n. 56, 211n. 25, 213n. 48, 214n. 58
Matthew, Alan, 95, 107, 142
Matthews, Fred, 9, 202n. 2
McAdoo, William, 59, 60–61, 207n. 56, 211n. 25, 215n. 64
McAfee, Ward, 15, 203nn. 9, 11, 17, 22, 204nn. 26, 28, 205nn. 37–38, 206n. 52, 206n. 55
McDonald, Angus D., 108–9, 123, 125, 126, 127, 132, 218n. 32, 220n. 51, 226n. 7, 228nn. 53, 57, 229n. 66
McGanny, Danny, 55, 126–27, 213n. 50, 219n. 42, 228n. 51
McGinnis, Felix S., 44, 80–81, 87, 88, 107, 108–9, 113, 114, 115, 123, 126, 127, 142, 221n. 74, 224n. 50, 225n. 1, 229n. 70
McWilliams, Carey, 16, 18, 203nn. 21–22, 204nn. 30, 33, 205n. 39
Meier, Albert E., 35, 208n. 82, 209n. 95, 223nn. 36–38, 225n. 82
Mercier, A. T. 229n. 70
Meyer, John R., 2, 140, 201n. 3, 231n. 20
Mohler, A. L., 220n. 50
Moline, Norman T., 217n. 12
Molotch, Harvey L., 203n. 8
Morgan, Edmund S., 10–11, 202n. 5 (chap. 1)
Morgan, Tom, 35
Motor Carrier Act of 1935, 122
Motor Carriers Association, 73; opposition to SPMT, 79
Motor Transit Corporation, 69; organization of, 92; ownership of, 93

Myers, William A., 204n. 33, 208n. 77

Nash, Gerald D., 206n. 53, 207nn. 67–69, 209n. 89
National Trailways System, 129
Natron Cut-Off, 85
Navajo, 88
Net revenue, Southern Pacific, 1911, 27
Newell, J. P., 233n. 6
New England Transportation Company, 78, 160
New York Central, 71, 121, 144; fare yields, 1922–30, 81 fig. 3.5; fare yields, 1922–35, 117 fig. 5.2
New York, New Haven & Hartford Railroad, 71, 78, 160
Noon Daylight, 231n. 31
Northwestern Pacific, 25 map 1.4, 127; agreement with Pacific Greyhound, 111; purchase by Southern Pacific, 111

Oakland, Antioch & Eastern, 53
Olin, Spencer C., Jr., 206n. 53
Operating cost, rail, 46, 137–39; factor inputs, 1923–41, 197 table 27; increase by steel trains, 57; labor, 1923–41, 199 table 28; safety improvements, effect on, 30; short/light vs. long/heavy, 138
Operating cost analysis, rail, 1925, 138
Operating cost index, rail, 1923–41, 197 table 26
Operating expenses: separation of, 50–51, 63, 168–69 table 2, 212nn. 34, 36
Operating ratio, freight, 1916, 51; 1920, 64; Southern Pacific, 1920s, 86
Operating ratio, passenger, Santa Fe, 160; 1933, 115; 1933, 1934, 118; 1935, 121; 1937, 1938, 1940, 132–33; 1940, 134

Operating ratio, passenger, Southern Pacific, 148, 160; 1920s, 86–87; 1929, 113; 1933, 115; 1933, 1934, 118; 1934, 1936, 1937, 125; 1938–41, 132; 1940, 134; 1930s–41, 148
Operating ratio, rail: defined, 42, 148; effect of rate discrimination on, 49; passenger, 160; passenger, 1916, 51; passenger, 1920, 63; passenger, ICC, 1932–41, 193 table 23; significance of, 45
Operating ratio, Southern Pacific, 43, 148; 1901–10, 49–50; 1910–17, 50; as indicator of success, 49–50
Operating statistics, rail: used by management, 13, 42–43, 50
Oregon Motor Stages, 78
Oster, Clinton V., Jr., 2, 201n. 3
Otis, Harrison Gray, 17
Out-of-pocket costs. *See* Costing methods, marginal costs
Overland Limited, 82, 85
Overland Route, 85
Overton, Richard C., 82, 220n. 49
Owl: combination with *West Coast*, 115

Pacific Coast Steamship Company, 31
Pacific Electric Railway, 57, 60, 123, 125; organization of, 23; passenger service elimination on, 1941, 127; passenger traffic, 1914–17, 56
Pacific Greyhound: challenge from Santa Fe, 110–11; conspiracy theory, 111–12; design improvement, 98–99; development of, 6; effect of Depression on, 94; effect on Southern Pacific, 1930s, 101; load factors, 1935, 1936, 223n. 30; Northwestern Pacific agreement, 111; passenger revenue, 1935, 1936, 223n. 43; passenger route changes, 101, 104; passenger service improvements, 101, 124; passenger traffic trends, 1930s, 99, 101, 105; profitability of, 6, 7–8, 133; Santa Fe opposition to, 122–24; Santa Fe Trailways, competition, 133; schedules vs. Southern Pacific, 103, 104; service supplied to Southern Pacific, 110; Southern Pacific, agreements, 109–10; wildcat sedan competition 105–6
Pacific Greyhound fares: basis for, 124; reduction of, 97–98, 108–9, 124; structure of, 104–5, 186 table 16, 187 table 17
Pacific Greyhound Lines, 79, 97; establishment of, 91–92, 93; load factors, 97; management structure, 93–94; ownership of, 93; routes, 1931, 100 map 4.1; routes, 1936, 102 map 4.2
Pacific Greyhound management: efficiency of, 111–12; importance of, to rail management, 91–92; strategy, 1930s, 95–96; structure reorganization, 1930s, 94–95
Pacific Greyhound operating statistics, 96–97
Pacific Greyhound profitability, 111–12, 134, 158; investigation of, 108; by route, 184–85 table 14
Pacific Railroad Act: of 1862, 12; of 1864, 12
Panama Canal, 31
Passenger, bus: characteristics of, 101, 107–8
Passenger cars: investment in, 1920s, 85–86
Passenger era, 1910–15, 23, 25–26
Passenger financial performance: view of E. P. Ripley, 58
Passenger, rail: characteristics of, 101, 107–8
Passenger rail fares: 1920s, 155–56; bus vs. rail, 105; ceiling, definition of, 120; discounts, 1920s, 89; effect of Depression on, 115, 117–18; effect of reductions on steamships, 81–82; increase, 1920, 65, 66; increase due to

Index

competition, 80–81; increase due to federal regulation, 60; rate freeze, 29; reductions, 79–80; reductions, 1933, 117–18; Santa Fe, reductions, 1933, 1934, 120; Southern Railway, 1920s, 119–20; Southern Railway, reductions, 1932, 119

Passenger rail revenue: effect of 1921 recession on, 66; growth of, 1934–41, 130 fig. 5.3; increase of, 1920, 66–67; as percent of income, 1911–20, 52 fig. 2.1; as percent of income, 1911–30, 72 fig. 3.1; as percent of income, 1911–41, 131 fig. 5.4

Passenger rail service, 1920s, 89–90; as civic responsibility, 3, 55; as corporate identity, 53, 65, 87, 88, 155; cost of, 2; cross subsidies of, 50, 54; decline, xiii, 2–6, 51–52, 89–90, 151, 153; domination of, 1; effect of automobile on, 67, 114, 153; effect of Depression on, 114; financial condition of, 1920s, 89–90; as freight promotion, 3, 53–54, 87, 132, 155; improvements, effect on cost, 157; intercity demand for, 52, 53; interstate demand for, 52 fig. 2.1, 53, 70–71; intrastate demand for, 52 fig. 2.1, 53; local, 25, 27, 70–71; photos 1, 2; luxury service, 54–55; luxury service restoration, 65; management response to stagnation of demand for, 156–57; market development failure, 159; profitability of, 3; public demand vs. ability to service, 202n. 4 (chap. 1); as public relations, 53, 155, 159; revenue, 195–6 table 25; revenue decline, 226n. 3; scheduling improvements, 1920s, 82–83, 182 table 12

Passenger rail service, Santa Fe: contraction of, 58; cutbacks, 59–60, 156; improvements, 156–57, 1920s, 87–88; trends, 88–89

Passenger rail service, Southern Pacific: indicators, 1920–30, 182 table 11; replacement with buses, 77–78, 156, 1927–35, 188 table 18

Passenger rail traffic: financial performance, 56–57; growth of, 9; growth in relation to population, 55; Santa Cruz and Salinas, 189 table 19; tripling of, 1899–1910, 21–22

Passenger rail traffic trends, 56–57; 212n. 40; 1920s, 70–71; automobile and effect on, 55–56, 66–67; bus fares and, 1933, 187 table 17; bus vs. rail usage, 1930s, 105; decline in demand, 1920s, 70–71; decline in 1929–33, 114–15; expenditures for rail, 205n. 42; fares, 1933, 187 table 17; interurban electric, 174 table 7; management strategy, 56–57; Southern Pacific 205n. 41, 1937–38, 125; steam, 1920, 1929, 175 table 8; yield trends, 1922–34, 194 table 24

Patterson, George Stuart, 48
Patton, Clyde P., 203n. 10, 217n. 14
Peck, Merton J., 231n. 20
Peninsular Railway, 56
Pennsylvania Railroad, 42, 71, 121, 144; fare yields, 1922–30, 81 fig. 3.5; fare yields, 1922–35, 117 fig. 5.2
Pickwick Corporation, 94
Pickwick Stages, 69, 209nn. 92, 96
Pioneer Yellowway Stages, 69
Pioneer Zephyr, 121
Pooling agreements: implementation of, 225n. 80; improved efficiency through, 64
Population, California: 28 fig. 1.2, 203n. 22; 204nn. 23–24; 205n. 39
Porter, Glenn, 39, 201n. 2 (intro.), 209n. 2
Pratt, Edwin A., 53–54, 132, 213n. 43
Preston, Howard L., 217n. 12

Preston, William L., 204n. 23, 205n. 39
Private control of railroads: return to, 61, 63
Public transportation: declining demand for, 35
Pucher, John, 201n. 1 (preface)
Pullman, surcharge, 60, 65, 155
Pullman cars: competition from tourist courts, 114; improvements to, 57; migration of 1887, 16; profitability of, 125; usage rates 210n. 23; weights of wood vs. steel, 214n. 59
Pullman Company, 44–45; coach improvements, 1930s, 118; contracts with railroads, 44–45; costing methods of, 144; revenue drop of 1940, 147; use of steel cars, 57
Pullman trains: cost increase, 65–66; elimination of, 126; expansion of service, 57; passenger demand for, 53, 70–71, 156

Quigley, C. E., 94
Quirk, 221n. 70

Rae, John B., 217n. 12
Rail competition: effect on development, 27
Rail decline: arguments for, 9–10; business community hostility as factor in, 10–11
Rail fares: passenger trends, 156; 1933, 187 table 17
Rail fare yield per mile, 1933, 186 table 16
Rail monopoly: effect on development, 27
Rail passenger revenue: 1911–41, 190–91 table 20; fare yields, 1922–30, 81 fig. 3.5; fare yields, 1922–35, 117 fig. 5.2
Rail productivity growth, 1839–1909, 1910, 46
Rail routes: ca. 1880, 12 map 1.1; conversion to bus routes, 86–87, 156

Rail safety improvements: effect on operating costs, 30
Rapport, Leonard, 201n. 2 (preface)
Rate discrimination, geographic, 30; effect on operating ratio, 49; prohibition against, 136–37
Rates: Southern Pacific request for increase, 30
Rate war: effect on development, 16–17; Southern Pacific and Santa Fe, 16
Refrigerator cars: effect on farming practices, 21
Regulation of rates, 15; effect on decline of railroad, 4–5, 151, 152; effect on rail management strategies, 5; opposition to, 15
Revenue, Pacific Greyhound, 223n. 43
Revenue, rail: increase, 1934–41, 130 fig. 5.3, 131 fig. 5.4; as percent of income, 1911–20, 52 fig. 2.1; as percent of income, 1911–30, 72 fig. 3.1; per passenger mile, 81
Revenue, rail vs. bus: East Coast, 1933, 179–81 table 10; West Coast, 1933, 176–78 table 9
Revenue, Southern Pacific, 1911, 27
Ridge Route, 34, 68, 103, photo 9
Rio Grande Stages, 227n. 32
Ripley, E. P., 58, 59, 220n. 50
Rolling stock: estimates on returns, 143
Rolph, Governor, 217n. 20

Sacramento River Canyon, 149
Sailing ships: competition with railroads, 14
Saint, 59, 87; passenger revenue from, 215n. 68
Salsbury, Stephen, 3, 202n. 5 (intro.), 203n. 15, 213n. 41
Sargent, Fred W., 159, 233n. 3
San Diegan, 129
San Francisco & San Joaquin Railroad, 19
San Joaquin, 104
San Joaquin Daylight, 128, 132
San Joaquin Line, 83–84, 109

Index 245

San Pedro: designation as harbor site, 17
San Pedro, Los Angeles & Salt Lake, 17
Santa Cruz decision, 91
Santa Fe, 20 map 1.2; bus acquisition by, 121–22; business support of, in *Santa Fe Case*, 126; challenge to Pacific Greyhound, 110–11; change in management view of local trains, 58; extension to San Francisco, 19–21; high speed coach emphasis, 133; infrastructure improvements, 130–31; lines in California, 25 fig. 1.4; Pacific Greyhound opposition, 122–24; profitability of, 129–30; San Francisco & San Joaquin purchase, 19; Southern Pacific opposition, 122–24; Southern Pacific rate war, 16; streamliners, increased use of, 1936–41, 128; switch engine hours, 229n. 65
Santa Fe Case, xv, 123–24, 126; cost accounting in, 142–43; effect on Pacific Greyhound management, 126
Santa Fe management strategy, 1930s, 133–34
Santa Fe passenger fare: increase, 1920s, 156–57; reduction, 1933–34, 120, 1938, 129
Santa Fe passenger operating ratio, 1933, 115; 1933, 1934, 118; 1935, 121; 1937, 1938, 1940, 132–33; 1940, 134
Santa Fe passenger service: as corporate image, 115, 132; as freight advertisement, 132; high speed service emphasis, 129, 133; improvements in, 121–22, 156–57; innovations in, 122; reductions in, 115
Santa Fe passenger traffic trends: 1911–19, 174 table 6; 1929–34, 118–19; 1939–41, 129–30
Santa Fe Railway, 15, 204n. 29. *See also* Santa Fe

Santa Fe Trail System: organization of, 121–22
Santa Fe Trailways, 129; competition with Pacific Greyhound, 133
Santa Fe Transportation Company, 122
Savage Act of 1907, 207n. 68
Schisgall, Oscar, 208n. 81
Scout, 88
Scrip books, 108
Section 4, 136–37
Seeley, Bruce E., 208n. 73
Seger, C. B., 220n. 50
Sharfman, Isaiah Leo, 203n. 13
Shasta Dam, 149, 160, photo 17
Sherman Anti-Trust Act, 30
Shoup, Paul, 78, 218n. 29
Signor, John R., 204n. 31, 221n. 56
Simmons, Jack, 3, 10, 202nn. 6 (intro.), 4 (chap. 1)
Skowronek, Stephen, 207n. 56, 215nn. 65, 73–74
Sleeping cars. *See* Pullman
Smith, Charles E., 160–61, 226n. 10, 233nn. 4, 6
Smith, Merritt Roe, 10–11, 202n. 5 (chap. 1)
Snell, Bradford, 5, 99, 202n. 8 (intro.), 222n. 14
Southern Kansas Stage Lines, 98, 227n. 32
Southern Pacific: anti-trust, 30; business opposition to, in *Santa Fe Case*, 126; conspiracy theory, 111–12; cost analysis improvements, 143; cost, fully allocated, 1911, 27; economy trade, 129; effect of Depression on, 94, 113, 114; effect of Pacific Greyhound on, 101, 109; expansion to Los Angeles, 14; expansion from San Francisco, 14; formal agreements with Pacific Greyhound, 109–10, 111; freight operating ratio, 1920, 1923, 86; freight traffic trends, 1937, 1938, 125; Great Northern Railway opposition, 78; growth of, 21–22; infrastructure improvements,

Southern Pacific (*continued*)
214n. 61, 1930s, 130–31; lines in California, 25 fig. 1.4; Northwestern Pacific purchase, 111; passenger revenues, 1935–36, 109; passenger service in central California, 26 fig. 1.1; passenger traffic, gross earnings for major trains, 146 fig. 6.1; passenger traffic, tripling of, 1899–1910, 21–22; purchase of EP&SW, 85; rate war with Santa Fe, 16; revenues, 1911, 27; Santa Fe opposition, 122–24; schedules vs. Pacific Greyhound, 1930s, 103, 104; short distance train replacement by bus, 133; speed comparisons ca. 1920, 1930, 182 table 12; speed comparisons ca. 1930, 1940, 191 table 21; speed increase, 1930s, 129, 133; streamliners, 124–25, 128; switch engine hours, 229n. 65; usage and profitability, 172–73 table 5; use of Pacific Greyhound buses, 109–10; Western Pacific opposition, 78

Southern Pacific Company, 22; mainlines, 24 map 1.3

Southern Pacific management: failure of, 134; failure to respond to passenger needs, 114–15; strategy, 133–34

Southern Pacific Motor Transport Company (SPMT), 78

Southern Pacific operating ratio, 43, 172–73 table 5; 1901–10, 49–50; 1910–17, 50; as indicator of success, 49–50

Southern Pacific passenger operating ratio, 148; 1920s, 86–87; 1929, 113; 1933, 115; 1933, 1934, 118; 1934, 1936, 1937, 125; 1938–41, 132; 1940, 134

Southern Pacific passenger service, ca. 1920, 74 fig. 3.2; ca. 1925, 75 fig. 3.3; ca. 1930, 76 fig. 3.4; ca. 1935, 116 fig. 5.1; as civic responsibility, 71–72, 126, 127; as corporate image, 128; elimination of, 126–27; improvements to, 118, 129, 132; indicators, 182 table 11; productivity consequences management strategies, 192 table 22; reduction in, 114–15; replacement by bus service, 1927–35, 188–89 table 18

Southern Pacific passenger traffic trends, 205n. 41; 1933–34, 118, 1937, 1938, 125; 1939, 1941, 130; 1911–19, 174 table 6

Southern Pacific/Union Pacific Overland Route, 59

Southern Railway, 119–20

Spady, Richard, 140, 231n. 22

Speed: passenger response to, 150

Spencer, Arthur C., 207n. 62

Spreckles, Claus, 19

Sproule, William, 55, 58, 78, 80, 123, 214n. 60, 220n. 50

Stanford, R. Patrick, 219n. 35

Star Auto Company, 37

Star Auto Stage Association, 36, 37, 209n. 96

Star Stage Association, 36

State Highway Act of 1909, 32

Steamers. *See* Steamship

Steam railroads: operation of, 1915–20, 215n. 69

Steamship, coastal: rate increase in, 60; competition with railroads, 31, 70; effect of railroads on, 81–82

Stenason, John, 231n. 20

Stetson-Eshleman Bill, 29

Stindt, Fred A., 225n. 78

Streamliners, 152, 161; efficiency of, 148; increased use of, 1936–41, 128; to increase speed, 121, 150; market failure of, 147–48; operating costs, 142–45; profitability of, 125; Santa Fe use of, 122; Southern Pacific use of, 124–25; tare weight of, 148; use of, as public relations, 159

Sunbeam, 228n. 57, 232n. 38

Sunset Limited, photo 4, 59; schedule

of, 104; streamlining of, 228n. 57, 232nn. 38, 40
Superbus, 99
Super Chief, 128, 132
Superintendent of transportation, 43
Switch engine hours, 229n. 65

Talcott, T. M. R., 47, 211nn. 26–27
Tare weight: costing, 136, 145, 148; effect on passenger operation, 148; increase in, 149, steel trains vs. wooden, 57, 214n. 59; streamliners, 148
Tatterson, George, 35, 36
Tedlow, Richard S., 210n. 11
Tehachapi Pass, 58, 84, 85
Tejon Pass, 19, 34, 84, 160
Terminal status: granting of, by Southern Pacific, 18
Thompson, Gregory L., 203n. 12, 232n. 37, 233n. 45
Tidewater Southern, 52, 206n. 48
Toll facilities, 68, 69
Traer, Glenn, 92
Traffic association, 80
Traffic officer, 45
Traffic-rejecting fare, 80
Train ferry, replacement of, 83
Transcontinental Passenger Association, 66
Transportation Act of 1920, 64, 87, 137, 216n. 4
Travis, W. E. "Buck," 35, 37, 69, 73, 79, 88, 91, 92, 94–95, 97, 99, 107, 108–9, 111, 123, 126, 209nn. 92, 95, 218n. 30, 223n. 29, 228n. 49, 229n. 70
Twin City Zephyr: load factors, 231nn. 28, 34

Uniform system of accounts, Interstate Commerce Commission, 42
Union Pacific: anti-trust, 30; combination with Southern Pacific Company, 22; connection with Central Pacific, 11; mainlines 24 fig. 1.3

United Railroads of San Francisco, 35–36
United States Railroad Administration (USRA), 59, 157; jurisdiction over steamship lines, 60

Valley Route, 106
Value of service vs. cost of service, 49
Vaughn, T. L., 98
Visalia Electric, 52, 206n. 48

Wagons: competition from, 14
Warner, Sam Bass, Jr., 11, 202n. 6 (chap. 1)
Weidel, Joseph, 142–43, 231n. 28
West Coast: combination with *Owl*, 115
Western Association of Short Line Railroads, 35
Western Pacific: opposition to, by Southern Pacific, 78
Weyl, Walter E., 54, 213n. 44
White, Arthur, 139, 210n. 19
White, John H., Jr., 214n. 59, 232n. 37
Wickman, Carl Eric, 35, 92, 94, 95
Wilcox, Edwin G., 227n. 48
Wildcat sedans, 105–7, 224n. 57
Wilson, T. B., 93
Wilson, Woodrow, 59
Winchell, B. L., 220n. 50
Wise, Marion J., 41, 219n. 32, 220n. 51, 226n. 7
Worthington, W. A., 229n. 70
Wren, Charles, 69, 79, 91, 94, 222n. 13
Wright, Richard K., 124, 227nn. 42–43

Yale, 31, 60; return of, to West Coast, 1921, 69–70
Yellow Coach, 98–99

Zephyr, 143
Zwick, Charles, 231n. 20

Historical Perspectives on Business Enterprise Series

Mansel G. Blackford and K. Austin Kerr, Editors

The scope of this series includes scholarly interest in the history of the firm, the history of government-business relations, and the relationships between business and culture, both in the United States and abroad, as well as in comparative perspective.

Regulated Enterprise: Natural Gas Pipelines and Northeastern Markets, 1938–1954
Christopher James Castaneda

Managing Industrial Decline: The British Coal Industry between the Wars
Michael Dintenfass

Henry E. Huntington and the Creation of Southern California
William B. Friedricks

Making Iron and Steel: Independent Mills in Pittsburgh, 1820–1920
John N. Ingham

Eagle-Picher Industries: Strategies for Survival in the Industrial Marketplace, 1840–1980
Douglas Knerr

A Mental Revolution: Scientific Management since Taylor
Edited by Daniel Nelson

Rebuilding Cleveland: The Cleveland Foundation and Its Evolving Urban Strategy
Diana Tittle

Daniel Willard and Progressive Management on the Baltimore & Ohio Railroad
David M. Vrooman